NICARAGUA, BACK FROM THE DEAD?

An anthropological view of the Sandinista movement
in the early 21st Century

Johannes Wilm

new left notes

Nicaragua, Back from the Dead?
An anthropological view of the Sandinista movement in the early 21st Century
author: Johannes Wilm
edited by: Angela Lieber and Shaine Parker
drafts commented by: Dr. Victoria Goddard, Dr. Casey High, Phil Hughes, Mariya Ivancheva, Dr. Stephen Nugent and Linus Strothmann

Copyright ©2011 Johannes Wilm
Published by New Left Notes
Tucson, AZ and Oslo, Norway
http://www.newleftnotes.org

You may copy, distribute and also sell this version of the book as often as you want, as long as you do not remove this copyright notice nor the author's name. The interviews and individuals quotes in this book were all originally in Spanish and have been translated to English by the author.

The copyright holders of the included photos/pictures are the individuals and organizations mentioned in the caption. Usage rights for purposes that go beyond the reproduction of this book either in its entirety or of entire chapters, must be obtained individually from the mentioned copyright holders. When no copyright holder is mentioned in the caption, the photographer was the author. The photos taken by the author can be used for other purposes without prior consent, as long as the photographer is mentioned in all forms of publication where the photos appear. For high quality versions please email photos@newleftnotes.org.

Library of Congress Control Number: 2011911633

Publisher's Cataloging-in-Publication data

Wilm, Johannes, 1980-
  Nicaragua, back from the dead? : an anthropological view of the Sandinista movement in the early 21st century / Johannes Wilm.
        xxxiv, 306 p. : ill., map ; 23 cm.
  Includes bibliographical references (p. 267-294) and index.
  ISBN: 978-82-8198-001-3 (pbk.)
  ISBN: 978-82-8198-002-0 (e-book)
1. Frente Sandinista de Liberación Nacional. 2. Political participation–Nicaragua. 3. Nicaragua–Social conditions–1979-. 4. Nicaragua–Economic conditions–1918-. 5. Nicaragua–History. 6. Revolutionaries–Nicaragua–History–20th century. I. Title.
F1526.W55 2011
  972.850544–dc23   2011911633

Why this book?

In the 1980s Nicaragua was almost constantly in the news. A revolution in 1979 catapulted the leftist *Frente Sandinista de Liberación Nacional* (FSLN) into power, and the President of the United States, Ronald Reagan, financed a bloody contra-revolution for most of the decade. The Sandinistas lost national elections in 1990, and that ended the last experiment of socialism on the American mainland. Little more was heard from the central American Republic in the following years.

The Sandinistas returned to power in 2007, but surprisingly little has been heard about them. In the few cases the media has brought attention to it, it has focused on certain aspects of some policies of the new FSLN government, such as abortion rights. What these portrayals all have in common is that they say the current government diverges from the program of revolutionary transformation of the 1980s. No-one has looked at current Sandinismo in its totality and how the country is progressing.

In this book I try to show what it means to be part of the Sandinista movement in the 21st century. This includes common points of reference all types of Sandinistas share, and how the web of different types of Sandinistas is structured in a way that emphasizes popular participation of people with very different backgrounds and perspectives.

The Sandinista movement puts a particularly strong emphasis on Nicaragua and the movement's own history over the last 100 years. In the 1980s they received military and economic support from Cuba and the Soviet Union, and now Venezuela plays that role. Sandinismo has changed with the change of alliances in ways that Nicaraguans seldom recognize.

Foreigners writing about Nicaragua in the 1980s looked enthusiastically at the revolutionary transformation, while in the 1990s everybody just saw decay and how the Sandinista movement fragmented. I show that most looking at Nicaragua in the 1990s incorrectly assumed that the Sandinista movement would disintegrate completely into identity politics, while really their work turned more clandestine in preparation for another takeover of the state.

The Sandinista movement includes people who believe in many different ideologies (nationalism, social reformism, Marxism and anarchism). Sandinismo did in the past include, and still includes, many of the individual aspects of identity politics in a way that may have led some anthropologists to believe it was the sole center point of Sandinistas' engagement with politics. I look at how the current unity of the movement depends on a limited number of common reference points in the last 100 years of Nicaraguan history, which are interpreted very differently by other groups, but which at all times emphasize the part of Nicaraguans in international relations. Although Liberals and Sandinistas both have groups of supporters, the models of political participation and how political success gets measured for the two groups is fundamentally different. Related to the internal ideological difference within the Sandinista movement is an informal structure of different groups of Sandinistas who engage in concrete actions to change society. Oftentimes this works without provoking conflict between different groups of Sandinistas, and is therefore not immediately noticeable to the outside observer.

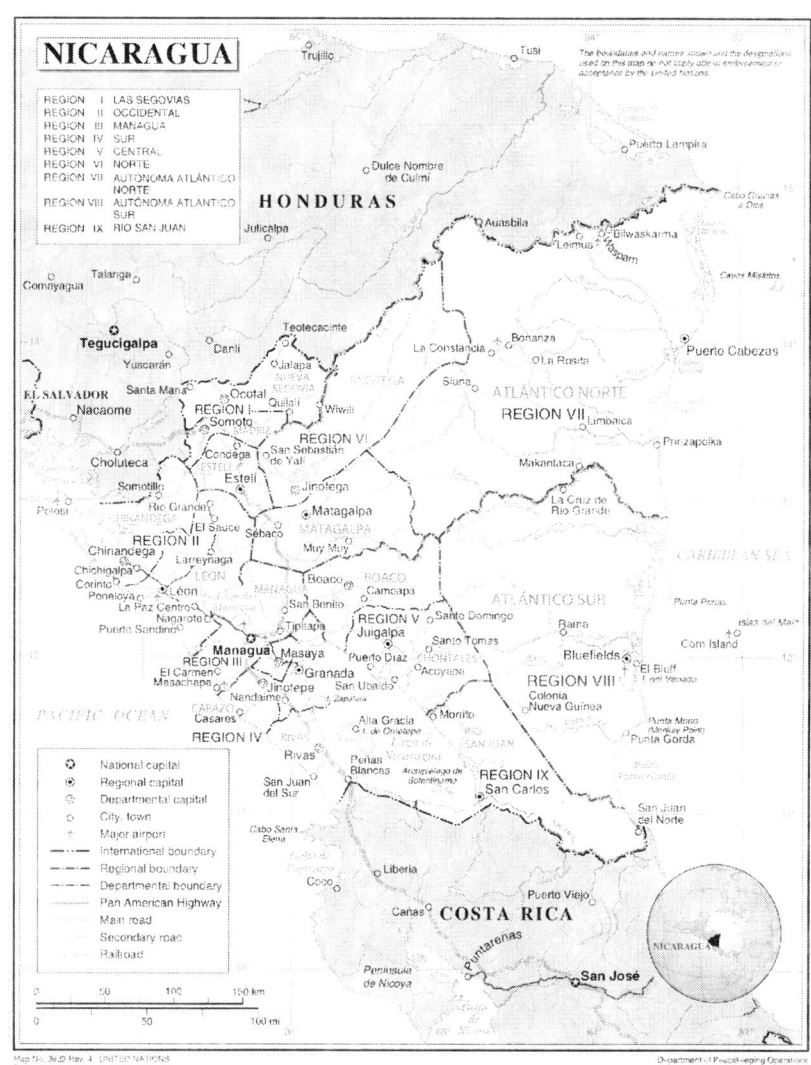

Contents

Abstract	iii
Introduction	xi
On Nicaragua	xi
How I ended up in Nicaragua	xiii
What is so interesting about Nicaragua?	xvii
Getting in contact with Nicaraguans	xix
Where I stayed	xxii
My initial blunders	xxiii
Social science literature on the Nicaraguan revolutionary experience	xxv
Revolution studies	xxvi
Post-Sandinista studies	xxix
Sandinista II studies	xxxii
1 Recent political history of Nicaragua and the Sandinista movement	**1**
Before 1920	1
Augusto Nicolás Calderón Sandino	4
Somoza	5
The organization of resistance against Somoza	6
The Sandinista years 1979–90	11
Foreign Involvement	12
The FSLN structure	14
Popular participation and direct democracy	17
The FSLN electoral defeat in 1990	17

	The FSLN as an opposition force	20
	The FSLN electoral victory 2006	23
	Subjective aspects of the history as it is presented	24
2	**The politics of history**	**25**
	What parts of Nicaraguan history are important?	26
	Political identities in Nicaragua	27
	The controversies around historical representations in Nicaragua	29
	From the 1850s to 1920s	29
	Calderón Sandino	31
	The Somoza years	39
	Under the Sandinista in the 1980s	45
	Reasoning the electoral failure in 1990	48
	Three neoliberal governments	50
	Governing without a majority	52
	Problems understanding the discussion of Nicaraguan history	53
	Concluding remarks	55
3	**Economic development, expectations and perceptions**	**57**
	Development theories	58
	Mainstream modernization development theories	59
	Counter-hegemonic development theories	61
	Nicaraguan economic history	67
	Economic policies between Zelaya López and the Somozas	69
	Economic policies under the Somozas	71
	Economic realities and policies under the Sandinistas of the 1980s	76
	Liberal economic politics	86
	Nicaraguan economics during the second Sandinista government	91
	Popular ideas about economic realities and models of the past	98
	The 1970s	98
	The 1980s	99
	The 1990s–2007	104
	The current Sandinista government	106
	Concluding remarks	112

4	**Shaping politics**	**113**
	Transport worker strike (May 2008)	114
	The MRS protests (May – November 2008)	117
	Award given to last Minister of Education of East Germany and alliance with Honduras (19 July 2008)	124
	The Georgia conflict	127
	León FSLN candidate for mayor clashed with police (September 2008)	129
	FSLN won local elections (November 2008)	130
	Parliament stopped working (November 2008 – February 2009) .	137
	Military coup in Honduras (June 2009)	138
	30 years of revolution and some advances (summer 2009)	139
	Concluding remarks	141
5	**Sandinista projects of change**	**143**
	The historic structure of the FSLN	143
	The principle of alliances	147
	The new FSLN as part of a Socialism for the 21st Century	152
	Ways of exerting power by individuals and groups	153
	Concluding remarks	182
6	**Historic relations with Eastern Europe**	**185**
	Nicaraguan particularities in the current global system	186
	Connections to a former center	189
	The experience in East Germany in perspective	207
	Dependence on Russia?	208
	Concluding remarks	209
7	**Factors that differentiate Sandinistas**	**211**
	Age as a defining factor	217
	The literacy campaign celebration	219
	The lack of ideological models among younger Sandinistas	220
	Little focus on theoretical knowledge among organized Sandinista youngsters	222
	Term redefinitions	224
	'Seriousness' and acceptance of younger Sandinistas . . .	230
	Current studies of political theory	232
	Professionals and Sandinismo	233
	MRS Sandinismo	238

Concluding remarks 245

Conclusion   **247**
    Developments since... 250
    ...and into the future 252
    What is to be done? 255

Glossary   **257**

Bibliography   **271**

Index   **298**

Introduction

On Nicaragua

Nicaragua is situated in Central America, between Honduras and El Salvador to the north and Costa Rica to the south, and is the largest of the five Central American republics. It extends over an area of roughly 130,000 km². Its climate is tropical though somewhat diverse, with rainfall ranging between 1,000 and 6,000 mm annually in different regions. Its soil is very fertile, and among the country's top agricultural exports are exotic fruits, meat, fish, coffee, tobacco and sugar cane (Taylor 1963). The total population is 5,666,301, of which 57% live in urban areas. The median age of Nicaraguans is 22.9 years (July 2010 estimate). In 1975 the population was estimated at 2,798,000, so population increase has been rapid. It was estimated that in 2010, Nicaragua was the poorest country in Central America and the second poorest country in the Americas (CIA 2011a; World population prospects 2008). Nicaragua is divided into 15 *departamentos,* mainly in western Nicaragua, and two *regiones autónomas* on the east coast. The departamentos and regiones autónomas contain a total of 153 *municipios*. Municipios and regiones autónomas have separate locally-elected governments, but departamentos do not. The borders and jurisdictions between the different regions and governments are not always completely clear. Although departamentos do not possess their own governments, they are used as administrative units by the central state, and Nicaraguans operate around them as significant units. Some of the political parties also use departamentos as organizational units.

Western Nicaragua is almost exclusively Spanish speaking, while on the eastern Atlantic coast, several groups speak creole languages and English in addition to Spanish. Transportation between the coasts is not very developed. A road between Managua in western Nicaragua and Bluefields, the capital of the *Región Autónoma del Atlántico Sur* (RAAS) on the east

In the port of El Rama passengers switch from boat to bus on their way to western Nicaragua.

coast, has been planned for decades and under construction for years. For now, the only way of going from one to the other is by taking a bus from Managua to El Rama and then a boat from there to Bluefields, or by flying directly from Managua to Bluefields. Transportation between western cities is relatively easy, with many bus lines of different speeds operating between major cities, and at least one bus line reaching to every major village. Transit between settlements on the east coast is still conducted exclusively by boat.

Most Nicaraguans live in western Nicaragua, where all the largest cities lie. In western Nicaragua there are nine cities with more than 100,000 inhabitants: the capital Managua (pop. 1,051,258), León (197,549), Masaya (160,551), Chinandega (158,185), Matagalpa (145,750), Estelí (125,684), Granada (119,083), Tipitapa (111,923) and Jinotega (108,806). The largest city in the regiones autónomas on the Atlantic coast was until 2011 Nueva Guinea (83,433), which is connected by road to Managua. In April 2011, President José Daniel Ortega Saavedra moved three municipios from the RAAS to the departamento Chontales by presidential decree, arguing they had little connection to the rest of the region culturally and that it was often difficult for these municipios' inhabitants to travel to Bluefields. The three municipios that were moved to Chontales included the two most populous of the RAAS, Nueva Guinea and El Rama (62,732), leaving Bluefields (50,960), the largest city in the RAAS and Siuna (73,888), in the *Región Autónoma del*

Atlántico Norte (RAAN), the most populous in the regiones autónomas (2010 estimates Serrano 2007; Martínez and León 2011, 96–99). Border crossing checkpoints are operated in the north entering into Honduras and in the south into Costa Rica, and the country can easily be crossed north to south within a day on the Pacific side, even when taking cheaper and slower local buses. It is less common for Nicaraguans than it is for their northern neighbors to seek work in the United States, and more Nicaraguans migrate south to Costa Rica[1], where wages are considerably higher. Most Nicaraguans believe that Nicaragua is the safest country in Latin America, and they are generally very proud of this.

How I ended up in Nicaragua

Nicaragua served as a major topic in European and US American news throughout the 1980s, but that is not how I learned to know the country. My journey started in Mexico.

In the second half of 2006 I traveled through Mexico. I wrote about the occupation of the Zócalo in Mexico City by the left-wing presidential candidate Andres Manuel López Obrador and blogged about the teacher uprising in the city of Oaxaca. In late November of 2006, the uprising in Oaxaca was quelled. That same month, I remember sitting at the university radio station in Oaxaca one morning with a group of protesters. I was with the last stand of the protesters, 13 of us. I was the only foreigner in the group, but I knew of two other young foreigners still in town. The group decided I should help them get out of town, and after first assigning me a young girl to help, changed their mind and asked me to help a teenage punk rocker from Mexico City named Daniel. I immediately went to take Spanish classes that morning before doing anything else. Looking back, it seems strange I would take the time to do that – or that Spanish schools and other businesses in Oaxaca remained open for business during the lifetime of the commune and subsequent fights between Oaxaca's inhabitants and the military. At the time it seemed natural to stick to at least some aspects of normal, everyday life.

---

1. 76% of foreign born people registered as living in Costa Rica in 2000 were Nicaraguans (Madrigal 2006). Mexicans, Guatemalans, Hondurans and El Salvadorians occupied the top four spots on the list of illegal migrants residing in the United States in 2009, while Nicaraguans did not appear in the top 10 (Hoefer, Rytina, and Baker 2009).

"Watch out!" a soldier screams at me as I make my way to the entrance of the *Universidad Autónoma "Benito Juárez" de Oaxaca* (UABJO, far right).

When I went to the university around midday, I found it surrounded by the military. I acted as if I were a journalist in order to avoid looking suspicious, and started taking pictures of the soldiers while I slowly made my way to the entrance. "Watch out!" one of soldiers screamed, obviously thinking I would behave like a normal journalist and listen to him. Once inside, I showed the pictures I had taken to the activists, to give them a sense of what was going on around the university. Daniel was ready – he had washed for the first time in weeks and looked like somewhat less of a rebel. We ran to the back entrance while the university radio played classical music through huge speakers placed outside the building. This seemed like a surreal soundtrack to accompany the end of the uprising. "Everything is fine," I joked while we hastily made our way across the university grounds, "Don't you hear the music?"

Many of those present in Oaxaca over the last few months of the uprising were killed or made to disappear over its final few days. Not Daniel, I thought. When we arrived at the back entrance to the university, a group of army trucks passed the corner and stopped momentarily. Daniel jumped back onto university grounds and hid behind a wall while I froze. Since it worked before, I pulled out my camera and started aiming it at them. It worked, I was again mistaken for a journalist, and the soldiers drove off rapidly without saying a word. There was a highway just outside

The university radio station represented the last stand of the Oaxaca commune. The building was secured by the checkpoint on the left and Molotov cocktails were stacked in case of a military attack on the building.

the gate, and while Daniel protested—he wanted a cab or some other mode of transportation he deemed safer—I winked the next bus over and we both boarded. After hiding him for a day in my hostel—during which time he spent half the money he had been given for a first-class bus ticket on booze—we took a cab and then a second-class bus to Mexico City. At the checkpoints along the way, Daniel pretended to be a tour guide for me and a US American activist from the hostel who I picked up along the way.

Reporting on what happened in Oaxaca without getting involved could have been an option for me, but it would have been one in which Daniel possibly ended up dead as so many others did. I had first met Daniel a few weeks earlier, when he sat—drunk—in downtown Oaxaca attacking me for being ignorant, as a European, about their local struggle. At that time he was convinced that I would not dare go onto the barricades at the university campus. He had arrived that morning from Mexico City and had still not seen any of it. In the end, I dragged him out from the center of town and onto these barricades. Although there were snipers and occasional abductions—most likely orchestrated by right-wing extremists in the area around the university—the atmosphere remained generally relaxed, with young people sitting around piles of burning trash listening to guitar music, and discussing what the future would look like once capitalism was defeated on a worldwide scale.

Capitalism did not get defeated, and once Daniel and I arrived in Mexico City, it was announced that the Mexican government had a list of 99 foreigners who had been involved in the actions in Oaxaca. Involving oneself in politics as a foreigner is illegal in Mexico, and I was fairly certain I would be on the list. I headed for the southern border, crisscrossing Mexico via Veracruz, then Ariega, Tapachula and San Cristobal, Chiapas. I

xv

hoped to avoid the Oaxacan authorities this way, and for extra security I used the name "Julius Nissen" for bus check-ins – my name was never verified. I tried to get across the border close to Tapachula, but due to either the bureaucracy or an actual arrest order existing—I could never quite tell which—my crossing was prevented and I returned to Mexican soil. I managed to cross into Guatemalan territory by land in Ciudad Cuauhtémoc – a much older border station where I assumed they would not have the technology to check my legal status in Mexico.

For a while I turned into part of the general backpacker crowd, and I headed south hoping to reach some friends in Brazil I had met at the *World Social Forum* in Porto Alegre, Brazil in 2005. When I arrived in Nicaragua some two weeks after leaving Mexico, the *Frente Sandinista de Liberación Nacional* (FSLN) had just won the elections, and everybody was discussing it. I could remember some posters about solidarity with the Sandinistas in a certain party office in Norway, but I had never studied the Nicaraguan situation. Third world[2] socialist experiments were doomed to fail, according to my own political framework. I expected any successful revolutionary attempts to take place in a leading first world capitalist country. Yet in Nicaragua, I was suddenly confronted with many people who hoped for and expected this revolution to come back after 'the 16 years of neoliberalism.' I needed to understand this better.

After entering from Honduras, I stayed one night in the northern mountain city of Estelí. The first thing I remember doing when arriving in Managua was visiting a shopping center—Metrocentro—and buying a history book. It was the only one there, and the shop assistant commented to the customers who came after me that she was surprised they had one. What a strange place I thought – everybody talks about history, but no history books are available.

I spent Christmas 2006 reading about the Sandinista struggle, from its beginnings in the early 1960s until its downfall in 1990, while also talking to the local Sandinistas on the island of Ometepe about what was to be expected after the recent victory of the FSLN.

It interested me what would happen to Nicaragua. I took a week of

---

2. Classifying countries as belonging to the first, second or third world countries can seem outdated, because countries in the third world have developed very differently in recent years, and the second world used to be the Soviet Union and its closest allies. Nowadays it may be more appropriate to say 'developing world' instead of third world, but Nicaraguans continue to talk about themselves as living in the third world.

Spanish lessons in León and my teacher made me form the following sentence: "When the gringo crosses the border, I will poke his eye out." The instructor commented on my being "a good anti-imperialist." I found the entire situation and experience of reality held by the Nicaraguans to be intriguing. What would happen? Would Nicaragua be able to go back to the 1980s both politically and culturally? Would all those I had met, many of whom had worked and hoped for 16 years to finally have their socialism back, have to face a reality – that socialism in the 21st century is impossible or fundamentally different from their 1980s?

After talking to people in most western Nicaraguan towns about the impending changes and hearing ever more exciting versions of what Nicaragua was to turn into, and attending Ortega Saavedra's inauguration festivities in early January 2007 (the crowds started leaving when Ortega Saavedra started talking about which policies from the 1980s would not return). I left Nicaragua in early January 2007, and would not return until April 2008. Things had changed. Apparently during the 16 years leading up to the Sandinista victory in the presidential elections, those most interested in history had wanted to forget it rather than read about it.

What is so interesting about Nicaragua?

My interest in Nicaragua concerned mostly the Sandinismo ideology and how it had changed from and related to the 1980s. It was important for me to understand what it means for an individual to be a Sandinista, and how this differs from being a Liberal or Conservative. This question related to many aspects of people's personal identities and went far beyond who they voted for or of which party they were a member. It was not restricted to ideological differences completely, as the variety of opinions/ideologies within the Sandinista movement proved to be gigantic.

I tried to find how the Sandinista public or Sandinista supporting public related to the FSLN, what they expected from an FSLN government, and how much Dependency Theory, Marxism[3], and anti-imperialism ideology were part of the views of most Sandinistas in comparison to the amount of neoliberalism and modernization theory. I also wondered how partic-

---

3. *Marxism* has since the middle of the 19th Century denoted the overall ideas present in the writings of German revolutionary and philosopher Karl Heinrich Marx (1818–83). The followers of Marx and further writings/theories that have been written since and go in the same direction are termed *Marxist*.

ipatory democracy worked under the Ortega Saavedra government. In this connection, my main concern was whether the role of the different types of organizing in non-governmental organizations, labor unions, and *Consejos de Poder Ciudadano* (CPC) that are somehow linked with Sandinismo was to legitimize those decisions of the President for which he had no parliamentary approval. Were these part of a long-term strategy to link the FSLN to the state beyond the current elections, or were these to extend the influence of and improved the communication from the base of society. It was also important to understand how the contribution in participative political processes by non-FSLN members was viewed. Were they systematically excluded?

As the current government was portrayed internationally as everything but revolutionary, I wondered whether there would be a push for radicalization from some lower level within the Sandinista movement. I could imagine the FSLN leadership would find itself two steps behind a population expecting "patria, socialismo o muerto"(Chavez at Ortega's inauguration ceremony Rodríguez 2007b) or that the FSLN leadership would turn out to represent a minority of educated radical scholars in an otherwise Liberal population.[4] If radicalization would come from below, I was wondering what parts of the program of the FSLN leadership it would go against and what channels would be used—CPCs, party apparati or government bureaucracy—and whether such attempts would be successful.[5]

Given Nicaragua's unique historic background of foreign interventions, I wondered how important international relations were for Nicaragua (most of all economically), and what importance generally was attributed

---

4. The discourse of Ortega Saavedra before the 2006 elections and immediately afterward was minimally radical. This changed before I returned to Nicaragua and so my initial ideas were somewhat outdated. I planned on including in my interviews some of the key terms from former times, such as 'vanguard,' and 'imperialism,' that were avoided by Ortega Saavedra around the elections. I had planned to ask respondents what they connected those terms to and how they felt about them, and then compare the responses. But because the words served as part of the official Sandinista government vocabulary at the time of my return, finding out how much people used such terminology worked more as a test of the degree to which they aligned with the government.

5. Similar to the previous question, I wanted to note reactions to key terms such as 'Contras' and 'neoliberalism,' yet again the word 'neoliberalism' had been given a negative connotation in the wording of government statements. Interestingly, no Liberal would ever mention 'neoliberalism' in a favorable light either. I recorded the degree to which former contra supporters and people still organized in the *Partido Resistencia Nicaragüense* (PRN) now participated in and cooperated with the current government.

to international relations by the Nicaraguan public. Given that the Sandinistas were back in power, I was interested in finding out how the international relations of the 1980s were seen today and what relevance was attributed to them in the current setup.[6]

Getting in contact with Nicaraguans

I realized that simply being in Nicaragua physically wouldn't be enough to get to know Nicaraguans and specifically Sandinistas. So I engaged in several different projects which allowed me to get in contact with different types of Nicaraguans. The four projects I spent the most time on were:

1. Looking for Nicaraguans who studied at the Wilhelm-Pieck school of political leadership of the *Freie Deutsche Jugend* (FDJ, Free German Youth) in East Germany during the 1980s.

    The school had been one of three schools in the Eastern Bloc that had educated young people (ages 16–25) from around the world who were believed to be the next generation of political leaders in their respective countries. All students studied 1 year and then returned to their native countries to engage in the local struggle there. Up to 10 Nicaraguans attended this school each year throughout the 1980s. In the early years they used false names due to security issues, and in the later years they promised not to exchange addresses. I was asked by an East German who had studied at the school to try to find his classmates who attended from 1985–86. I put up posters throughout the town of León and went to Managua to be recorded on national television with my campaign to find all the Nicaraguans who studied there. I started the search in late July 2008, and received calls from former students for the next 10 months. Altogether I found 37 students, although some could not be verified. I usually traveled to whatever town or village they lived in with my video

---

6. The last question came up both as part of the ongoing politics in which a more Central place was attributed to Russia during my time in Nicaragua (see also — *The Georgia conflict*, p. 127) and when the Ruben Dario medal was given to former East German minister of education Margot Honecker (see also — *Award given to last Minister of Education of East Germany and alliance with Honduras (19 July 2008)*, p. 125) on 19 July 2008. When looking for former students from the Wilhelm-Pieck school of political leadership (see also — *Connections to a former center*, p. 189), I wanted to assess the relevance of the international relations of the 1980s and its effect in ordinary conversations today.

camera, and sometimes stayed over night or stayed in touch for a longer duration of time. My questions to them concerned what they had done before going to the *Deutsche Demokratische Republik* (DDR, German Democratic Republic); why they went; what they remembered of the trip; what they did after returning and what they did now; and what they thought of the current political situation in Nicaragua.

2. Collecting the life stories of the founders of the organization 'Amigos.'

    Bayardo José Fonseca Galo, the uncle of my main informant[7], Carolina Fonseca Icabalzeta, was very active in the student movement prior to and during the 1979 revolutionary insurrection. He did not hold any important political position in the new Sandinista administration. He wanted to start an organization of people like him who were politically active previously, but who now did not belong to the inner circles of the FSLN. The stated purpose of the organization Fonseca Galo wanted to start was to spread knowledge about Sandinismo and engage in social projects for the betterment of society–thereby advancing the general cause of the party without directly getting involved in it. Fonseca Galo maintained contact with an extensive number of friends across the country with whom he had close contact and who he wished to recruit to this new organization. I accompanied him around Managua to interview some of those who had agreed to join, and was sent by Fonseca Galo to El Rama and Chontales to meet with and interview others he was interested in recruiting. The primary questions I posed to Fonseca Galo's contacts were: To what inner-party tendency they belonged before 1979; what their role in the insurrection and the 1980s was; how they survived the 1990s; and what their involvement or stance on the current situation was.

3. Helping to create a new national information system for the Nicaraguan *Ministerio Agropecuario y Forestal* (MAGFOR) for all of their

---

7. An 'informant' is an anthropological term for someone who helps an anthropologist gain information about something. Usually that is just everyone one has major conversations with, the people one interviews in formal settings and those who help one to set up interviews and get to know more people. That is how I am using it here. It does not have connotations as meaning a type of 'spy' as its colloquial usage implies.

Bayardo José Fonseca Galo is on a mission to reengage former revolutionary fighters in Sandinista politics.

data through the NGO *Servicio de Información Mesoamericano sobre Agricultura Sostenible* (SIMAS).

From January 2009 to September 2009 I worked on an information system for the MAGFOR. This project involved engaging with the free software movement, situated in Managua. I also taught courses on the use of open source software at the *Universidad de Managua*'s León campus (UdeM León). The free software movement provided the principal driving force behind the idea of the need for social/political change, but the project also involved engaging with the Sandinista bureaucrats who ran the ministry and the largely Sandinista agriculture professionals who organized the project of renewal in the NGO SIMAS. Through my interactions with this particular cross-section of Nicaraguan society, I gained a deeper understanding of middle-class professional Sandinistas' views of Sandinismo, and the policy plans of those formally involved in government. I found it interesting to note and highlight the relations between the open source movement and this more technocratic use of IT, as they would initially seem to represent two competing political visions within Sandinismo.

4. Work as a political journalist.

In addition to the above, I tried to be present whenever a political event occurred as a sort of reporter with a video camera, oftentimes publishing my results on the Internet. This gave me the opportu-

I thank Nicaraguan activists of all types who have shown me what Sandinismo is about. These Sandinistas surround me during a day of marches in León. At first I am afraid they will hurt me, but they then explain that they want to thank me for a photo I shot at an earlier event which proves their innocence in a case of a destroyed university door (see also — *Tendency*, p. 227). Luckily no group or individual has ever been angry enough at me to attack me physically, and almost all of the time members of all groups have been very helpful in explaining their perspective to me. *Photo: Bernhard Gruber*

nity to come in contact with the principal actors. In particular, I developed a network of contacts in the Sandinista administration of León quite early from this.

Where I stayed

I arrived in Nicaragua on 6 April 2008. For the first month I stayed in the *Bello Horizonte* neighborhood in Managua, where I rented the garage of a friend of a friend of a friend of mine. The family consisted of the mother, a teacher not particularly fond of any political ideology, and her son, a disc jockey who was not involved politically, but who felt closest to the party *Movimiento Renovador Sandinista* (MRS). During my stay there, he began dating a Palestinian who had very strong Sandinista views. After a month I moved to León, the second largest city in Nicaragua, where I stayed downtown in a house owned by Rigo Sampson Davila, a member of the FSLN. His father was a former mayor of León and currently worked as director of the local university. I stayed at Sampson Davila's house until late August 2008. From September 2008 until February 2009, I stayed across the road from Rigo Sampson Davila at the house of María Mercedes, a former activist in the 1980s struggle against the Sandinistas who lost two brothers in the fight to protect Nicaragua from the Sandinistas. One brother had served as a member of the *Guardia Nacional* (GN), the other one as a member of the Contras. From February until June 2009, I rented a house with Bernhard Gruber, an Austrian civil worker, in a somewhat poorer area (San Felipe), a few blocks from downtown León. The area did not have the same party politics as the center of town, but political questions came up nevertheless. During this phase I spent less time in León than I had previously. From July until September 2009, I stayed at a hostel in Managua and did most of my research there, working with young Sandinistas, and also was involved during this time in the production of an information system for the ministry of agriculture.

My initial blunders

Just like anyone entering a field for the first time, I did not do everything correctly from the start, and I made some assumptions based on my earlier research that did not make sense later. One of the things I had not understood was how the political discourse and the relationship between news media and political groups in Nicaragua worked. I did not understand that at times things were said as part of a tactical game. I investigated the MRS party for several months in the beginning before I understood very few Sandinistas felt represented by them (see also — MRS Sandinismo, p. 238).

With time it became easier for me to distinguish when statements were made out of tactical concerns and when they represented the speaker's real opinion. When an informant told me one of the tactically planted stories, I immediately interrupted and quickly explained how the point he was currently making did not correspond to other facts I had already discovered before an even greater distortion on his part would have made it impossible for him to admit his error without losing face. With this I demonstrated I was not just a tourist with little to no knowledge about Nicaraguan reality. Some would then react by telling me another tactically planted story, but at least as soon as I had interrupted the informant a second time and pointed to the disconnect from reality, the conversation would start over with a more realistic approach. Arguably I could not have avoided going through a phase of learning about the nature of tactically planted stories, and they do say a great deal about the nature of the contact between Nicaraguans and many foreigners, which generally speaking is of a temporary nature. On many occasions none of this had to do with me personally – the same stories were told internationally at conferences, and just about anywhere in Europe or the United States when talking to people with some knowledge about Nicaragua. FSLN activists generally claimed it is part of a *Central Intelligence Agency* (CIA) tactic to destabilize the country by spreading stories against the government. That may be true in some cases, but does not explain why members of all political groups were engaged in this activity.

Another issue was the question as to which informants could give the most accurate information. As is likely the case in most countries, the amount of contact individual members of society have with foreigners is not evenly distributed. Some people reside in a position to meet more foreigners, and others are more inclined to seek them out. Fonseca Icabalzeta was pointed out to me by a German friend of mine who had met her when she worked in Nicaragua a year earlier. Fonseca Icabalzeta, aged 29–30 years, studied in Managua and her entire family consisted of active Sandinistas. She claimed to have only two foreign friends, and the information and contacts she provided seemed to be with good intentions and not with the idea to make me see Sandinismo only one way. Rigo Sampson Davila, son of the ex mayor of León and member of the FSLN, was also an early contact. He works for a Norwegian study abroad program, speaks English and owns the house I first stayed in. I was told by a co-student from my time at the University of Oslo that "he would be good to talk to." His exposure to foreigners was clearly above-average. Although I lived in his house for three months, I never formally interviewed him. I understood the criticism he had of the FSLN through numerous conversations and with time it seemed to me his viewpoint of wishing for a more centrist Nicaragua, and seeing the problems of Nicaragua rooted in its ethnic makeup, were very much informed by his class position and income level. That situated him beyond and above most ordinary Nicaraguan economically. While

Sampson Davila seems no less authentic than Fonseca Icabalzeta, his ideas of Nicaraguan politics are spread rather one-sidedly to every group of Norwegian students who spend their time in Nicaragua. Their picture of what Sandinismo entails is, likely to be skewed.

More severe problems arise when a heightened amount of foreigner contact is connected with economic need. Most foreigners I met were either traveling through or conducting social research, and the latter type was specifically targeted by some Nicaraguans. Such a case was María Elena Bustillo. I met her during my first trip to Nicaragua, while she was selling postcards in the central square of León. After I left, she tried to contact me via video chat, with the clear objective of monetary help. For various reasons, that never happened. Upon returning to Nicaragua, I met her while strolling across the central square and I visited her in her house during the first few days and even filmed what happened there. She had turned from being very enthusiastic about the FSLN to being rather disappointed. For a while, I helped her out economically by letting her wash my clothing. Yet within the first few weeks, I came to understand she managed to be in contact with most research based foreigners, and quite a number of them had been dragged to her house to see just how poorly she lived. I could actually not make out to what degree she was actually living in the house she showed to foreigners, or whether it was just a shed to show tourists and awaken their sense of empathy. Given the total amount of money she managed to get from all the various foreigners—usually larger amounts allegedly to be spent on improvements for the house—it did not make sense that she was not able to climb economically. After discovering the nature of the relation we had, I broke off most contact with her. When short-term research students would come into town, I advised them to go and speak to her, and to at least some of them she functioned as quite a capable guide and cultural translator, putting them in contact with whomever they needed to talk with.

Social science literature on the Nicaraguan revolutionary experience

Quite a lot has been written by other anthropologists on Nicaragua and the Sandinista movement since the triumph of the revolution. After I returned from Nicaragua the first time, I started researching all that I could find in

Europe. Other works I did not find before returning to Nicaragua. A lot of this is interesting for historical comparison, yet in the end I felt something was missing about Sandinismo as it is today.

Revolution studies

After the FSLN won the revolutionary insurrection in 1979, Nicaragua was the site of many anthropologists investigating a concrete revolution throughout the 1980s. A number of anthropological studies were conducted on the FSLN and the Sandinista movement. Three documentary films show the early years of the revolution and the experiences of individual members of society: one on the experience of the revolution, one on the literacy campaign, and one on the FSLN and the Contras (Schultz 1980; Tercer Cine 1981a, 1981b). Enriquez (1997) explored how certain collectivization programs worked better than other agrarian programs under FSLN rule to make the farmers identify with the FSLN and its project for transition. Bourgois (1986) displayed that the Miskito minority, and the black population were heavily recruited by the CIA for Contra operations. These groups live mainly on the Nicaraguan east coast in the two semi-independent regiones autónomas and its members are generally subject to even higher levels of material deprivation than the general population. The study of these areas is quite apart from the study of the central and Spanish speaking part of Nicaraguan, and focused on the bilingual language situation and patterns of their internal organization. A work that I discovered much too late, which would have been very useful in preparing me for Nicaragua is the book *Nicaragua* by Walker and Wade (2011), the former of which published previous versions under the same title and other books on Nicaragua since the early 1980s. The book is written in an extremely readable journalistic style and the perspective of Dependency of Nicaragua to the United States, that is presents is also very much the same way I see the relationship here. For obvious reasons, the authors have a much closer personal relation to the Nicaragua of the 1980s than me. For me, the 1980s is a backdrop to the current events, whereas for them the focus lies in this period, although they also describe the history since then.

Of particular importance in popular discussions abroad about the Sandinista revolution of the 1980s is what was called the *mystique* of the revolution. The academic version of this have been the studies about the

Nicaraguan Miskito refugees wait for food in a camp in Honduras during the 1980s. The treatment of the east coast Miskito Nicaraguans was one of the darker chapters of the Sandinismo of the 1980s. Consequently, the *Central Intelligence Agency* (CIA) recruited heavily among them and anthropologists studied them (Bourgois 1986). *Photo: UNHCR File*

emotions in connection with the revolutionary process (Reed 2004). I find this field a bit problematic. Talking about the Nicaraguan revolution as mystique seems to make Nicaragua more exotic than what it needs to be. In part, it seems to me that westerners coming to Nicaragua try to find something exotic/mystique even when things are not very different from their home of origin. I clearly remember one situation when SIMAS had an open day event, presenting the different project of which they were involved to representatives of donor organizations. Among their methods of disseminating information to the public were filming interviews with individuals and uploading them to a website, recording audio plays and spreading them by radio, having radio DJs read price data of agricultural goods over the airwaves and putting the same data on an advanced website where users would be able to compare the data better. Several of these methods were experimental on a world scale. A Danish representative of an aid organization raised her hand and said that in Africa they used street theater and dances, and suggested SIMAS also start using this method. The Nicaraguan colleague seated beside me, Carlos Alberto Rocha Castro, rolled his eyes at this suggestion, and started laughing when I whispered to him

The Sandinista Carolina Icabalceta Garay complains about the lack of revolutionary *mystique* during the current Sandinista government.

that maybe we should make a street dance about agricultural prices rather than put them on the Internet. Nobody said anything out loud – possibly because the Danish woman who spoke represented funding.

It is this sort of assumed exotic qualities of Nicaragua and Nicaraguans I try to avoid. This is how I understand how the term 'mystique' was and is used by First World anthropologists and other social scientists in relation to the Sandinista revolution. I try to keep my descriptions clean and open for comparison for the readers from the First World, and let them relate it to their own lives. The term also appears in Sandinista daily speech, in which it seems to be equivalent to the existence of a willingness to work voluntarily. In this sense it is used by Sandinista Carolina Icabalceta Garay who complained of it in the current phase of the revolution:

> I think there was more mystique during the 1980s than now...Oh yes. Neoliberalism has done that much of Sandinista militancy has been monetized a bit. It's all about costs and benefits, more than the passion of the 1980s. I think that has simply been lost. That is a gigantic loss, the loss of these values...

I do recognize the importance of this second sense of the term when describing how the current Nicaraguan government makes use of paid protesters (see also — *Use of paid protesters?*, p. 178). I have avoided using the term mystique in my own analysis in order to not produce more confusion surrounding its usage.

Another subject of a lot of attention in literature on the Sandinista revolution was the reform of the health care system as part of the revolutionary process (Donahue 1989; Ripp 1984; Garfield 1984; Bossert 1984; Williams 1984), a subject that continues to be relevant. Ripp (1984) suggested that from a Marxist viewpoint, the study of the health care systems can serve as a replacement for participant observation among just a handful of informants, as the analysis of the class antagonisms within the health care system will automatically say something about class relations in society in general. This line of thinking may be what made it popular to study individual aspects of Sandinismo rather than the phenomenon as a whole.

Post-Sandinista studies

In recent years, a number of works on Nicaragua have been published. Most of these concern the time between the Sandinista governments. The period was labeled 'Post-Sandinista' when it was not known that the Sandinistas would return to power again. Much involves new types of social movements and the sense of destructiveness of this period.

Babb wrote about the situation of Nicaraguan women and the imagery of revolution in the post-revolutionary period (Babb 2001, 2004). In Recycled Sandalistas she focused on poor households in Managua in the 1990s, when government programs to help these were rolled back. Babb concluded that the consequences were very different for men and women. Women were forced back to the household, to take care of children and family and were actively discouraged from participating in the wage labor workforce. She showed how some women are able to fight back. She compared the situation with that of other post-revolutionary regimes. Generally, the *International Monetary Fund* (IMF) instituted the same program as imposed on many other Latin American countries, but with harsher consequences for the general population (Babb 2004, 35-36). Many of those who worked in the public sector saw themselves forced to work in the informal economy. That oftentimes meant setting up a store in their home, especially for women who stayed at home to watch the children (Babb 2004, 36). Simultaneously, what Babb (2004, 36) called 'still mobilized mass-organizations,' groups she obviously believed would fade away with time, managed to win concessions in negotiations with the Liberal governments. In this connection Babb (2004, 37) focused on how the Sandinista women's organization *Asociación de Mujeres Nicaragüenes Luisa Amanda Espinoza* (AMN-

LAE) lost support from some sectors, and how a new penal code in 1992 obliged women who were pregnant due to rape, to give birth to the child, and outlawed homosexuality. Babb described a dysfunctional society and combined it with discourses on development and how the fundamental premise under the Nicaraguan discourse at the time was that the country was in pain. Those from poor households related this much more to their own lives than an abstract entity (Babb 2004, 175–202). As she saw it, non-partidarian movements were about to start growing out of the rubble of neoliberalism, including, peace, environmental and indigenous organizations in what she saw as an "altered national context [that] supported more pluralist approaches" (Babb 2004, 203–239).

This seems similar to what Amin (1990) thought, when he argued that the goal of national independence as a common theme which could be used to gain political support throughout the third world were exhausted by 1990. He also believed a lot of the subsequent movements would treat single issues, again much in line with Babb (2004). According to Amin (1990) this was not so much an expression of the end of more fundamental criticisms of the system, but it meant that national liberation in itself was not a goal that would reach far enough for the masses. These new movements would still seek to confront capitalism and the notion of exploitation, yet they would do so in more isolated cases. Given this perspective, the time of party politics did not come completely to an end, but had to be readjusted to the new subjectively experienced necessities of the people of the south.

The study of health care continued from the Sandinista period, though rather than looking at the build-up of the health care system, the focus was on its break-down, looking at such things as the abolition of 'therapeutic abortion' mentioned above and the preparations to remove it (McNaughton, Blandon, and Altamirano 2002; McNaughton, Mitchell, and Blandon 2004). Another focus of study was the study of land rights following the revolution (Abu-Lughod 2000; Everingham 2001). Everingham (2001) wrote on changing property rights in Nicaragua after the electoral defeat in 1990. In his perspective, the privatization of lands after 1990 were done in a way that favored certain influential groups. Further, this made land disputes in the following years inevitable, made the poor even poorer and prevented the full establishment of democracy (Everingham 2001, 34). He looked at the specifics of Nicaraguan law and the history of the various decrees that ordered the expropriation of land in the 1980s (Everingham 2001, 63–65). His conclusion, possibly inspired by a politically

Liberal viewpoint, was that the heads of states and international political experts were right in arguing that the level of uncertainty of property held, was the most important factor in determining the overall level of poverty of peasants within a society and which made Nicaragua stand out particularly badly (Everingham 2001, 83–84).

Similar studies about various aspects of the perceived break-down of society were written by several anthropologists: Rodgers (2008) about the horrific lives of the members of street gangs of Managua, Metoyer (2000) focusing on women's organizations, Quesada (1998) focusing on embodidness, Field (1998) focusing on the rebirth of indigenous identities in western Nicaragua, Tatar (2005) who claims to show that the FSLN never really represented the insurrectionist movement of 1978/79 and Lundgren (2000) who looked at those who received professional education during the Sandinista regime and how they negotiated their previous alignment with the FSLN in times of neoliberalism when these were frowned upon.

The anthropological study of the Miskito could be conducted somewhat apart from this national context, possibly due to the physical distance from Managua, language differences and that Sandinismo was not very popular in the 1980s among the Miskitos. Jamieson (2002) wrote about wealth differences in a little village at the Laguna Perla and the importance of ownership of the equipment to catch sea bob in determining such differences in the early 1990s. In his analysis he did not mention the change of government in 1990 or the importance existence of the Sandinista movement had for such class relations. This would have been unthinkable had the study been conducted on the Nicaraguan west coast.

Still relevant?

I prepared myself for life in Nicaragua by reading several of the studies from before 2007. I was aware that some changes had taken place, and that I would not find the country in a process of neoliberal self-destruction. Yet given that most of these studies were conducted only a few years in the past, I expected them to still be more or less relevant. I quickly noticed that gigantic changes had taken place. There was not the plethora of different independent social movements Amin (1990); Babb (2004) had predicted. Although a rather large number of formally independent theme based organizations existed, I understood early on they were always related to party politics. The connections were not always immediately obvious, and many times the 'political line' was to deny any party connection. Other times the connection was concealed even from some of the lower level participants. Yet, it could always be found if one was persistent enough. Most organizations that declared themselves independent were linked to the FSLN. I also found such groups connected to the *Partido de Resistencia Nicaragüense* (PRN, the party of the former Contras) and the MRS (see also — Power through combining parliamentary and activist work, p. 170).

Relations between Miskitos and Sandinistas had changed markedly from the 1980s, with Sandinistas gaining much more support on the east coast than previously. I went to the east coast only once, a trip during which I was able to interview representatives of the FSLN in Laguna Perla and Bluefields who were in power. The trip gave me more insight into the current state of relations as it helped my formation of a general analysis of the current Sandinista scheme. Among other things, the FSLN representatives in Laguna Perla now believe that their main problem of gaining local support is with mestizos as the party has gotten an image of being the party of indigenous and Miskito in this area.

The situation in land rights was quite different from what researchers encountered just a few years earlier in that some land was again given out, although not on the same scale as in the 1980s. And it still involved much confusion about who is actually to be seen as the owner of any property due to changing property rights and interpretations of laws by the various governments. Political deals made around the handing over of power by the Sandinistas to Chamorro were still being used to explain the repartition of land by the government. As a historical background, studies on land rights are highly informative and relevant in understanding today's situation. Different from the descriptions of Everingham of the time of Liberal governments, the confusion I witnessed, tended to favor the poor rather than the rich land owner during the second Sandinista period.

Sandinista II studies

The second period of Sandinismo, starting in 2006–07, has received less study than in the previous periods. One study that came close is that of Gooren (2010), who was in Nicaragua in 2005–06, before the elections. He has a small section on Nicaragua after the elections, which seems to be mostly based on citations from online sources. Gooren focuses on Ortega Saavedra's election campaign and looks specifically at the religious aspects of it, a field of which I have much less knowledge. The part of his study that focuses on more general aspects of the election are the same ones mentioned by the international media and which in Nicaraguan politics form the propaganda of the MRS: Talking about an alliance between *Partido Liberal Constitucionalista* (PLC) and FSLN known as 'el pacto' to split all positions of power between them since 1998 while leaving out that there have been many other alliances in Nicaraguan politics since then, many of which run counter to this particular alliance (see also — *El pacto*, p. 149), and giving a skewed view on the issue of therapeutic abortion (see also — *Therapeutic abortion*, p. 148).

Other studies go into specifics, such as general health care (Bartoszko 2009; Helgheim 2009). There is a difference in how this is done when compared to studies of the 1980s which generally had a positive and participative undertone. The Bartoszko study has a generally critical undertone in her presentation of the subject matter. She was in Nicaragua in the very early part of the second Sandinista government in 2007. Bartoszko sees a discrepancy between the nationalist Sandinista discourse which promotes the idea of an inclusive society and a health system which, in reality, works with principles that exclude and are based on principles of privileges for certain groups. Helgheim (2009) focuses on the more specific issues concerning the changes in the legal framework of therapeutic abortions in 2006 and especially the Sandinista involvement both in the negotiations forbidding it and later in undermining the prohibition of it.

Bartoszko also writes about adult education and the renewed literacy program that was very important to the Sandinista administration in 2007–09 (Pytko 2008; Bartoszko 2010). Bartoszko argues that while literacy programs are offered by the new Sandinista administration just as they were in the 1980s, they are not seen as being of any concrete value to those who receive them. Programs, filling more immediate needs are seen, not as being complementary to the literacy campaign, but rather as opposites. The point of learning how to read and write is lost for many of those who cannot capitalize on this knowledge in the form of an actual job.

The tradition of political studies continues in the form of studies of the CPCs (Bochove 2008; Pallmeyer 2009). Bochove (2008) was present at several meetings of the CPCs of León and compares it with other instruments of direct democracy that were created in the years preceding the Sandinista takeover and similar institutions in Bolivia. His objective is to see whether they do in fact bring more direct democracy to the local and municipal levels of Nicaraguan government. He concludes they do in fact change one aspect by excluding foreign organizations from participating in the structures the way previous organizations had allowed. At the same time, they are more directly connected to only one party (the FSLN), and the fact that at departamento level they are organized by FSLN personnel, makes them less democratic to Bochove (2008, 47–48)

All of these studies helped me, especially their investigative parts and field material. I met Bochove at a CPC conference in León in spring 2008 and although I have been present at a number of different CPC meetings, I had not compared them to other similar institutions. I lived with Helgheim during her stay in León. It was through conversations with Helgheim that I first understood how exactly the Sandinistas undermined the anti-abortion law they passed.

Each of these studies focuses on only one individual program of the new Sandinista government, and not always over a very long period. I hold that it is only when taken in its entirety that certain aspects of incoherence and general patterns of decision structures first show. While Pytko (2008) makes references to an overall Sandinista discourse, this discourse she takes for granted, and the interactions between a particular aspects of policy of the current government and the entirety of Sandinismo are not further analyzed. In all these studies, the historic period and economic positions of Nicaragua are not taken much into account, nor are the formal and informal negotiations with the world beyond the Nicaraguan state. It is as if Nicaragua and the FSLN are free to do whatever they want, disregarding any power structure that goes beyond the nation state.

It is in this area that I choose to locate this study – viewing the Sandinista project or projects, including all its programs, as one general program for social change. The comparison I seek to make with the Sandinista project of the 1980s is less concerned with individual details, such as whether certain government programs have changed names or have slightly different parameters, as much as how the overall logic according to which they are employed, structured and executed has changed. Parts of the Sandinista project go beyond pure parliamentary decisions and presidential decrees, which are largely ignored by the existing literature. In an overall analysis, this part has to be considered.

First Chapter

Recent political history of Nicaragua and the Sandinista movement

In order to understand anything about the Sandinista movement, one has to know something about Nicaraguan history over the past 100 years. This is when the political groups that exist today were formed. During my time in Nicaragua, it was frequently pointed out to me that without knowing this history, I could forget about understanding anything about what goes on today. Such a history can of course be presented in many different ways. The focus I place on it here is the one that is emphasized by most Spanish-speaking Nicaraguans today and it is presented in a way that I believe to be uncontroversial in Nicaragua. Additionally, I have added some points about general political developments on a global scale that may aid in understanding the specifics in Nicaragua.

Before 1920

From the middle of the 19th century up until at least the 1920s, the two main political groups in Nicaragua were Liberals and Conservatives. Most historic characters can be classified as belonging to one of the two groups. Although the terms 'Conservatives' and 'Liberals' originated in European political discourse, one should not mistake them as necessarily meaning the same as what is common in Europe. Until the 1930s, the United States usually favored Conservative leadership in Nicaragua, and intervened militarily several times on the Conservatives' behalf. Liberals and Conservatives were and are political identities that are not always directly linked to

Timeline of Nicaraguan leaders

1893–1909	Liberal President José Santos Zelaya López
1909–26	A series of Conservative and Liberal presidents seldom referred to, in combination with constant interventions by the United States
1926–29	Conservative President Adolfo Díaz[1]/ US Marines
1929–33	Liberal President José María Moncada Tapia / US Marines
1933–36	Liberal President Juan Bautista Sacasa / Director of the *Guardia Nacional* (GN), Anastasio Somoza García
1936–56	Dictator Anastasio Somoza García[2]
1956–63	Dictator Luis Anastasio Somoza Debayle[2]
1963–79	Dictator Anastasio Somoza Debayle[2]
1979–80	Five-person Junta of National Reconstruction: José Daniel Ortega Saavedra (FSLN), Sergio Ramírez Mercado (FSLN), Moisés Hassan Morales (FSLN), Violeta Barrios Torres de Chamorro, Alfonso Robelo
1980–81	Five-person Junta of National Reconstruction: Ortega Saavedra (FSLN), Ramírez Mercado (FSLN), Hassan Morales (FSLN), Arturo Cruz (Conservative), Rafael Córdova Rivas (Conservative)
1981–85	Three-person Junta of National Reconstruction: Ortega Saavedra, coordinator (FSLN), Ramírez (FSLN), Rivas (Conservative)
1985–90	FSLN President Ortega Saavedra
1990–97	UNO President Barrios Torres de Chamorro[3]
1997–2002	Liberal President José Arnoldo Alemán Lacayo
2002–07	Liberal President Enrique José Bolaños Geyer
2007–	FSLN President Ortega Saavedra

[1] Although Díaz called himself president, the legitimacy of his presidency is disputed.

[2] The official positions of the Somozas vary, as they sometimes controlled the country as presidents and at other times as leaders of the *Guardia Nacional* (GN).

[3] *Unidad Nicaragüense Opositora* (UNO).

Sources: Ministerio de Educación (2011); Pozas (1988, 58)

Events and figures often referred to in Nicaraguan history

1856	Andrés Castro Estrada threw stones at invaders from the United States
1912	General Benjamín Francisco Zeledón Rodríguez fought US troops occupying Nicaraguan territory
1923–25	Augusto Nicolás Calderón Sandino worked in oil sector of Mexico
1926–27	Calderón Sandino and his rebel army teamed with Liberals to fight Conservative and US forces
1927–34	Calderón Sandino and his rebel army fought US forces by themselves
1934	Calderón Sandino was killed during peace talks with the Director of the *Guardia Nacional* (GN) Anastasio Somoza García
1956	Liberal Rigoberto López Pérez killed by Dictator Anastasio Somoza García
1959	León students massacred during rally
1961	Leftist FSLN founded under the name *Frente de Liberación Nacional* (FLN)
1963	FLN name changed to FSLN
1975	FSLN split into three ideological factions
1976	FSLN founder Carlos Fonseca Amador killed
1979	FSLN reunited and triumph of Revolutionary Insurrection
1979–90	FSLN control of Nicaraguan state and society
1990–2007	Known as 'the 16 years of neoliberalism'
2000	FSLN regained position of mayor of Managua
2007–	FSLN reelected to state power

Sources: Ejército de Nicaragua (2009); Cuenca (1992); Evans (2007); Bahen and Hernández (2007); Barbosa (2005); Valenta (1985); Equipo Correo (2010); Palmer (1988); Ministerio de Educación (2011); Equipo Envío (1990); Equipo Envío Nitlápan (2006a, 2006b)

social class. Until 1979, the presidency went back and forth between these two groups. Liberals and Conservatives still exist in Nicaragua, although the group of Liberals has fractured into several parties in recent years, all of which claim general adherence to the traditions of the historical Liberal movement.

The first notable person commemorated today for being historically significant is Nicaraguan soldier Andrés Castro Estrada, who fought filibuster invaders from the United States in 1856 by throwing stones at them. He is seldom described as connected with one of the political groups, although he most likely was Conservative. The action he is remembered for is throwing a stone at one of the US Americans during a battle. The second person remembered today is Liberal President José Santos Zelaya López who governed Nicaragua between 1893 and 1909 and was responsible for the construction of a railway and for drafting a constitution that gave women the right to abortion in the case of a pregnant woman's life being in danger. Generally, he promoted a program of modernizing Nicaraguan production. The third person often remembered today is the renegade general and Liberal politician Benjamín Francisco Zeledón Rodríguez, who in 1912 fought against the US troops occupying Nicaragua (Ejército de Nicaragua 2009).

Augusto Nicolás Calderón Sandino

Augusto Nicolás Calderón Sandino[1], the Nicaraguan who the Sandinista movement was later named after, worked in the Mexican oil sector in the state of Veracruz for 3 years. In 1927 he returned to Nicaragua. Nicaragua was invaded several times by US Marines after the end of the Zelaya López presidency, and in 1927 the country was again occupied by the United States, which intervened in an electoral issue between Liberals and Conservatives, favoring the Conservatives (Jansen 2004).

Calderón Sandino founded a small army, which joined the Liberals in

---

1. Calderón Sandino was born 'Augusto Nicolás Calderón' because his father did not recognize him as his son until adolescence. When his father did recognize him (socially speaking), he started signing his name as 'Augusto C. Sandino,' although, in legal terms, his status in relation to his father had not changed. He has later been referred to as 'Augusto César Sandino,' whereby it is unclear whether he himself started using that name around 1927, or whether it was just assumed that the initial 'C' stood for César, given the historical precedent of 'Augusto César' in the Roman empire (Sánchez 2007).

Left, Augusto Nicolás Calderón Sandino, standing in the center, on his way to Mexico, where he found work and political support in the 1920s. *Right*, some decades later, Anastasio Somoza Debayle (*left*) and his brother Luis Anastasio Somoza Debayle (*right*) ruled the country. Calderón Sandino was assassinated by their father in 1934. *Photos: Wikimedia*

a struggle against Conservative forces and US Marines (Ejército de Nicaragua 2009, 36). In 1928 the Liberals decided to sign a peace treaty with US forces and Conservatives, which let the Conservatives keep the presidency and forced both sides to disarm. Calderón Sandino refused to abide by the treaty. He and his army continued fighting against the Conservative regime and the US American presence in Nicaragua. Their stated goal was to make every US soldier leave the country (Jansen 2004). Calderón Sandino and his men claimed their struggle was 'anti-imperialist' and that they fought for 'nations' right of self-determination.' The group consisted largely of peasants, and some of its leaders were illiterate, which led to many difficulties in debates on theoretical issues (Fonseca Amador 1969, 30). It was not easy to determine whether Calderón Sandino and his group shared an overall ideology (Jansen 2004; Fonseca Amador 1969).

Somoza

The United States left Nicaragua in 1933, after training an army of Nicaraguans called the *Guardia Nacional* (GN) during its last year of occupation. At its head the United States put the Nicaraguan General Anastasio 'Tacho' Somoza García. The stated plan of the United States was for the GN to control uprisings against the constitutional order (Ejército de Nicaragua 2009, 35). Calderón Sandino was assassinated by Somoza García's men during peace talks between the GN and Calderón Sandino in 1934, while the terms for the decommissioning of Calderón Sandino's group were being discussed. Calderón Sandino's associates were thereafter strongly suppressed. The revolutionary movement died down for several years, and 40 years of dictatorship commenced (Palmer 1988, 92–94).

Somoza García utilized the GN to establish himself as dictator, and he formally took over the presidency for the first time in 1936. He and his two sons ruled Nicaragua until 1979, although formal sham elections were held throughout the period of the dictatorship. Most of the time a Somoza was officially president, with a few minor interruptions. Throughout this period, one of the Somozas controlled the armed forces. This era is now referred to as the period of 'Somocismo.' Somoza García acted as dictator of Nicaragua until 1956, when he was assassinated. His first son, Luis Anastasio Somoza Debayle, was in charge until 1967. His second son, Anastasio 'Tachito' Somoza Debayle, ruled Nicaragua until 1979 (Ministerio de Educación 2011).

The Somoza dictatorship was brutal. It included torture and execution by firing squad of political opposition groups. It was also riddled with contradictions, as the Somoza government regularly broke the laws it created whenever it seemed the convenient way to secure dominance (Borge Martínez 1980). Some controversy exists today as to whether it was really the wish of the United States to establish a dictatorship during the early Somoza years. The opposing argument is that the majority of US policies toward Nicaragua pointed to reestablishing democracy until 1948. Washington even cut off diplomatic relations with Nicaragua for an entire year: from 1933 to 1944 US-embassy personnel were told not to influence Nicaraguan politics. From 1948 on, however, the United States did not complain about Somoza, and shifted its policy to supporting him openly (Clark 1992).

The organization of resistance against Somoza

Towards the end of the period of Somoza García, the struggle against the dictatorship commenced. Somoza García was shot and killed by the Nicaraguan poet Rigoberto López Pérez of the dissident Liberal party, *Partido Liberal Independiente* (PLI), in 1956 in an attempt to end the dictatorship (Evans 2007). Another often-mentioned part of the resistance against Somoza in the early years was a student protest march in León on 23 July 1959. The students were protesting a 'massacre' of another protest organized by Conservative students which had happened just prior to that. The León protest march was attacked by the GN, leading to four deaths among the students (Manzanares Calero 2002; Barbosa 2005).

The Soviet Union initially opposed revolutionary attempts in nonindustrial societies. Its line during the *Second World War* (WWII) was not to attack Latin American governments which cooperated with the United States and the struggle against Nazi Germany. This profoundly influenced the principles of the *Partido Socialista Nicaragüense* (PSN) when it was founded in 1944 (Fonseca Amador 1969, 31). The most famous Somoza-era revolutionary, Carlos Fonseca Amador, was originally a member of the PSN. After a visit to Cuba from 1955 to 1956, where he allegedly learned about guerrilla tactics and studied anti-imperialism and Calderón Sandino, he and his contemporary revolutionaries decided to break with the doctrine of nonaggression, and an organized struggle against Somoza formed (Palmer 1988, 94–95).

In 1961 Fonseca Amador and other students founded the party which later became the *Frente Sandinista de Liberación Nacional* (FSLN). Their stated goal was overthrowing the Somoza dictatorship. During the first two years of its existence, the party was known as the *Frente de Liberación Nacional* (FLN) (Valenta 1985, 165). The idea to include the name of Calderón Sandino in the name of the FSLN in 1963 allegedly came from Fonseca Amador (Alegría and Flakoll 2004, 146). Tomás Borge Martínez, Interior Minister during the 1980s and one of the founding members of the FSLN, claims the image of Calderón Sandino was a natural historic reference point for any revolutionary group (Tomás Borge Martínez, cited in Alegría and Flakoll 2004, 148) with a strategy like that of the FSLN.

The FSLN divided into three tendencies

The FSLN fought an 18-year continued struggle, largely underground, until it took over state power in 1979. Fonseca Amador functioned as the chief ideologue of the party for most of that time, with an ideology of combining peasants' and workers' struggles. Fonseca Amador advocated the unity of opposition to Somoza among radicals and Liberals. In some texts Fonseca Amador (1969) refers to himself as a Marxist and claims the FSLN represented a Marxist line without the Marxist-Leninist baggage associated with the PSN.

The FSLN at first tried to organize using Ernesto 'Che' Guevara's so-called *foco-strategy*. Instead of starting by organizing large amounts of people among the urban proletariat, the discontented and alienated peasant farmers made for an easy breeding ground of ideologically-clear revolutionaries, and once having grown in the countryside to a level where small

A portrait of Carlos Fonseca Amador is used on a 2004 poster commemorating 25 years since the triumph of the Sandinista revolution. *Source: FSLN*

and mobile insurrectionist cells could attack the GN in several strategically important points, organizing an urban insurrection would be easy (Childs 1995, 597). In the following years 1963–67, the strategy did not work very well and many Sandinistas were killed. In most countries in Latin America, similar movements were wiped out by military forces supported by the United States, but the FSLN managed to survive (Palmer 1988, 97).

In the last years before the 1979 insurrection, the strategies and ideologies within the FSLN diversified as more people joined (Miranda, Ortega Saavedra, and Gorman 1979; Perez 1992). Between October 1975 and March 1979, the party consisted of three ideological tendencies or wings, each of which had slightly different ideas about what revolutionaries should do under the given circumstances (Equipo Correo 2010, 13):

- The *Guerra Popular Prolongada* (GPP) tendency, to which Fonseca Amador belonged, believed a prolonged struggle in the mountains in combination with labor struggle in the cities would be the only way to succeed, and that peasants formed an essential part of any revolutionary movement. It represented the views most closely resembling the initial ideology of the party.

- The Marxist-orthodox *Tendencia Proletaria* (TP) argued that, in the decades after WWII, Nicaragua had developed capitalism and with it an urban proletariat had grown. They believed now was the time to focus on the classic Marxist strategy of organizing the urban proletariat, and they mainly aimed their organizing at this sector of society.

- The third tendency, the *Tendencia Tercerista* (TT) to which current President José Daniel Ortega Saavedra belonged, was focused on the need for immediate action. It defended the practice of insurrection in the countryside and the city simultaneously – as it had already been established. But it did so without combining it with most of the ideological considerations the other two tendencies entertained (Miranda, Ortega Saavedra, and Gorman 1979; Perez 1992, 115–116).

An interview with Ortega Saavedra, half a year before the takeover of power in early 1979, reveals how fragile the coalition within the FSLN was at the time. Ortega Saavedra argued in the interview that the TP was just a small group of academics, quite distant from the initial ideas of the FSLN, and although they were close to the centers of production, they spent most of their time propagandizing and not organizing. About the GPP, Ortega Saavedra said, they were isolated in the mountains, and they did not have real influence either. According to Ortega Saavedra, the unity of the FSLN at the time derived from common actions rather than commonality in ideology. Simultaneously he explained that the TP was complaining about insurrectionist actions organized by the TT, but he believed they would accept them bit by bit. During the entire period of their existence, 1974/75–79, members of all three tendencies tried to come up with a unifying strategy (Miranda, Ortega Saavedra, and Gorman 1979, 115).

In the 1986 published version of *Carlos, el amanecer ya no es una tentación / Carlos, now the dawn's no fond illusion,* which Borge Martínez originally wrote while incarcerated in 1976, the author showed that differences in strategic outlook made up the disagreement between the TP and the GPP. Disagreements also existed between the leading figures of the GPP. Fonseca Amador stated during internal meetings that the industrial working class would be destined to lead a revolution if it was to be victorious, but that the peasant class should not be discounted due to their prevalence in countries such as Nicaragua (Fonseca Amador, cited in Borge Martínez 1976, 39–41). Fonseca Amador's statement could just as well have been made by a member of the TP and was controversial. This gives some idea about the broadness of the scope of the tendencies.

In the later years of the Somoza regime, opposition to Somoza also grew among some bourgeois sectors of society. Pedro Joaquín Chamorro, editor of the newspaper *La Prensa*, was arrested together with 27 other civil leaders for conspiring against the Somoza government after calling the 1974 elections fraudulent (Tijerino 2008, 296). On the 15 December 1974, Chamorro started organizing a group opposing Somoza. The group involved Socialists, Liberals and Conservatives. They agreed on their opposition to Somoza, but not all of them were prepared for insurrection from the bourgeois part of society. Chamorro was killed by Somoza's forces in 1978 (Tijerino 2008, 296–299). The alliance with oppositional parts of the bourgeoisie was also part of Ortega Saavedra's program. Different from some of the pro-capitalist modernization Marxists, this alliance was to be 'tactical and temporary.' Ortega Saavedra was asked in an interview how one could avoid that the United States would support one's capitalist alliance partner, who with that help then could take control entirely over the process. Ortega Saavedra answered, that the answer was to ally one-

Sandinistas enter Managua on top of a bus in 1979. After an insurrection that lasted all of 1978 and for the first half of 1979, the Sandinistas took control of the country as dictator Anastasio Somoza Debayle fled. Photo: Marcelo Montecino

self with capitalists, but not with the traditional capitalist parties. Henry Ruiz, speaking for the GPP agreed, but believed a prolonged struggle would make it in the interest of the bourgeoisie to do away with "Somoza ..., a bastion of imperialism"—and set the interests of the national bourgeoisie against those of imperialism (Miranda, Ortega Saavedra, and Gorman 1979, 117–118).

In March 1979, a conference was held in Havana, Cuba, in which the three tendencies reunited (Equipo Correo 2010). At this time the FSLN was given a structure of nine *comandantes,* who formed a national directory in which each of the tendencies was represented with three people. With that step taken, the tendencies officially ceased to exist. The composition of the national directory remained the same until the 1990s (Perez 1992, 117).

The Sandinista years 1979–90

In July 1979, after an 18 month insurrection against the dictatorship of Somoza Debayle (Leogrande 1996, 329), Somoza Debayle fled and the Sandinistas took charge. The 1980s were, before the taking of power by the

Ortega Saavedra government in 2006, the only time in the Sandinista movement's history in which it held power at a national level and its ideology converted into the ideology promoted by the state. The Sandinista regime was led by a junta rather than a democratic-representative government during the first five years. This junta was made up of three FSLN representatives and initially two bourgeois anti-Somocistas. It established a (politically) left-leaning, but not fundamentalist, power base (Pozas 1988, 58).

Foreign Involvement

Initially, Sandinista leaders tried to forge ties to the US administration in order to gain access to funding. The United States under the rule of President James Earl Carter initially cooperated to a very limited extend, while pressuring its Western European allies into not cooperating with or supporting the Nicaraguan government. US legislators compared the Sandinistas in Nicaragua to the Communist Party in Cuba to explain why they could not support Nicaragua under a Sandinista-led government (Berrios 1985, 112). From a US American perspective, the two cases were somewhat similar: Just as in Cuba, the revolutionaries initially were not against the United States or opposed to capitalism, but non-acceptance and lack of assistance from the United States led to their radicalization. Carter's limited initial support may be seen as a way of trying to avoid a Cuban-type situation (Leogrande 1996, 330).

Under President Ronald Reagan, the United States' position towards Nicaragua became increasingly negative. From 1981 to 1990, the United States more or less openly tried to overthrow the Sandinista regime. The United States funded so-called 'Contras' who maintained a civil war against the Sandinistas during much of the 1980s. Those involved with the Contras often claim the FSLN established a dictatorship in 1979 (Hüeck 2006, 9). Reagan's support for the Contras ultimately culminated in the Iran-Contra affair, in which the President circumvented legislation designed to hinder him from financing the Contras. This prohibition was put into place by the *US House of Representatives* (USHR) in 1984 (Leogrande 1996, 329–338).

Starting in the late 1960s, the Soviet Union invited Latin America to cooperate with the *Council of Mutual Economic Assistance* (CMEA), the economic network binding Soviet-allied countries together. This allowed for countries receiving aid through CMEA to gain greater economic indepen-

A mural in León depicts the conflict of the 1980s – the *Central Intelligence Agency* (CIA) is a snake that destroys the Sandinista literacy program.

Solidarity posters from the *Deutsche Demokratische Republik* (DDR, German Democratic Republic). *Source: DDR Archiv*

dence from the United States (Berrios 1985, 111). The Soviet Union was not officially involved in the Nicaraguan revolution, and only established official contact with the FSLN shortly after the triumph of the revolution.

During the Somoza dictatorship until July 1979, Nicaragua and the Soviet Union did not entertain political or economic relations. Diplomatic ties were established on 18 October 1979. Soviet embassy personnel did not arrive before January 1980. In March 1980, the Sandinista leaders went to Moscow for the first time and signed cultural, technical and economic agreements with the Soviet Union, followed by similar agreements with Bulgaria, Czechoslovakia, and the *Deutsche Demokratische Republik* (DDR, German Democratic Republic) (Berrios 1985, 112). The agreements were in trade and interpersonal exchange, which gave university scholarships to Nicaraguans to study abroad and allowed for professional experts to be sent to Nicaragua from Eastern Europe. This relationship lasted until the electoral defeat of the FSLN in 1990.

The FSLN structure

From working as a rather small organization in the mid 1970s, the FSLN quickly changed its operational model into that of a larger political party with significant political power.

The modern concept of political parties first came into being in the 1800s. Among socialist and social democratic parties, two basic concepts evolved: Mass parties, which try to grow membership as much as possible, and small Leninist Vanguard models. Largely, mass parties resemble trade unions in their membership and are made up of broad parts of the working population. These parties mostly accept quite different views

Left, Sandinistas like José Daniel Ortega Saavedra risk their lives in a training camp in 1978. *Right,* Ortega Saavedra rules the country as a member of the Junta of National Reconstruction in 1979. The Sandinistas went from being a small rebel group to a state-controlling political party in very little time. Also in photo on right, Sergio Ramírez Mercado stands behind Ortega Saavedra. Ramírez Mercado was also a member of the Junta, was vice president 1985–90, and in 1995 co-founded the opposition party *Movimiento Renovador Sandinista* (MRS). Photos: Pedro Meyer

among their members even on their core issues. The life of the majority of the members of these parties is not exclusively centered around party membership. Parties following the Leninist vanguard party model try to only gather the ideologically most schooled and trained persons within the party. Other supporters are not permitted full membership status. The process for joining a party operating according to the Leninist model is complicated, and may involve several months or even years of probation, before membership status is obtained (Lenin 1902, chapter 4).

The ruling parties in the Soviet allied countries and small communist parties in countries that were allies of the United States up until the dissolution of the Soviet Union, all tried to follow the vanguard party in theory, while Social democratic parties in the west during this period followed the mass party model. Some East European ruling parties ended up having a membership in the millions and were therefore mass parties and vanguard parties at the same time.

The FSLN was structured using elements of both models, similar to how revolutionaries in El Salvador organized at the time (Harris 1988, 24), and similar to the revolutionary parties in Cuba and Grenada during the insurrection period of the revolution. The FSLN operated according to a relatively open membership model before taking state power (Harris 1988, 24). After the insurrection, the FSLN turned to a vanguard party model with very limited possibilities of joining the party. The party was made up of a self-selected and disciplined elite of revolutionary cadres/members. Many key positions in the state were controlled by cadres of the party. This vanguard party was augmented by a network of mass organizations linked to the revolution. The *Unión Nacional de Agricultores y Ganaderos*

A common sight in Nicaragua 1989: Celebrations of the 10 year anniversary of the revolution. Photo: Tiare Scott

(UNAG) and the *Asociación de Trabajadores del Campo* (ATC) organized larger groups of the population, and were two of the main organizations which fulfilled this role (Harris 1988, 24).

The need to include democratic rights in socialist, anti-imperialist struggles received a lot of attention across Latin America in the 1970s and 1980s (Santos 1977, 188) after being absent for many decades (Harris 1988, 18–19). Discussion on how to set up a political party focused on keeping internal political structures democratic (Lowy, Michael and Denner, Arthur 1987, 460–462). An essential part in what set Nicaragua apart from other Soviet-allied countries[2] was the government's position on the issue of democracy. The Sandinistas did not forbid opposition parties, and free elections were held in 1984 and 1990. The FSLN had a goal of always permitting oppositional parties, while expecting these to eventually whither away, as they believed they would no longer fulfill a social purpose Borge Martínez (1980, 96–97).

---

2. Nicaragua officially formed part of the nonaligned bloc of countries, and Ortega Saavedra (1979, 44) described it as a misunderstanding that the country would form part of the Soviet bloc. Nevertheless, connections with the Soviet Union were close enough for outside observers to describe the country as Soviet-allied.

Popular participation and direct democracy

After taking power, besides focusing on politics of social justice, Sandinistas focused on politics of popular participation, which they thought essential in the creation of a new type of society (Ortega Saavedra 1979). Besides the Sandinista mass organizations, an institution of popular participation was created in the 1980s, the network of the *Comités de Defensa Sandinista* (CDSs). The CDSs were a network of neighborhood committees spanning the entire country and they involved around 500,000 people. It mirrored a similar Cuban institution employed since the 1970s with the stated goal of preventing bureaucratization of the state (Harris 1988, 22). The CDSs were organized as an institution of direct democracy, with the members at the base not representing anyone other than themselves. Everybody was allowed to participate voluntary. The CDSs were represented in the *Consejo de Estado* and integrated into the dealings of the government at ministerial level through 'coordinating committees' (Irvin 1982, 41).

The FSLN electoral defeat in 1990

In 1990, national elections were held and the FSLN was voted out of power. The elections were part of a peace agreement with some of the groups of Nicaraguans who fought militarily against the Sandinistas during the 1980s. Violeta Barrios Torres de Chamorro, won the presidency as a leader of a coalition called the *Unidad Nicaragüense Opositora* (UNO) which included 2 left-wing groups, and 12 right-wing parties from Conservative and Liberal origins, several of which at some level had been cooperating since the mid-1980s, but at all times fought between themselves. The campaign of Barrios Torres de Chamorro was strongly supported by the United States and surprisingly won with 55% compared to Ortega Saavedra's 41%. Most Sandinistas seem to have thought that electoral defeat was impossible at that stage. With that, the end of the war was a certainty and 26 June 1990 the Contras officially ended their demobilization (FRD 1993).

The government change in Nicaragua in 1990 was one of several cases in which the United States successfully overthrew a socialist government. Access to agricultural production and direct foreign investments under the Sandinistas may have constituted reasons for intervention. The Nicaraguan market for products from the United States was fairly limited due to the overall level of poverty. An additional reason for intervention

The Sandinistas lost the presidential elections of February 1990 to the Unidad Nicaragüense Opositora (UNO), a coalition group of 14 different parties of both right and left. One main promise of the election campaign of the opposition was that they could bring peace to Nicaragua (FRD 1993). Photo: UN Photo by Steen Johansen

may have been the fear of a Sandinista-like ideology spreading to neighboring Central American republics, in which revolutionary movements formed simultaneously with the founding of the FSLN in Nicaragua. This could have an effect on Mexican politics, and with time, the Soviet Union could possible have been able to build an alternative to the *Panama Canal* through Nicaraguan territory. This will always remain mere speculation, as long as files on the analysis by the United States of the Sandinistas are inaccessible.

In the early 1990s socialist regimes in Eastern Europe were not replaced by US allied puppet dictatorships with orders originating directly in Washington, the way United States historically had done. The countries were turned into allies by integrating the country's leaders with the internationalized global elite. Elitist and liberal, but democratic regimes were put in place and formal democratic state apparatuses established. Extensive ideological rhetoric was employed on the popular classes to change their aspirations and dreams to be in line with that of western countries. In the western hemisphere the same strategy was used on both

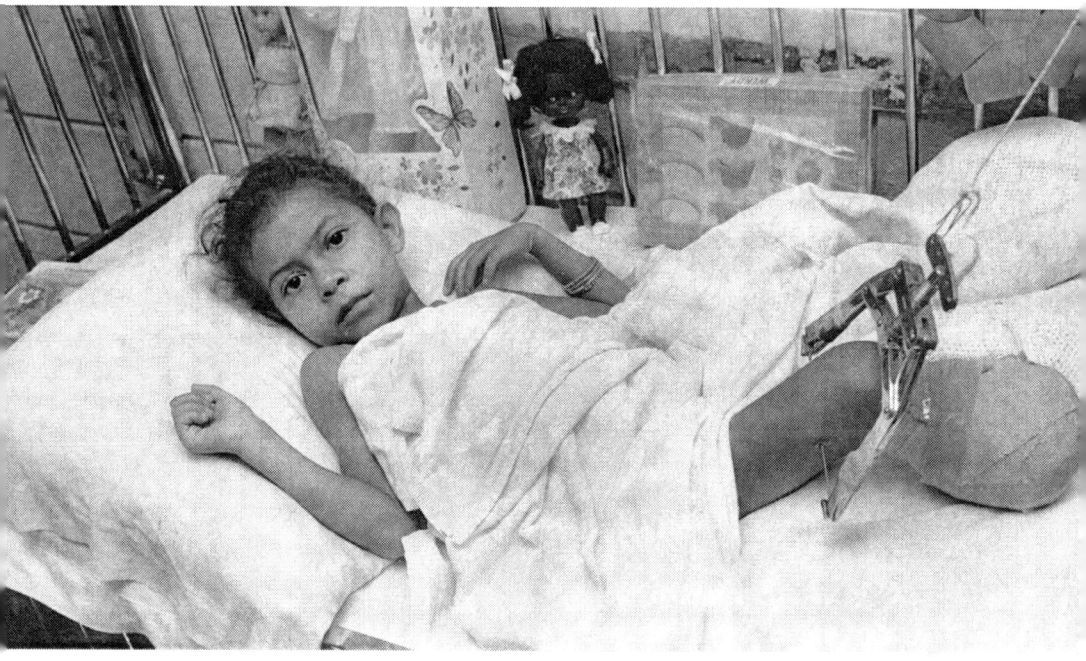

Elda Uri Sanchez, age 7, was the victim of a Contra placed mine in road near Pantasma, Jinotega on 20 October–November 1986. The war against the Contras grew increasingly unpopular during the 1980s, and the prospect of ending it by voting for the opposition is often mentioned as the main factor that made people decided not to vote for the Sandinistas in 1990. *Photo: Witness for Peace*

Nicaragua and Haiti. The United States seems to have sought to control these countries through obtaining hegemony in civil society (Robinson 1996, 642–643).

The Sandinistas negotiated a treaty with President Barrios Torres de Chamorro to keep the leader of the army, Humberto Ortega, for half her governing period, until 1993. Barrios Torres de Chamorro was only able to govern because she made deals with the Sandinistas. She started to privatize many services and abolished the Nicaraguan railway system. The next president, José Arnoldo Alemán Lacayo (1997–2002), was very anti-Sandinista. It is said he required public employees to enroll in his *Partido Liberal Constitucionalista* (PLC). The President of the United States, Bill Clinton, suspended aid to Nicaragua after a hurricane during the Alemán Lacayo years, when it was discovered the aid never reached its final destination. President Enrique José Bolaños Geyer (2002–07) was vice-president under Alemán Lacayo, but once he took over as president, Bolaños Geyer charged Alemán Lacayo with fraud. The FSLN at first helped Bolaños Geyer remove Alemán Lacayo's immunity, but then once the PLC split over the issue and Alemán Lacayo was in prison, switched back and forth between Alemán Lacayo and Bolaños Geyer, voting with the party of either one,

After the opposition won the elections of February, in March 1990 the *United Nations Security Council* (UNSC) voted to send armed personnel to aid the demobilization efforts of the Nicaraguan Contras (UN 1990). By 26 June 1990, the demobilization had officially been completed (FRD 1993). *Photo: UN Photo by Steen Johansen*

depending on the issue (Ministerio de Educación 2011).

At some point in the 1990s, as a product of the Sandinistas trying different strategies to continue to exert power, it seems the Sandinista movement grew into a more diversified group with several individuals and subgroups each coordinating their own projects independently of the FSLN leadership. In a 1999 interview, Ortega Saavedra described the party as looking like an 'anarchist party' – apparently meaning that it was full of highly studied but not always agreeing activists who now ran their various projects relatively independently. He admitted the 'marked contradictions' of class in society reflected in the FSLN – some of the FSLN members were now to be counted as part of the ultra rich (Gaynor 1999). I understood what Ortega Saavedra meant after visiting several projects—of land grabbers or groups organizing children's activities—organized by Sandinistas and in the name of Sandinismo, but without the party formally being aware of their existence.

The FSLN as an opposition force

In the years after the FSLN lost power, the concept of the vanguard party was questioned. In 1994, a power struggle between an orthodox pro-

Three different presidents ruled Nicaragua while the Sandinistas were in the opposition (left to right): Violeta Barrios Torres de Chamorro (1990–97), José Arnoldo Alemán Lacayo (1997–2002) and Enrique José Bolaños Geyer
Photo: Wikimedia Photo by Oliquez85, OAS Photo by Roberto Ribeiro, OAS Photo by Juan Manuel Herrera

vanguard faction around Ortega Saavedra won against a faction which claimed they wanted to change the party so it would be a more open, and an electorally oriented party. After Ortega Saavedra won, the opposing faction lost top posts it held in the party newspaper Barricada. Since 1990 the paper operated rather independently of the party (Jones 2002).

The losing faction started a new political party—the *Movimiento Renovador Sandinista* (MRS)—which in theory was to be more open to alliances with other political groups, devoid of vanguard concepts (Smith 1997, 106) and more of a party of the social democratic kind. Most of the FSLN members of the national assembly left the FSLN and joined the MRS. In the next elections in 1996, the FSLN won many more members of the national assembly than the MRS. Other than these few years, the FSLN always held a substantial number of members of the national assembly. These members of the national assembly were essential for finding majorities for each of the three Liberal presidents. Additionally the FSLN continued to hold substantial power in labor unions, and until 1998 in other mass organizations. During this period, the FSLN could theoretically stop orders made by any one of the Liberal presidents. Each one of the Liberal presidents committed to signing a number of political contracts with the FSLN over the years, in order to avoid such interferences (Smith 1997).

In 1998 the FSLN newspaper Barricada closed down, because the government decided not to fund advertisement in it any longer. Government

In early January 2007, María Elena Bustillo (left) and her son show me the poor area where they live in southern León, far away from the rich downtown neighborhoods, a few days before the return of José Daniel Ortega Saavedra to the presidency. Nicaragua had severe problems of poverty and income disparity during the years of Liberal governments and they tell me of their hope that this will come to an end now.

advertisement accounts for 70% of all advertisement in Nicaragua. The state acting as a major advertiser is very common in Central America. All newspapers have experienced a sharp decline since 1990. Between 1994 and 1997, the number of newspapers sold fell from 68 per 1000 inhabitants to 30 per 1000 inhabitants. Much of this was due to overall economic problems. The literacy rate fell from 88% in the 1980s to 66% in 1995. Local companies were drained of capital and could not invest. The few people still reading the advertisements were too poor to buy most products (Kodrich 2008, 63–71).

It is widely reported after losing the elections of 1990, Ortega Saavedra met with all the solidarity groups and told them to continue to help, but to stop sending the help to the government and send it to a net of Sandinista-dominated NGOs, created for that purpose, and to send it to the already existing 'mass organizations.' The NGOs consist mostly of professionals and very seldom do they publicly portray their NGO as being part of the Sandinista movement. The internal communication network between FSLN, Sandinista mass organizations and Sandinista NGOs was frequently mobilized in order to stop the Liberal governments from acting contrary

President José Daniel Ortega Saavedra (right, on top of car) and his wife Rosario Murillo (left of Ortega Saavedra) are on the campaign trail in 2006. Photo: José Garth Medina

to Sandinista ideology. This approach, famously called 'governing from below,' is what the Sandinistas claim to have done during the 16 years of neoliberalism. The ties between FSLN and mass organizations were officially given up in 1998 (Font 2009, 279).

The FSLN electoral victory 2006

In the fall of 2006, the FSLN won the presidential elections for the first time since 1990, and Ortega Saavedra is inaugurated as president on 6 January 2007. He did not win a majority of votes to become president. Only 38.07% voted for Ortega Saavedra according to the official count. That is less than he received in previous elections. In 2001, 42% voted for Ortega Saavedra (2001). The figure for 1996 is 37.75%, and for 1990 40.8%. Each of the national elections of Nicaragua in those elections was won by a Liberal candidate (Equipo Envío 1990; Equipo Envío Nitlápan 1996, 2006a).

Part of the explanation for the electoral victory in 2006 was a combination of a split vote among Liberal voters between the candidates of the *Alianza Liberal Nicaragüense* (ALN, 29%) and the PLC (26.51%) (Consejo Supremo Electoral 2006). The other part was the electoral reform in the 2000. The reform added a special provision that specified in the case of one candidate gaining at least 5% more than the second best scoring candidate, only 35% of the total vote are needed in order to be able to declare victory. Previously, 45% of the total vote were needed to gain the presidency without a second round. The reform was pushed through by a permanent alliance of PLC and FSLN as part of an agreement to split all major posts in the country in-between them. This political maneuver is known as 'el pacto' (La Prensa 2005; Equipo Envío Nitlápan 2006a). Taken together and if the election results of 2006 were not manipulated, the FSLN electoral victory of 2006 was only due to a lack of unity among Liberals and advanced political negotiating on the part of the FSLN and not due to increased popular support of Ortega Saavedra and the FSLN.

Subjective aspects of the history as it is presented

The political history of Nicaragua as presented above is and cannot be complete, as no history can ever be complete. I mention the events I believe most important to the Nicaraguans I spoke to. It is a simplified version, in that most Nicaraguans are able to list a much longer list of historical events that are important to them. Some of the commemoration celebrations are only held locally in a certain village or city. These are mostly left out, partially due to lack of awareness of all and for reasons of space. History does figure prominently in many aspects of Nicaraguan social life and in all the following chapters we will look at this phenomenon more closely.

Second Chapter

The politics of history

In the preceding chapter we looked at some of the highlights of the past century in Nicaragua. In this chapter we will look at how this history is seen by different groups of Nicaraguans. The same event can be seen in several different ways. Other events are focused upon only by one or a few groups. Sometimes it is possible to see the same event as having been caused by either Nicaraguans or non-Nicaraguans. In most cases, the version which emphasizes Nicaraguan historical agency is preferred by all Nicaraguan groups I met, even though they disagree on most of everything else.

I will here give an overview of the discussion about political history and historical agency in Nicaragua. The term 'historical agency' has been used in various ways within the field of anthropology. I use the term in the way Graeber defines it, "the capacity to make history," with history defined as "the record of those actions which are not simply cyclical, repetitive, or inevitable" (Graeber 1996). The understanding employed here is generally looking at agency on the level of the individual. What it means to have 'power' is a bit more complicated. Having historical agency implies power the way it is used in Nicaragua, but also countries or groups (or foreign individuals) can have power without having historical agency in that what they do is not influencing the course of history, but rather makes it stay on its inevitable course. That is what I here choose to call that they act 'mechanically.'

For this chapter, I draw first and foremost upon the general political journalism I undertook, which gave me an insight into how non-Sandinistas tend to explain historic realities, and I conducted interviews with old revolutionary fighters who started the organization 'Amigos,' as they tended to be the most thorough in their explanations of the recent historic realities of Nicaragua.

What parts of Nicaraguan history are important?

While Nicaragua has a colonial past, just as the rest of Latin America, it is the much more recent past that is most important to Nicaraguans. No one group dominates all aspects of social life. Several groups exist, each of which dominates in at least one sphere, with each representing a different account of the past. The importance that is attributed to economic centers within the Nicaraguan history, specifically the United States, has taken on a life of its own which—no matter what Nicaraguan group one chooses to follow—is completely different from any version of history that may have been imported from the United States or Europe.

The revolution is the most important factor in determining the current Nicaraguan situation, the way most Nicaraguans seem to see it. Besides Nicaragua, Mexico and Cuba have a history of successful revolutions on which the state institutions and the populations continue to focus, while the other countries in Northern Latin America do not have such a history (Wilm 2009). Likely that is what has led to some similarities in the understandings of the importance of history. The Nicaraguan revolution is the youngest and consequently more people from the insurrectionist period still live, and Nicaragua experienced more abrupt political changes since the revolutionary beginning than Mexico or Cuba. Also this seems to be a factor for the continuing extensive discussion of history in Nicaragua (Wilm 2010). Also before Sandinismo and the Sandinista revolution, Nicaragua had a long history of having several unconciliatory groups with radically different political goals fight for power. This may constitute an additional factor as to why political-historical discourse is so prevalent.

What makes a lot sense in the case of Nicaragua is to look at how history is employed to differentiate and legitimize different groups. While Nicaraguans are extremely informed about Nicaragua's particular history, the meaning of different events within Nicaraguan history are highly contested, and Nicaraguans are generally very familiar with them and discuss and argue the points. Anyone who has been in Nicaragua in recent years will have noticed this, and the anthropologist Tully (1997, 302) wrote about the practice of discussing history as a central part of Nicaraguan popular culture in the mid-1990s.

It is important to note that this history telling, which largely happens orally, is not about telling myths. Although an apparent 'rebirth' of indigenous identities among the majority of Spanish-speaking Nicaraguans flowered during the 1990s (Field 1998; Tatar 2005), it has not altered the overall standards of what is accepted as valid history among Nicaraguans. Instead of myths of ancient times, the telling of the past in today's Nicaragua generally lives up to the same standards of quality as the western academic discipline of history. My contacts were generally willing to use academic standards for falsification and validation of stories of the past, once they accepted me as a person generally knowledgeable in the area. What is accepted as a believable history seems to be similar or the same as in other parts of the western world, so creating abstract models of what constitutes credible tellings of the past within Nicaraguan society seems to make limited sense.

The following sections give a basic overview of some of the main historical points that are discussed. Even more about the theme of history telling can be found in the following chapters, and should give the reader an idea of the magnitude of this phenomenon.

Political identities in Nicaragua

Individual identities in the Spanish-speaking part of Nicaragua contain a very important political aspect. A typical introduction of a person introducing himself to a group of Nicaraguans he has never met would be: "Hi, I am Jorge, Sandinista and worker." This Jorge need not be a member of one of the Sandinista parties in order to state this. He could be participating in an explicitly Sandinista cooperative or some other organization which is not directly linked to the Sandinista parties. He could also not be member of any group and just voting for one of the Sandinista parties or even not voting at all and just trying to follow what he sees as Sandinista principles in conducting his life. Nevertheless he could claim to be a Sandinista if he feels he is one. The same sentence could also be said by the members of any of the other groups. The identity aspect of belonging to one of the groups is similar to what Adler Lomnitz and Melnick (2000, 82–82) describe as 'party subcultures' in Chile, in that their origins lie in party politics, but that they are somewhat freed from the day to day politics and instead are more about personal identity and a feeling of belonging. The groups in Chile are mostly defined through descriptions of their consumption patterns, dress and speech. One can easily identify similar subcultures in much of Europe, and to a somewhat more limited degree also in the United States of America. Yet as we will see, in Nicaragua belonging to a the group around a political party seems somewhat closer related to current politics.

The two groups with most political influence in Nicaragua are currently the *'Liberals'* (mostly connected with the *Partido Liberal Constitucionalista* (PLC) and the Sandinistas aligned with the party *Frente Sandinista de Liberación Nacional* (FSLN). Two other fairly large groups are Sandinistas aligned with the party *Movimiento Renovador Sandinista* (MRS) and *'Somocistas.'* Somocistas are the only larger group which generally will not speak about themselves as a group. Smaller groups are the *'Conservatives'* and those affiliated with the *'Contras'* (from 'contra-revolutionaries'), who fought against the Sandinistas in the 1980s and who now tend to use the term *Resistencia* to describe themselves rather than Contras, which still is used by other Nicaraguans to describe them. In addition, countless tiny groups of people, mostly without formal organization, cross all of the above categories in very local ways.

What all groups have in common is that they refer to a group that was in power in Nicaragua some time during the last century, with very abrupt and mostly not very democratic shifts between them. For the Sandinistas several different phases exist in which they are thought to have exerted power and which are referred to with differing importance by different Sandinistas. That is an important factor as to why history lives in everyday life. When a Nicaraguan is currently affiliated with one particular group, it normally also means that in his interpretation/discussion of the past he will emphasize certain historical moments in a way which makes his particular group seem significant.

Ideological differences between the groups mean there are differences in how historical events are understood and how history progresses. An idea of dependency between the core and peripheral countries manifests itself in most accounts from members of all political groups, but with different amount of emphasis placed on it. In general Sandinistas have a strong overtone of Dependency Theory included in any history telling (Velasco 2002). That applies also to written historical works that originate within the Sandinismo project, written by high-ranking activists of the FSLN such as Román, Fonseca Amador, and Fonseca Terán (2008d). Pronounced supporters of the Contras or the Somozas seem to largely agree on the exploitative aspects the first world has towards countries like Nicaragua. Liberals and Conservatives emphasize this aspect less.

The controversies around historical representations in Nicaragua

I present some of the main points of how history is discussed by my informants and, through that, give an idea how these themes are discussed generally in Nicaragua today. The point I make with this is that, although some parts of Nicaraguan history remain highly controversial and are presented in very divergent ways generally linked to the ideological group of the person telling it, all versions seem to put agency in the hands of Nicaraguans and very seldom acknowledge that some thought or action originated outside the borders of Nicaragua.

From the 1850s to 1920s

It is generally accepted today, from the 1850s to the 1920s the United States could invade Nicaragua without having to face too much resistance. This worked until the advent of the anti-imperialism movement of Augusto Nicolás Calderón Sandino in the 1920s. Among Sandinistas, the invasions of the United States are not presented as a result of a conscious decisions. Instead, the United States merely acted mechanically like any empire would have. Those portrayed as having historical agency are those Nicaraguans who—ultimately unsuccessfully—opposed the interventions of the United States or those who are claimed to be responsible for inviting the US military to Nicaragua.

Sandinistas today generally identify with the Liberals of this time period. Those Liberals and Conservatives to whom I spoke with generally do not have much to say about the time period. Sandinistas claim the Liberals invited the filibuster troops from the United States who Andrés Castro Estrada fought, and that the Conservatives brought the intervening troops from the United States which then removed President José Santos Zelaya López. When I asked Carolina Fonseca Icabalzeta when US interventionism in Nicaragua started in the 20th century she answered:

> That was in 1909/10, when the Conservatives invited the

Fernando Fonseca sees a connection between his grandfather who fought with President José Santos Zelaya López and rebel-leader Augusto Nicolás Calderón Sandino and his own engagement with Sandinismo. This connection is not so much one of having discussed politics but rather of growing up with someone with experiences of political exile with corresponding friendships and connections.

United States to intervene against President Zelaya [López].

Her father, Fernando Fonseca, proudly explained how his grandfather had first fought with Zelaya López and how that also was part of the foundation that inspired some of his later deeds as a Sandinista:

> As a family we have an ancestor [...] my grandfather, who [fought] in the revolution of Zelaya [López]. [...] But after he while he lost faith in Zelaya [López] because he saw his project as unrealistic and later opted for [Calderón] Sandino, as a Liberal. So as a child I was influenced by my grandfather. Not because he made me... convinced me of anything, but rather because I saw how certain people came to visit him. They were very old and came from Honduras, because he had been exiled in Honduras for 11 years.

Two of the three main national heroes from before 1920 recognized by the Sandinistas today were Liberals – Zelaya López and Benjamín Francisco Zeledón Rodríguez. Those Sandinista informants who I pressed on an opinion about the party political affiliation of Castro Estrada, admitted he was most likely a Conservative, but generally not much focus is put on his party affiliation. All three from this time frame are now celebrated by the

Guimar Aminta Arias, President of the *Instituto Nicaragüense de Fomento Municipal* (INIFOM), explains to me how the Sandinismo of today will bring development to Nicaragua. As in all government offices under the current government, three pictures hang on the wall: (left to right) a full-body Augusto Nicolás Calderón Sandino, a depiction of Andrés Castro Estrada throwing a stone at a US filibuster soldier, and a full-body of Nicaraguan writer Rubén Darío (1867–1916).

Sandinistas for their acts of defying the United States, and not by Liberals or Conservatives. Castro Estrada is pictured as throwing a stone at a US American soldier. Oftentimes he stands next to Calderón Sandino, as part of the branding on many government products and websites under the current FSLN government. The explanation by Sandinistas as to why they focus more on these persons than other political groups, generally centers around their nationalism and struggle against intervention by the United States.

Calderón Sandino

Calderón Sandino is today regarded as the founder of the modern-day anti-imperialist struggle in Nicaragua by just about all Nicaraguans, although anti-imperialism in the form of native American struggle against European invasion existed earlier. According to Fonseca Amador (1969, 29), Calderón Sandino's actions were part of a Nicaraguan tradition of violent resistance as a response to the very violent exploitation, and this tradition was not the same as what existed in other parts of Latin America. Perhaps as an explanation, Sandinistas oftentimes recount how Calderón Sandino, at 17, watched the lifeless body of Zeledón Rodríguez dragged through the streets after his death (Calderón Sandino 1929), and how this had a profound effect on Calderón Sandino's view of the world. Yet, anyone who stays in Nicaragua for a few minutes and takes his first taxi ride will very likely hear about Calderón Sandino and how he initiated the struggle, as it is one of the most discussed themes, both among Liberals and Sandinistas. A great deal of the ideology and organizational model of those calling themselves Sandinista has changed since the days of Calderón Sandino. The concept of imperialism as a force negatively influencing the people in Nicaragua and other third world countries, continues to play an important role as part of the Sandinista ideology (Ortega Saavedra 1979), but also many Liberals seem to have taken parts of it to themselves. Calderón Sandino in this sense is strangely less controversial amongst Nicaraguans than one may think given that one of the two groups invokes his name and the other does not.

Sandinismo and the forgotten debate on Imperialism

Although the Sandinistas today often refer to Calderón Sandino and all that he did, the version they focus on is somewhat tainted. One of the more important concepts connected with Calderón Sandino is that of 'anti-imperialism.' In his 1933 proclamation *To abolish the Monroe doctrine*, written to defend the establishment of a small rebel army to rid the country of US occupation soldiers, Calderón Sandino specifically named imperialism as the enemy:

> ...[D]eeply convinced that the grotesque Yankee imperialism, day by day is infiltrating the domestic and foreign policy of Central America, turning our cowardly leaders into mummies – the vibrating spirit of the Indo-Hispanic race becomes at this time the Autonomous Army of Central America to save its racial dignity, flinging militarily, politically and economically away from its territory the Wall Street bankers, even if to do this we will have to leave our bodies dead, lying face up towards the sun (Calderón Sandino 1933).

When I first read of Calderón Sandino and his reference to the term 'imperialism' and 'anti-imperialism' I was reminded about the discussion of the same terms in Europe just a few years earlier. 'Anti-imperialism' was a concept developed in the international socialist movement only a few years before Calderón Sandino's entry into Nicaraguan politics (Lenin 1917c; Luxemburg 1913; Bukharin 1920). Around the *First World War* (WWI) and the time of the creation of the Soviet Union, the issue of imperialism was highly debated in various forums worldwide. Different Marxist theorists pointed to slightly different aspects. To a certain degree Marxist theoreticians clearly disagreed, but in the end their common framework was that they saw the entire world as part of one single capitalist system, which evolved and now spanned the entire planet and had an exploitative character.

Closely linked, was another term often used when discussing Calderón Sandino, that of a 'nation's right to self determination' (Lenin 1914). This concept was somewhat more controversial, and critics said it is not always clear what constitutes a nation and why these nations' interests—which are seen as nothing more than a product of the establishment of capitalism—should be part of socialists' program for change (Luxemburg 1908-1909). Altogether the theories of 'anti-imperialism' and 'nations' right to self-determination' do deliver the ideological groundwork for the organizing of revolutions in third world countries such as Nicaragua with the objective of not only overthrowing the local government, but also hurting the international capitalist system, so it is not that strange that Calderón Sandino would make use of these.

Ortega (1980, 53), brother of Ortega Saavedra and leader of the armed forces during the 1980s, claims in his writings that Calderón Sandino was about applying concepts and ideas present at the time to Nicaraguan reality. Fonseca Terán (2010a, 48) defends the same hypothesis, that Calderón Sandino referred to the international debate occurring at the time, when he invoked the term 'imperialism.'

Interestingly, while my initial idea seems supported by those written by Nicaraguan sources, I never hear about the influence of the European debate in conversations with Sandinistas or other Nicaraguans. It is oftentimes argued that Calderón Sandino's anti-imperialism came 'naturally' through living under such exploitative conditions and seeing what happened to his country. This interpretation of the ideological origin of Calderón Sandino's struggle places all historical agency in Nicaraguan hands and it leads away from any possible European or outside influence.

In the case of third world countries, the concepts of anti-imperialism and of the right to self-determination were and are attractive concepts not only to left-wing revolutionaries who want to change the entire structure of society, but also for those from the elite who are quite pleased with their position within their own society, as the perpetrator of most exploitative mechanisms is placed outside the country. Potential political support from the local bourgeoisie may be a factor why leading Sandinistas chose to leave out the connections to international radical movements the term had in the past, when speaking about anti-imperialism in a Nicaraguan context.

Calderón Sandino – nationalist or socialist or ?

In the many conversations I had with Nicaraguans of all types, Calderón Sandino sometimes is portrayed as having gained knowledge about radical politics through his stay in Mexico and meeting left-wing ideological groups of different types. Others deny all ideological connections to Mexico. The denial of Mexican involvement is generally assumed by those Sandinistas who put a lot of emphasis on the nationalist character of the early Sandinista movement, who prefer to focus on the nationalist aspects of Sandinista ideology.

The disagreement is part of a wider disagreement among Sandinistas today as whether Calderón Sandino was a nationalist or a socialist, and if he was a socialist explicitly or implicitly. Most Sandinistas I met who believe he was a socialist, believe he was so implicitly through his belief in anti-imperialism, having lived under very exploitative circumstances in Nicaragua and reject his alleged learning experience in the Mexican class struggle (Leiva 1982, 165). Part of the proof employed to defend this view is that Calderón Sandino, at one point in time, is said to have claimed land for his soldiers, to be run as cooperatives. This, they believe, gives some insight into Calderón Sandino's general view on how society should be run.

In contrast to this stands Somoza García (1976, 150–151), who portrays Calderón Sandino as a communist by linking him to communist contacts in Mexico. Calderón Sandino tried in some of his letters to combine liberalism with communism and Christianity, calling Jesus of Nazareth a revolutionary and communist (Calderón Sandino, cited in Somoza García 1976, 251–255). Calderón Sandino made this alleged statement without any reference to any of the greater socialist theoreticians. Some of the most well-studied of my Sandinista informants claim that the documentation of

Somoza García is a falsification, yet among Sandinistas, similar viewpoints about the character of Calderón Sandino remain present.

Fonseca Terán, who describes himself as a 'Marxist–Leninist,' focuses on the involvement of cadres sent by the Communist International in Calderón Sandino's group. In addition, Fonseca Terán mentions that Calderón Sandino made an international call for workers to join the labor union associated with the Communist International (Fonseca Terán 2010a, 48–49). This view is the one which makes Calderón Sandino most explicitly a socialist. It is generally agreed that Calderón Sandino was not a studied Marxist, but those who follow less prominent radical ideologies within Sandinismo, generally try to base their belief in the actions of Calderón Sandino. Carolina Icabalceta Garay, a Sandinista and history teacher in Managua, sees herself as an anarchist:

> When [Calderón] Sandino worked in Mexico, in the petroleum company [...] there was a lot of presence of the labor union movement which was very influenced by the anarcho-syndicalism that came from Europe. I think [...] that the anarcho-syndicalists have greatly influenced the political left of Latin America. Yes I know that in the Sandinista party, when you speak of anarchism you receive a reaction like "argh, crazy-talk! Marx and Lenin!" I really think that's sad, because one has to learn from all.

Icabalceta Garay did not try to say that Calderón Sandino was an anarchist, but it is clear that she thinks he must have been influenced in his political thoughts by this ideological tradition. In some of the written literature I find similar claims. Muro Rodríguez et al. (1984, 42) describes how Calderón Sandino encountered anarcho-syndicalists and socialists groups while working in the Mexican oil sector some years earlier. This may have provided him with direct access to the European debate on anti-imperialism and nations' right for self-determination. Icabalceta Garay is the only one of my informants who used the precise word 'anarchist' to describe herself. However, this exact passage is essential for most who claim that Calderón Sandino had a left-wing ideology of some kind. Instead of anarchism, it is generally whatever ideology they follow themselves they claim Calderón Sandino picked up in Mexico in this way. It is as close to an admission of foreign influence on the thoughts of Calderón Sandino as one can get among Sandinistas.

Some Nicaraguans today claim they adhere to the original Calderón Sandino and the vision of anti-imperialism he held, but that he did not hold the socialist views that Sandinismo later entailed, and this misrepresents Sandinismo during the time of Calderón Sandino. Some of these people today identify with the Contras. I also meet Sandinistas with this same view. These generally think the current government should act more nationalist and less socialist.

One focus point when it comes to Calderón Sandino's possible rejection of radicals, is his treatment of the El Salvadorian Marxist Farabundo Martí. Martí, according to most descriptions, fought together with Calderón Sandino against occupation of the United States. The stories diverge on how their cooperation ended. Rigo Sampson Davila, who is said to represent the right-wing of the FSLN, explained the issue to me as that once Calderón Sandino discovered Martí's Marxist belief, he told him to leave the country within a day or so. Sampson took that as proof that Calderón Sandino was not particularly fond of Marxism or socialism. Fonseca Terán (2010a, 48–49) describes the situation as a product of the Mexican communist party thinking which complied with the newest party line of only working with movements who explicitly worked towards socialism, and that Calderón Sandino honored Martí upon his death in 1932, and made it clear that he never was in disagreement with the ideology of Martí. The difference in opinion on who Calderón Sandino was and how he should be classified using today's political categories seems to be present at all times in the self-presentation of anyone who claims to be a Sandinista.

In all versions of Calderón Sandino's encounters in both Mexico and with Martí, the ultimate decision making power is portrayed as lying in the hands of Calderón Sandino and whatever may have come from outside Nicaragua only came as inspiration and a starting point for his own ideological development. Historical agency lies again with a Nicaraguan. The difference in opinion as to what ideology Calderón Sandino really held, is not reflected in the way Sandinistas generally present what Sandinismo means to them. An example this can be seen at the start of the interview with one of the members of 'Amigos', Víctor Cienfuegos, previously a revolutionary fighter now in charge of a social club for common people in a poorer area of Managua:

> I think that in order to understand Sandinismo, to understand the nationalist character of Sandinismo, one needs to understand the figure [Calderón] Sandino. One needs to know

Víctor Cienfuegos believes Sandinismo is most of all about giving "Nicaragua back to the Nicaraguans."

where [Calderón] Sandino came from, what Sandino fought for. Because we, the Sandinistas, follow [Calderón] Sandino. He is the base, and we also have [ideological] fathers, [like] Carlos Fonseca [Amador], who also formed Sandinismo. [...] Generally, people come who don't know the history. They come and ask us very basic, very fundamental things [...about] the spirit of Sandinismo, the nationalism of Sandinismo. [...] So we are continuing this nationalism of [Calderón] Sandino. We are not communists, not orthodox [Marxist-Leninists], nor do we have anything to do with internationalism. We are very nationalist. [Calderón] Sandino was a guy who was nationalist, who fought to give Nicaragua back to the Nicaraguans. [...]

As this passage from the interview shows, Cienfuegos seems to be irritated by the fact that foreigners do not know the real Calderón Sandino, yet his own definition of Calderón Sandino and Sandinismo is very specific and is not shared by all other Sandinistas. Observing the difference in ideas about what Sandinismo means for different Sandinistas may very well have been what led other foreigners to ask him what it means for him in the first place. The description of Cienfuegos once more falls into the pattern of placing only Nicaraguans into the center of all attention. Possible foreign influences on Calderón Sandino or Sandinismo are not considered.

Calderón Sandino – a foreign agent?

A version of the history of Calderón Sandino not getting any attention, is one in which the concrete actions of Calderón Sandino may have been much more influenced by another country. While some Sandinistas put some focus on the ideological influence from Mexico, no Nicaraguan I have met, no matter what ideological camp, ever focuses on the possible importance of economic support for Calderón Sandino from the Mexican government. While all other aspects of Calderón Sandino receive a lot of attention, any possible connection with Mexico is at best portrayed as being of an ideological kind.

Historian Toynbee (1927–1930, 21–90) argues that the main cause for Mexico considering involvement, besides the ideological support it gave to leftist groups in all of Latin America, was that Mexico could play a role that it could not in the conflicts with the United States at its northern land border. Culture, language and geographic proximity allowed Mexico to play a much stronger role in Central America than it could at the US-Mexican border.

Some of my informants attacked Toynbee for representing a tradition of British and US American historians and for being heavily influenced by the propaganda of the governments of those countries. His book has been translated into Spanish in Nicaragua and sold as one of very few books on Nicaraguan history at one of the very few university book shops in Managua. One of my informants, a young and critical intellectual who belongs to the group running the website http://barricada.com.ni, referred to the book when I confronted him about the issue of possible Mexican financing of Calderón Sandino. I tried to question a small group of Sandinistas in Managua with the version of the events as presented by Toynbee and it did not seem to surprise any of them much.

It can be concluded that some Managua students have heard about this theory. Although they generally discuss history a lot, none of those

I meet sees a point in pursuing this particular theory or ever pointing to it. Given that just about all aspects of Calderón Sandino are questioned and quite a lot of Nicaraguans strongly oppose Calderón Sandino or the Sandinismo that grew out of him, it is surprising this version of events has received so little attention. Different from all the other accounts, it would place historical agency outside the borders of Nicaragua.

The Somoza years

Sandinistas today generally see the Somozas as a puppet of the United States. Somocistas focus on the difference in leadership style between the three different Somozas. According to the Somocista version, each Somoza governed and had an alliance with the United States, rather than that the United States governed through the Somozas. It is important to note here that while the Somozas were three different dictators, Somocistas are those Nicaraguans who either ideologically were and are in favor of the Somoza-regimes, those who materially benefited from it, and those who fall into both groups. Largely both groups are treated as if they were the same, although that is not always the case.

The Sandinista version of Somocismo lends little historical agency to the individual Somozas or to the United States. The actions of the Somozas are just mechanical and follow the general pattern of how empires behave. The Somocista version of events does lend much more agency to each Somoza. That is why they were free to be different in their government style. It would seem another purpose of their leadership styles was to show they were not all-out dictatorships. In neither version is historical agency admitted to lie outside Nicaragua. Historical agency does not exist or it lies with a Nicaraguan and within the national boundaries.

First oppositional voices

Some events, such as the assassination of Somoza García, are today commemorated by Sandinistas of both FSLN and MRS, who often claim that López Pérez and the 1950s social movements represent their own beginning. Similar to the treatment of times before Calderón Sandino, FSLN Sandinistas commemorate people who were members of other political groups in the time before the forming of the FSLN, while Nicaraguans who serve as members of these groups now, often do not commemorate

This memorial to four student activists killed in 1959 can be found in downtown León. Behind the heads of the students, a red-and-black flag is drawn. Today these colors are associated with the *Frente Sandinista de Liberación Nacional*, but the party was not founded before 1961.

them. Individual Nicaraguans and movements that went against the otherwise given order, i.e. those engaged in historical agency, are universally celebrated by the Sandinistas as part of their past.

One such date is the 23rd of July in León, when the students who were killed on July 23 1959 are commemorated in the form of a gigantic street party in downtown León. This celebration follows a number of other important celebrations in June and July, during which mainly Sandinista historical events are commemorated. The high point of these celebrations is the triumph celebration of the triumph of the insurrection on the 19th of July. The 23rd of July is the first day when the Sandinista red-and-black can be seen less than during all the previous events.

There are always some disputes as to how these events should be commemorated. Both years I was present, the event was eventually taken over by FSLN Sandinistas who claimed the student movement was exactly about what FSLN Sandinismo stands for today and who then went on to put on the popular FSLN Sandinista music which one hears for most of the early summer.

The initiative to put less emphasis on the FSLN in such commemorating events that cannot directly be linked to the FSLN, generally comes from students connected to the MRS who claim to see a historic parallel between the Somoza dictatorship of the past and what they claim to be the José Daniel Ortega Saavedra dictatorship of the present. They claim to

Armando Martínez is a cobbler proud to never have left the Sandinista movement. He became involved with the *Frente Sandinista de Liberación Nacional* (FSLN) around 1952–56 after visiting an event commemorating Augusto Nicolás Calderón Sandino in 1948. Martínez does not seem to see a fundamental difference between the organizational efforts of the early and later years of resistance against Somoza. Others claim that the FSLN wrongfully takes credit for the opposition movement before it was founded.

see a historical connection between themselves and these activists of the past.

Organizing for revolutionary insurrection

It is my experience from discussing with many Sandinistas who were active in the early years that although the FSLN represented a break from the Soviet-allied *Partido Socialista Nicaragüense* (PSN), the influence of Marxism nevertheless could not be neglected within the FSLN. They used several concepts from Marxist terminology—most prominently 'class war'—in their descriptions of how and why they were organizing.

The emphasis on the importance of the Soviet Union in the pre-revolution years differs among Sandinistas. Very few portray it as Fonseca Amador following a new model that came from the Soviet Union. Most see it as Fonseca Amador having the historical agency and it was him who changed his strategy because he was annoyed with the previous strategy of left-wing revolutionaries, because it gave no hope to any revolutionary effort in Nicaragua. Fonseca Amador (1964) described himself as a radical and an anti-imperialist who had some respect for the Soviet Union and its achievements.

German Bravo Urbina's initial involvement with the Sandinistas during the time of Somoza came about because all youths, also those not involved with the opposition, were repressed. Many Nicaraguans I talked to became Sandinistas only after they had been wrongfully accused of being one.

German Bravo Urbina, whose mother operated a Sandinista safe house and who was fundamental in running arms in the last period before the revolutionary triumph, according to Bayardo José Fonseca Galo (brother of Fernando Fonseca and uncle of Fonseca Icabalzeta), explains he started involving himself in Sandinista politics "because all youths were repressed, independently of whether they were actually guilty or not". Many of those who see themselves as Sandinistas today, explain they initially became opposed to the Somozas because they suppressed all youths. The repression, due to false accusations of subversive activity, led, according to their own accounts, to getting involved in precisely such activity. According to this version of events, the reason for the revolution can be found entirely within Nicaragua and not in the Soviet Union or anywhere else.

The state under Somoza presented those organizing against the government as 'terrorists' as one can notice when looking at old news clips. While that term is not used much any more, Somocistas today generally focus much on the amount of chaos the Sandinistas brought through their actions.

The FSLN as an underground movement

Palmer (1988, 93) claims that Fonseca Amador spent much of his time between founding the FSLN and his murder by the GN in 1976, appropriating

Calderón Sandino to the Sandinista movement. As a conversation starter, I often asked informants what they thought of the idea that Calderón Sandino as known today is largely the product of Fonseca Amador. Surprisingly I received no protests when making this claim, neither from Sandinistas nor others. Some Somocistas today claim it is unknown whether Fonseca Amador's death was due to any wrongdoings of the Somoza regime or whether the Sandinistas were complicit, either by committing the murder or by informing the GN of his whereabouts, in order to martyr him for the movement. Most others seem to believe the official story. Many MRS Sandinistas claim that if Fonseca Amador had survived, he would be a member of the MRS rather than the FSLN. This theory is based on the fact that Fonseca Amador had a background from the university, which most MRS Sandinistas also have. Given his generally left-wing agenda, which the MRS abandoned, it seems rather far-fetched.

Fonseca Amador is generally portrayed as being a person of great thoughts and fundamental principles by all those seeing themselves as Sandinistas. The Sandinismo of Fonseca Amador stands in contrast to the day to day Nicaraguan politics in which horse trades of every kind are fairly common. The FSLN put Calderón Sandino, who had been displayed as an outlaw and an enemy of order in the Somoza-rhetoric (Palmer 1988; Jansen 2004), up among Ernesto 'Che' Guevara and other revolutionary leaders as one of the great inspirations of any revolutionary (Palmer 1988, 91–92).

The tendencies that emerged in 1975 remain present today, at least unofficially, in that they represent different views of the past. Most of my informants who were politically active before 1979, can still easily be classified according to the tendency they followed then. For many of them, their tendency in this period continues to be integral in explaining how they define Sandinismo. I am able many times to correctly guess to which one they belonged.

When I interviewed Margarita Guevara Montano from Managua—another one of Fonseca Galo's connections—she explained what the Sandinista struggle was about in the late 1970s in her view:

> At that time there were masses of people who did not know how to write or how to read. But of course they had their own experiences with Nicaraguan political life. [...] And so we students took it upon ourselves to organize the popular masses; the peasants, the factory worker... most of all the

Margarita Guevara Montano started organizing factory workers for the Sandinista revolutionary insurrection at age 19. She believes that factory workers had mostly experienced repression in different spheres, but lacked clarity in their analysis of these phenomenon.

> factory workers. They had experiences with repression, but they lacked clarity in their political analysis. They knew they were repressed, but not why...

I guessed correctly that Guevara Montano belonged to the *Tendencia Proletaria* (TP). Generally speaking, most of those who were active at that time give their own tendency a more fundamental role in the process than the other ones. Many of those identified with the TP now claim that those from the *Tendencia Tercerista* (TT) had no clear class analysis, many coming from bourgeois backgrounds, and the majority of them left the FSLN in the 1990s and are now members of the MRS. When they left it was at least in parts as protest against Ortega Saavedra – a former member of the TT.

Strategic alliances

A large part of Sandinismo today, is the concept of strategic alliances with other non-Sandinista sections of the population to achieve a concrete goal – a strategy borrowed from the TT. The criticism from abroad and from foreigners since 2006 largely centers around the alliances of the Ortega Saavedra government with right-wing political sectors. The origin of these policies of alliances must be seen in the years of the three tendencies. The TT not only cooperated with right-wing groups, but also cooperated with the PSN to form a common front, and invited other similar groups of

The controversies around historical representations in Nicaragua   45

organized laborers to do the same (Miranda, Ortega Saavedra, and Gorman 1979, 117). The three tendencies in the party made it possible to attract proletarians and peasants simultaneously, but I have never spoken to a Nicaraguan who puts much emphasis on a tendency to which he did not belong.

It struck me during many conversations, how those formerly belonging to the TP today often speak of the alliance with bourgeois sectors of society that the TT argued for, as meaning the TT itself consisted of members of the bourgeoisie. I have not been able to investigate whether this concept of what the TT stood for or consisted of has changed over time, or whether it was just always assumed if one spoke for cooperation with bourgeois sectors of society, it was because one belonged to that part of society.

Under the Sandinista in the 1980s

When speaking to non-Sandinistas about the 1980s and how the government was set up, they generally leave out the initial years with the junta and the fact that non-Sandinistas participated. Those with a background from the MRS are often, but not always, more critical towards what they claim to be an authoritarian government style. Nevertheless, both MRS and FSLN Sandinistas generally look upon this phase positively. Sandinistas generally view the elections of 1984 as being the first free elections. The next ones, in 1990s, which the FSLN lost, generally are portrayed as a choice between "an end to the war or continued freedom." Those against the Sandinistas generally point towards the 1990 elections being the first free ones. The international context wherein the decision was made to have a multi-party system is not mentioned.

Direct democracy or surveillance society?

The *Comités de Defensa Sandinista* (CDSs) that existed in the 1980s are described in very differing ways.

According to Liberals and some Sandinistas is that they took control of absolutely every local decision to the point where the individual could not decide anything independently. Another accusation against the CDSs is that they made out an extremely tight surveillance network that would report anything its members deemed inappropriate to the government. These accusations mainly remind me of westerners speaking of the

Staatssicherheit (StaSi) of the *Deutsche Demokratische Republik* (DDR, German Democratic Republic).

On the other hand, those who liked them explain that together with popular militias and trade unions, the CDSs made it harder to influence parts of the upper party hierarchies to fundamentally change the political course of the country during Sandinista reign, because major decisions had to be carried by a popular majority. Corrupting the upper strata of political society was how it was done in other countries where aid packages from the *International Monetary Fund* (IMF) were given in return for privatizations and investment access for foreign companies (Irvin 1982, 41). In this sense, those positive to the CDSs describe them as having been a way for the general public to have a say in politics, and they in effect forced the government into more rapid implementation of already promised reforms in such areas as aid for the peasants, health, education and housing programs (Irvin 1982, 42).

Some of the wording both sides use when describing the CDSs is even the same. Nicaraguans of all types say they functioned as the 'eyes and ears' of the revolution (Mayorga 2007), but while supporters read this as positive, those opposing it see it as a negative. Another allegation is that Marxists/Sandinistas allegedly used them to control and radicalize the revolutionary process. Sandinistas in favor of the CDSs generally see that as a heroic action which also included 'educating' the non-Sandinista members of the CDSs and the neighborhoods about the revolutionary process, while other groups see it as fundamentally undemocratic.

Whether the CDSs and the general setup of government were the result of foreign influences is not generally discussed. No-one asks why Nicaragua would adopt a government instrument from Cuba and whether the plan to do so ultimately originated in Nicaragua, in Cuba or in the Soviet Union. Nicaraguans either blame the FSLN Sandinistas for these instruments of government or credit them for it. In that way, no matter whether they are in favor of or against the setup of the government of the 1980s, historical agency is at all times placed in Nicaraguan hands.

Sandinista relations to foreign powers

The Soviet Union still holds a very central place for most Nicaraguans since its involvement with the country in the 1980s. To the Liberals it serves as a scare and the FSLN Sandinistas see it as a power for good. Most MRS

Celso Celestino García López is a Sandinista from El Rama, where the Contras were strong during the 1980s. The confrontation between Sandinistas and Contras he attributes to capitalism.

Sandinistas I have met, do not mention the Soviet Union at all. I have only heard two basic versions of the relationship to the Soviet Union by both Sandinistas and anti-Sandinistas. According to one version, the Sandinistas were allied with the Soviet Union the entire time. The other version claims that the alliance with the Soviet Union was something certain Nicaraguan leaders decided upon right after the revolution. No emphasis is put on agency on the part of the Soviet Union and no president or important decision maker from the Soviet Union are ever mentioned. Also, it is not questioned whether the main decision concerning the possible cooperation between the two countries could have been taken in Moscow and not Managua.

The relationship between the United States and the Sandinistas in this period is generally explained as the result of one of three: According to some MRS Sandistas it was Ortega Saavedra who overstepped the line to what the United States could not accept – such as first promising to not send aid to the *Frente Farabundo Martí para la Liberación Nacional* (FMLN) in El Salvador and then doing just that. According to those who identify with the Contras or the Somocistas, the US government gave aid to the Contras after they had made an appeal for support and after the Sandinistas had instituted a bloody dictatorship which the United States "could no longer ignore."

The third position can be seen in what the Sandinista Celso Celestino García López from El Rama told me. In El Rama the Contras were somewhat stronger than in Managua and León, and he explained to me the reason for the confrontation between Contras and Sandinistas as: "It was the capitalist system which made us fight, poor against poor. Neither side benefited from the war." This is much in line with how most FSLN Sandinistas portray the actions of the United States and of Contra revolutionaries. For the FSLN Sandinistas, the actions of the United States and the Contras are mechanical and go against any revolution in the third world. They are done without any consciousness (historic agency) behind it, due to a combination of world capitalism and imperialism.

In all three versions, the United States seems to lack agency, while Nicaraguans are those who changed the path of history.

Reasoning the electoral failure in 1990

The electoral failure in 1990 was internationally seen in connection with the falling apart of the Soviet Union and the Warsaw Pact. Castro Ruz (1990) tried to explain the logic of the election campaign by the Violeta Barrios Torres de Chamorro camp in 1990:

> ...[T]hey said to the people: the economic crisis will end, if the opposition wins, the economic embargo [by the United States] will end, if the opposition wins, large sums of money will come. In addition they added: the Sandinistas are not able to resolve the crisis; the Sandinistas will not receive help from the United States; the Sandinistas cannot continue to receive the help, the cooperation they have received hitherto from a number of socialist countries, because – they said – your friends [the political establishment of Eastern Europe] have been overthrown. (my translation, Castro Ruz 1990, 282)

Castro Ruz may be right in that international circumstances were the most important argument to vote against the FSLN at the time. Few of my Nicaraguan informants talked about such external influences on the elections. The Liberals I spoke to generally saw it as a victory of democracy against antidemocratic forces, which were responsible for a war and for sending young Nicaraguans into this war during their military service. Those informants I discussed with what a Sandinista victory in 1990 might have meant, commonly held that the war might have started again. The explanation Sandinistas give for the electoral loss is generally implicit, and only when I asked directly did they say it directly. The main point given by Sandinistas seems to be that the United States was aware of the Nicaraguan people's strength and that a Liberal, more or less democratic government was the closest they could have to the direct dictatorship they really wanted.

For Sandinistas it seems a given fact that the majority of Nicaraguans wanted Sandinista policies and only voted against the FSLN out of this fear of more war. Icabalceta Garay in her explanation was a little more complex. Instead of blaming the election results on the change in international circumstances, she explained how she and her compatriots did not notice what the sacrifice of participation meant for many Nicaraguans at the time:

> We signed up for the popular militias, we signed up for the CDSs, we signed up for the harvesting of coffee and the help that needed to be done voluntarily…many of us. We did that with a lot of love. Yes, it is true there was some institutional pressure, I think. I wasn't able to observe those who felt forced to go, there was a line to follow… Given that I went voluntarily, I didn't notice those who went without wanting to do so. Yes, there were some autocratic, dictatorial measures. I think it's hard to determine how much of this was a culture of colonialism and dictatorship which preceded us, and how much of this was the reality of war which changes everything and which is the exact opposite of development.

Icabalceta Garay accepts some collective guilt for the Sandinistas, but then rapidly defuses much of this into cultures of dictatorship and colonialism and the general logic of war. The Sandinistas are presented as a group that acts or reacts; whereas other Nicaraguan groups are seen as being part of a culture that seems to have come into being mechanically. In her case, groups outside of Nicaragua are not even mentioned. The difference between the explanation of Castro Ruz (1990), which is consistent with most European explanations, and Nicaraguan explanations is that in Nicaraguan explanations, historical agency lies in the hands of Nicaraguans while in the international explanations events in Nicaragua are more or less dictated by worldwide developments.

Three neoliberal governments

'The 16 years of neoliberalism' and not being in power, (really closer to 17 – 1990 until 2007) are treated as a dark part of history by FSLN Sandinistas. FSLN informants do recognize at least in part distinct periods during those years. In that sense, the concrete political reality is portrayed as a combination of mechanical empire type politics from the United States irregardless of who heads the United States, and the concrete stupidity and corruptness of the Nicaraguan in possession of the presidency at any given time.

The MRS Sandinistas point out that Humberto Ortega made sure to leave his position in 1993 with as much money as possible and that he started his business in Costa Rica. That generally is mustered as evidence to show that José Daniel Ortega Saavedra is corrupt through and through and has no principles. When I point out that they are two different people, Humberto Ortega being José Daniel Ortega Saavedra's brother, I am often reminded other Sandinista leaders also are said to have walked out with great amounts of money after losing the 1990 elections; however, without showing what advantages José Daniel Ortega Saavedra may have gained. This is generally used to discredit the morals of FSLN Sandinistas. FSLN Sandinistas often point out that the MRS Sandinistas were still part of the party in 1990, and then claim it was really the current MRS Sandinistas who became rich in that period, and that's why they gave up on the struggle of the classes.

The term of the first government, that of Barrios Torres de Chamorro (1990–97), generally is viewed by my Sandinista informants as a time of economic sellout, and a disarming the country. Barrios Torres de Chamorro is not generally seen as having been corrupt, but people around her are seen as such. Barrios Torres de Chamorro is often accused of having sold out the Nicaraguan railway in a heartbeat and to have forgiven the debt the United States needed to pay Nicaragua as war reparations, something people from all sectors of Nicaraguan politics continue to be angry about.

The second presidency, that of José Arnoldo Alemán Lacayo (1997–2002), is generally viewed by Sandinistas as a time of outrageous corruption and economic sellout of the country in a way that Barrios Torres de Chamorro had not been able to accomplish. One favorite tale is that Alemán Lacayo at a party sat in a small pool with all his ministers, and relived himself into the water. He then announced that anyone who would get up, would be out of the government and everybody sat still. Whether true or not, it gives one an idea of how Alemán Lacayo is perceived. Of all the figure heads of the political right, Alemán Lacayo seems to be generally respected by FSLN Sandinistas as having a 'real' following. "He represents the petty bourgeoisie, so it's better to make a deal with him than with [the banker] Montealegre," I am told at the municipal office of the FSLN León. Those views seem to be shared by many FSLN Sandinistas.

When speaking of the presidency of Enrique José Bolaños Geyer (2002–07), informants of all types focus on his helping to imprison Alemán Lacayo. He is seen as much less of an activist type and more of a laissez faire type president in that he is said to have claimed he could not do anything about power outages in major population centers. Although the influence of especially the United States is acknowledged, no similar focus is paid to the difference between the presidencies of Bush Sr., Clinton and Bush Jr. The actions of the United States generally are portrayed as being the same at all times and not the result of historical agency. The fact that the United States chose to support a dictatorship up until 1979, and after 1990, a series of formally "democratically" elected presidents with a very different record on human rights issues receives little attention. Such a focus could possibly be seen as lending historical agency to individual factors outside of Nicaragua.

The FSLN out of power(?)

For many Sandinistas, their strategy of continuing to exert some power despite having lost the elections seems to have been legitimate in that they feel the country was hijacked by the political right and under the control of the empire. Others seem to be rather irritated by this intervention on the part of the Sandinistas. The Sandinistas are criticized for their strategy during their time in opposition as having undermined the democratic rule of law. The criticism comes from the current Liberal opposition and is reported in much of the right-wing media. This criticism is also heard from Liberals in the streets. "In Nicaragua it's always the Sandinistas who govern," one anti-Sandinista taxi driver told me, "If they don't govern from above, they govern from below. Be sure to write that in your book!" The difference in views can be seen as being based upon two different views in concern to agency. While Sandinistas see the period as lacking historical agency if it were not for their actions, Liberals see this as the

Rigoberto Irurzum Alonso Moreno from Managua was 9 years old in 1990. He is one of many Sandinistas who sees no problem in Sandinismo governing against a majority in parliament, because in his view, the opposition in parliament failed to improve the country sufficiently during their time in government.

period in which they legitimately were to govern and the interference by Sandinistas was uncalled for.

Governing without a majority

FSLN Sandinistas generally portray the whole liberal-democratic setup as being foreign to Nicaragua and the third world in general, and nothing more than a way for the United States to ensure continued oppression of Nicaraguans. According to them, it took 16 years to understand how to work the system, so the political right in the end had no other choice but to hand power back to them. They believe all election results when the Liberals were in charge to be fraudulent. Some FSLN Sandinistas use that to explain how the they could score below 50%. Another very common explanation for why it is acceptable to govern against a majority in parliament from FSLN Sandinistas comes from Rigoberto Irurzum Alonso Moreno, a Managua friend of Fonseca Icabalzeta from university, who is not a member of any political party, yet counts himself as Sandinista:

> There is no opposition in Nicaragua that wants the best for the country. [...] 40% are Sandinistas. The other 60% had 16 years to fix this country, and they could not manage to do it. So now it's our time to try again.

FSLN Sandinistas, with their explanations, put an emphasis on the need to take historical agency upon themselves. The appearance of Venezuela on the international stage as a means of financing another Sandinista experiment of state power does not receive much attention. Explanations are sought only within Nicaragua, even though FSLN connections to Venezuela are well-known.

The two groups who emphasize change between the 1980s and now are the MRS Sandinistas and the Contras. The Contras generally approve of the current government and disapproved of the old one, and the MRS Sandinistas feel the opposite. The Contras now generally explain that the Liberals in the 1990s did not help them in any way, and it is only now with the current FSLN government that their voice is heard. Sometimes it is explained that Ortega Saavedra finally understood how to listen, other times they admit it was them who finally understood who their real friends are. Noticeably absent from both MRS and Contra explanations as to what the difference between the 1980s and now constitutes, are foreign powers such as the United States, Venezuela and the Soviet Union. When a Liberal or a MRS Sandinista does focus on Venezuela, it seems to be a portrayal very similar to that which the Sandinistas have of the United States: An empire that acts mechanically. The historical agency and choice to follow Venezuela lies under all circumstances with Ortega Saavedra and other Nicaraguans and not with Hugo Chavez or other Venezuelans.

Problems understanding the discussion of Nicaraguan history

Some readers may argue that Liberals, Conservatives, Somocistas and Contras are not fundamentally different groups. It seems easy to cross from one to the other. Historically they are somewhat distinct (Hüeck 2006, 9), and in my experience people classify themselves as belonging to one of them specifically rather than to a mix of all of them. It seems it has more to do with their personal preferences of what they like to be identified with rather than with any clear ideological distinctions.

Calderón Sandino and the FSLN up until 1979 are generally presented as individualists and makers of history, while the general populace is left out. After 1979, there is more focus on the collective involvement, rather than the involvement of single individuals. The extent to which the FSLN changed its policies according to popular demand are not mentioned. This is not by accident. When talking to people who experienced the time from before 1979 until now, it is very common for them to tell me first how they started their involvement in the movement, then what they did at the precise time of the insurrection and maybe what their own position was in the 1980s. After that, their own persona tends to get lost and I am presented with a general history of the country – "We lost. Then Violeta Chamorro...". For some, this collective history sets in right after insurrection, while others focus on their own lives during the 1980s. Any distinction between self and Sandinista state seems to be nonexistent in their explanations. For many, this likely has to do with their personal experience being intensely negative or positive. For others, it may be seeing themselves as being of little importance in comparison to what happened around them.

More confusion lies in the fact that several of the main historical actors also figure as historians who publish written material, mostly on periods preceding their own time. This underlines the importance generally given to historical descriptions, and I have found it confusing to try to find out when an explanation is part of political argument in the present for a certain cause and when it is the most objective description a certain political actor manages to produce.

The material presented here may at times resemble a patchwork of very different ways of citing historical accounts. That is mainly due to the different nature of the sources. Some points or accounts are the same or very similar and I have heard certain points made many times by Nicaraguans who declare themselves to belong to some certain faction. Usually the setting for gathering this type of information were informal interviews, i.e. when sitting in a public bus, sharing a cab or just randomly being approached by unknown Nicaraguans in the street who felt they needed to explain 'historical facts' to me. I have included most of that material in a generalized form. Other points I first hear in this manner, before I decide to investigate further by asking more questions in the same direction to members of the same faction or approaching those from another faction with it, to hear their reaction. The next time I confront someone from the first faction with that reaction to get a counter-reaction, etc. Many of these accounts are described with a particularly concise answer which I felt beneficial to the reader.

Other types of data contain written accounts, which are cited according to common citation standards. It is not to be understood that these written accounts represent the real and objective history, while the spoken accounts represent an imperfect and partisan account. Both types are really of the same quality, and I have treated the material similarly. In addition to what is discussed within Nicaraguan society, I have in some cases included material which goes beyond the explanations given by Nicaraguans in order to show what alternative accounts of the same phenomenon could be given if Nicaraguan agency were not prioritized. Terms such as 'Liberal,' 'socialist,' 'Conservative' and 'anarchist' are used by my informants and within Nicaraguan society and they are not always used in the same way, I chose not to use these same terms to try to classify informants, historical actors or ideologies. I use broader categories such as 'left-wing' and 'right-wing' to describe some informants who I believe need to be classified further within the Sandinista movement.

Concluding remarks

The internal power structure and implementation of democracy and participative ways available to the population have been common problems for revolutionary movements that drifted away from their original path. The exception of the former might exactly have been Nicaragua, as the loss of the FSLN in the 1990 elections showed. After all, the red-and-black of the Sandinista flag does represent anarchism in many parts of the world, but the question of popular participation in the actual decision making process was an essential issue in Nicaragua. The acceptance of a popular majority may have been the main cause why the Sandinista movement was not discredited completely after the fall of the Soviet Union the way many similar movements fared. It is likely one important cause of different accepted versions of history being present in Nicaragua.

A pattern that can be seen throughout the entire current presentation of Nicaraguan history is the absence of agency on the part of foreign powers. All parts of history are universally attributed to Nicaraguan actors. Even when a foreign power is clearly involved, it does so because a Nicaraguan actor has mobilized it to do so, according to the thinking of Nicaraguans. In other examples, agency is transferred to individual revolutionary leaders in tales of a revolution at a later stage when the revolution is taken as part of a nation building project under much more institutionalized conditions than those the revolutionaries lived under. Under the regime of the *Partido Revolucionario Institucional* (PRI) from 1946-2000[1] in Mexico, Mexican schools taught about the Mexican revolutionary Emilio Zapato (Gilbert 2003) to justify the Mexican government's current political line (Gilbert 1997), much in the same way that the FSLN taught about Calderón Sandino in the 1980s and also has started to do so currently.

The PRI is seen by much of the left as a party that may have been socialist once, but by the time of their electoral defeat had degenerated and just clung to an image of revolutionary icons while having lost much of the meaning behind them. Icabalceta Garay made the same connection:

> Sometimes I think—as a Sandinista it hurts me—I feel like the
> PRI – the Mexican revolutionary party. It hurts so much, but
> yes I know there are ugly things, bad things that happen.

The difference between Nicaragua and Mexico is that in Nicaragua it is not only the FSLN that follows this pattern of transferring all historical agency to Nicaragua and Nicaraguans, it also holds true for all other Nicaraguan parties. As we have seen, Sandinistas today focus very little on the financing Calderón Sandino may have received from Mexico. The *Frente de Liberación Nacional* (FLN)/FSLN 1961-90 quite clearly followed that strategy and was financed by Eastern Europe and Cuba. They are viewed as acting completely on their own and without any links to these powers. Similarly, the Somocistas see the Somozas as acting on their own without any US influence, and the Contras see their actions as rather unrelated to decisions made by Washington. The same holds true with the Liberals for their time in office. Even when a foreign power is mentioned as having provided resources or troops, it is qualified with a story on why some Nicaraguan individual or group convinced them to do so.

Given the emphasis on Dependency Theory, which in other contexts is accused of placing all agents in the hands of first world actors, in the Sandinista ideology, it requires more of an explanation as to the purpose of generating their version of history.

---

1. The party operated under other names since 1929.

Third Chapter

Economic development, expectations and perceptions

An interesting feature of Nicaraguan political discourse I have found is the part dedicated to economic aspects. In this chapter we will look at the changing economic situation of Nicaragua and the plans for economic development and how these are judged by the Nicaraguan public.

The Somozas from the 1950s until 1979, the Sandinistas until 1990, and the Liberal governments up until 2007 represented very different approaches to achieving economic development. Each one of these was connected to a theory of how development could be achieved for third world countries, that was popular at the time at an international level. This is not always acknowledged by all Nicaraguans. Nicaraguans tend to put more emphasis on the wishes and views of the Nicaraguan government at the time than on international trends. At the same time, Nicaragua does switch between different theories for how development can be achieved more so than other countries, and it can be argued that this switch is the result of decisions made mainly by Nicaraguans and not foreign powers. The three development models represent three basic setups of the economy: The Somoza period in which a national bourgeoisie is built up, the country develops economically but income gaps are high, the Liberal period in which foreign capital is given access and controls most of the economy, and the Sandinista period in which it is a stated goal by the state to diminish income gaps while increasing overall production levels.

Most foreigners initially think that all Sandinistas are in favor of a Soviet-style command economy and all Liberals favor laissez faire style capitalism. Nicaraguan reality is a bit more complex, and most Nicaraguans seem to favor at least some state intervention and some level of decentralized decision making on issues relating to economics. As part of this chapter, I show how Nicaraguans use very different criteria for judging the success of the three governments. The Sandinistas of the 1980s are judged by where their policies could have led, had foreign intervention ceased and the Sandinistas not lost the 1990 elections. The Somozas and Liberals are instead judged by what the economic reality for Nicaraguans was during the time they were in power.

While the discussion on political history showed us how in many aspects Sandinistas and other groups legitimize themselves through their historic past, in the aspect of economic policies, Sandinismo stands out in that it is legitimized through possible improvements in the future, rather than the past.

In the first part of this chapter, I outline the international discourse about development on a world scale since the *Second World War* (WWII). In the second part of this chapter, I focus on how the economic situation of Nicaragua and its government's economic policies changed between the Somoza government until today. I also show what theories were employed when creating these policies. In the fourth part, I look at the differences in how Nicaraguans judge the different historic periods and the governments that stood and stand behind the economic policies.

The research for this chapter mainly took place among Sandinista professionals and ministry workers and the founders of the organization 'Amigos.' These groups were happy to engage in discussions about economic policy in the past, and the professionals who were still working were the most interested in relating it to the current government and what possibilities exist today. Both groups discussed it at a very theoretical level. They helped me find important Nicaraguan literature on the subject. This help does not show in terms of quotes as much as coherence in my presentation. I would have to read about a particular fact many times and then discuss it with informants before I would understand whether it is generally seen as important.

Development theories

Since WWII, a few theories on how development can be achieved by third world countries have been central. These influenced the debate on the strategies for achieving development that have been used in most third world countries, including Nicaragua. Before we look at the concrete policies different governments implemented as part of their development program, we look at general theories of development which formed the basis for these policy decisions.

Mainstream modernization development theories

The international trend in the two decades immediately after WWII, was to apply policies in third world countries that copied the historical models set by western countries. The United Nations and others tried to employ this theory in their development programs around the world. This theory is known as "modernization theory." The countries of the third world were simply "behind" and had to play catchup to reach the same level of modernity that the first world enjoyed. Strategies built upon this theory emphasized investments in state and private sectors coupled with transfer of technology from the first world (Wallerstein 1999; Smukkestad 1998).

For the countries that allied with the United States, models such as the phase model of US American economist and political theorist Walt Whitman Rostow (Rostow 1956, 1960) (see also — *Mainstream modernization development theories*, p. 60) were developed and employed. These models operate with the idea that a particular 'impulse' of some kind needs to start a phase of development which will generally modernize a country. According to these models, if the impulse to start development originates from outside the country—true in all cases of modernization initiated through the United States—the modernization phase needs to be oriented towards creating export goods to sell on a world market.

Export oriented strategies for development mainly build on the model of the British political economist David Ricardo (1772–1823). Ricardo's model proclaims that even if a country is less productive in all sectors, it will still gain from entering a free trade agreement with more developed countries. The important part is that the given country should stop producing a range of goods and instead focus only on one good which it is relatively better at producing and then focus on exporting it. This is termed as a certain country having a 'comparative advantage' of producing within a certain field. According to Ricardo, the country should then import all goods in which it does not have a comparative advantage (Ricardo 1821; Smukkestad 1998).

1. Traditional society	At this stage industry hasn't made its entrance yet, and almost all production is conducted in the traditional way. That does not mean that society is static. Changes can happen, but none of these will fundamentally modernize the country or increase living standards substantially.
2. Preconditions for take off	At this stage, mechanisms of mass production are introduced. The point of all efforts of development policies must be to reach this stage.
3. Take off	This is the tipping point, when one really can say that the new production mode takes over. This happens due to an impulse. The impulse can be internal, as the 1848 revolution was in Germany, or it can be external, such as the high demand for Swedish products throughout the 19th century on the international market.
4. Drive to maturity	Now the system matures and working methods are standardized and the cooperation of the various economic actors formalized. At this stage foreign trade really starts to become important.
5. Age of mass consumption	Now domestic demand reaches a level where it makes economic sense to produce for it. All the basic needs of the population are being covered.

Rostow's phase model: **After the *Second World War* (WWII), the US economist Walt Whitman Rostow created an overview of several phases of economic development which he believed a country needed to move through in order to reach the status of a fully developed country (Rostow 1956, 1960). Rostow's model is merely one of several similar phase models that were created between 1945 and 1968, which were seen as as explaining development in the view of the United States and its allies (Wallerstein 1999, 193).**

Neoliberalism

A current version of modernization theory is neoliberalism, the theory behind the policies universally employed by capitalist states since the time of Ronald Reagan, President of the United States in 1981-89, and Baroness Margaret Hilda Thatcher, Prime Minister of the United Kingdom in 1979-90. This current version continues along the lines of modernization theory, but puts a lot of emphasis on the exchange model of Ricardo (1821) and general classical economic theory (Sandbrook 1995, 278). They believe trade is good for all involved parties at all times, also those who overall are less efficient in production, measured in required labor time per produced unit (Ricardo 1821, chapter 7).

Secondly, and differing from early modernization theory, those arguing the case for neoliberalism hold that too much state intervention in the economy is an evil. For the economy to turn 'healthy,' government should not have 'too much' of an engagement in the development and economics of its respective subjects, and government oversight needs to be rolled back. Neoliberalism is strongly in favor of selling public property as a way to cancel national debt. Much of this theory is seen by neoliberals as being of universal principles and as one that should be used by governments independently of time and space and not beholding to specific peripheral or semi-peripheral countries. Associated with the neoliberal approach are the *World Bank* (WB) and the *International Monetary Fund* (IMF). Throughout the 1980s it set forth a number of *Structural Adjustment Programs* (SAPs), that were supposed to accommodate both development and get rid of the debt these countries had run up.

Opponents hold that the proponents of neoliberalism in reality have a goal of extending exploitation of the third world—which was necessary after the economic problems in the 1970s resulting from the oil crisis—and very often the neoliberals are directed not by rational arguments but their own economic interests.

Counter-hegemonic development theories

For socialist revolutionaries, development generally is seen as equivalent to the introduction of socialism. The classic model according to which Marxists handled revolutions in the 20th century in peripheral countries was to follow Russian revolutionary Vladimir Ilyich Lenin (1870-1924) in asserting that the conditions for completely socialized means of production—

that which is commonly termed 'communism'—would first have to be built up. In this period, which Lenin calls 'monopoly state-capitalism,' the state would take control of and rationalize production in order to prepare the country economically and culturally for socialism. This could in some cases also happen as part of an unforeseen consequence of general capitalist development, such as in the case of Germany, where state-control was largely introduced by the rulers during the *First World War* (WWI). Lenin believed this opened the possibility for socialism as a next step and argued Soviet Russia should copy it (Lenin 1917a, 1917b, 1921) as a first step towards socialism.

When Lenin formulated the model, other socialists such as Polish-German revolutionary Rosa Luxemburg (1871–1919) challenged him on the way this transition period was to be organized. Lenin (1921) believes one should use all dictatorial means necessary to 'hasten' development along, while Luxemburg (1922) holds that parliamentary democracy and freedom to organize—also for the opposition—have to be in place if the revolution is to represent freedom in any meaningful way. Many Marxists have since come to the conclusion that no generalized model of a transition period toward socialism can be made (Harris 1988, 13). In the cases where socialists have organized such a transition period, they varied heavily in political content and in the length of time they have lasted. Yet some form of monopoly state-capitalist transition periods were organized in most countries which underwent socialist experiments in the following decades. In Cuba the period officially lasted 4 years during which private property was nationalized (Harris 1988, 9) while in Nicaragua during the 1980s it never came to that.

Socialist versions of modernization theory

In the first few years after WWII, Soviet-allied countries followed a similar modernization model as that which the west employed, with the Soviet Union as the leading country rather than the United States or Western Europe (Wallerstein 1999, 194). Instead of directly switching to socialism, many Soviet-allied Marxists believed third world countries which had not developed an internal capitalist system would have to do so first. Karl Heinrich Marx himself stated at one time that "[t]he country that is more developed industrially only shows, to the less developed, the image of its own future" (Marx 1867, Preface). In line with this reasoning, these

Marxists argued that the overthrow of the system by a socialist revolution is not a possibility until one has a large proletarian movement. Until then, radicals will just have to participate in regular elections (Palmer 1988, 96). Even participation in labor unions will not help any, as the members of these are mainly artisans, pre-capitalist workers who one never should hope to work for a socialist revolution (Gould 1987, 354). Marx qualified his statement as only applying to western Europe and he said other parts of the world would not necessarily have to go through such a phase of capitalism (Marx 1881). This was apparently not acknowledged by Soviet-allied countries immediately following WWII when they set up their plans for where they thought revolutions would make sense or were possible.

Some Marxists in other parts of the world went even further along these lines. The British communist Bill Warren (1980), who operated within the Marxist paradigm, declared that capitalist development is contradictory and he concluded that in the third world, there was still had what he called 'the continuing transformative potential' of capitalism and imperialism. To support his claim, he pointed to the growth in manufacturing output in third world countries in absolute numbers (Warren 1980, 241) and also the growth of manufacturing as a percentage of the *Gross Domestic Product* (GDP) in several third world countries between 1950 and 1973. Similarly, in today's China, the *Communist Party of China* (CPoC) also makes use of the Marxist framework, despite all changes the nature of the regime has undergone in recent years, and argues the party's responsibility lies in following 'the three representations': "representing the demands for the development of advanced social productive forces, the direction of advanced culture, and the fundamental interests of the greatest majority of the people" (Holbig 2006, 18) – meaning Radicals should support the demands of engineers and capitalists for further capitalist development rather than follow peasants and workers and other groups with which Leftists traditionally have been connected.

The Soviet Union never went quite as far in dismissing socialist ideals for the sake of development as these two examples show, and there was one difference to be noted in how the Soviet Union related to the countries in which it directed development in comparison with how the United States and western European powers did it: The Soviet Union did not have current or former colonies and those third world countries who they were allied with in practice, were generally encouraged to seek a status as nonaligned countries rather than formally allying with the Soviet Union (Wallerstein 1999, 194). That may be why the idea that the Soviet Union would support a country with a capitalist structure is seldom mentioned.

Dependency Theory

With the gradual realization that modernization theory did not bring the welfare to the masses the way it was promised or at least expected in much of the third world, criticism of mainstream theories of development started to appear in the 1950s. One of the more prominent group of critics was known as *Dependency Theorists*. Their main target for criticism is the underlying premise in mainstream development theories that the development in one country works independently of external influences from other countries (Wallerstein 1999, 194).

Under the heading *Dependency Theory* various approaches emphasize that a constant stream of wealth is transferred from the developing third world countries (periphery) to the developed first world countries (core). Some theorists hypothesize operating with a middle layer of semi-periphery, acting as a buffer zone between core and periphery societies (Wallerstein 1974, 229–233). The fundamental difference between first world and third world, they see, is what is produced. Third world countries generally sell raw material and produce agricultural goods, whereas first world countries produce industrial goods. The two then trade one-another's products with each other. Over time, they note, the price of raw material and agricultural products goes down in comparison to the price of manufactured goods. This means the third world can afford less and less of the industrial goods they are importing from the first world, and this leads to obvious economic problems for the third world (Prebisch 1950; Singer 1950). They also argue that much of the high standard of living of the masses of the first world is a product of this transfer of wealth, and the various types of powers the countries of the first world have (media, military, political, etc.) are actively employed to keep this state of affairs in place.

One of the most well-known group of non-radical followers of Dependency Theory are called *Structuralist Dependency Theorists* and they were linked to the *United Nation's Comisión Económica para América Latina y el Caribe* (CEPAL) during the later *Cold War* (CW) years. They supported programs of import-substitution[1] in order to build up a home industry in

---

1. Import-substitution schemes denote government policies which put heavy taxes on

the various third world countries. They hoped that by producing some of their own machinery, these countries would be able to diversify their production and over time be able to do away with the exploitative links to more central first world countries that existed through the import of machinery.

Radical Dependency Theory

Political radicals appropriated Dependency Theory a few years later. Their geographic background was quite diverse and so were their audiences. In western countries, *The political economy of growth* by Baran (1957) was one of the most popular early texts written in this category that inspired several of the later writers. Followers of what with time became known as Radical Dependency Theory extend the idea of exploitation through terms of trade within a country. They hold that inside third world countries the local elites, situated in urban centers, exploit people further away from those centers, and they often have closer personal ties to and share interest with the interests of the western elites, compared with the rural and poorer population of their own country (Johnson 1981; Gunder Frank 1969).

Although the idea of extraction of surplus from the third world is essentially the same as it is for other Dependency Theorists, it is expressed in Marxist terminology and analyzed accordingly. Baran (1957, chapter 5) argues that the only reason Japan is not as underdeveloped as the other countries of Asia is that the country was never subjugated by the west and turned into a colony, the way just about all other countries of the third world had been at some stage. The attention to the importance of third world exploitation originates, for these radicals, from Marx's discussion of what the process of 'primitive accumulation' of capital was that made it possible for some Europeans to already have built up capital at the time when industrial capitalism was just starting. Marx (1867, chapter 26) argues a great part of that came from the forceful exploitation of the third world – through wars, slavery, forceful land grabbing, etc., all actions that today's capitalist would see as highly illegal and unethical, at least in the first world. Luxemburg (1913) argues this exploitation by force of the third world still continues to provide an influx of money to western capitalist countries even now that capitalism has started and capitalism is dependent

---

the import of certain key industrial products in order to provide for the establishment of such an industry at home.

on this. More recent Radical Dependency Theorists add to this, that when one produces either for a mass market in a foreign country in export enclaves or luxury products through import-substitution for the ultra rich in one's own country, the size of the available market is disconnected from wage levels, and so great profits can be made by lowering wages (Biderman 1983, 7–8).

Among several other reasons, that is why many Radical Dependency Theorists do not believe in import-substitution and according to Kay (1989, 126–127) take the fact that Latin America generally becomes more dependent and has national elites that react with acts of repression on popular movements as indicators that the national capitalist classes do not play any progressive role. According to this logic, a national capitalism that brings the same benefit to the population as has been the case in the first world is not possible, and the remaining options are either a fascism based dictatorial system or some type of socialism. Some Radical Dependency Theorists from Latin America, like Theotonio Dos Santos and Vania Bambirra, explored the idea of an independent capitalist development in dependent countries. If only one builds up machinery and heavy industry by nationally owned capital, they stated, accumulation processes could work without exploitation from other countries (Dos Santos (1978) and Vania Bambirra (1973), cited in Kay 1989, 151–152). Five years later, Bambirra (1978, 19) seemed to differ with her earlier statement as she declared that the Cuban revolution had shown socialism was the only way forward for Latin America because the national bourgeoisie did no longer see any perspective in nationalist-capitalist autonomous development.

The criticism of mainstream development theories continued to develop among Radical Dependency Theorists and more recent works seem to give less specific advice to third world countries. Amin (1980) attacked modernization theorists mainly on the basis of their belief that current developments in the third world mirror those of the center regions some decades or centuries earlier. At this time, he claimed developments in the third world are fundamentally different in that when development in the third world is capitalist, it mostly aids the international capital based in the countries central to capitalism. This type of a more general view does not in the same way as previous writings give a clear answer as what actions people in a third world country can take to evade dependency. This change was probably caused by the failure of the Soviet Union and failed attempts at revolutions by third world countries in the second half of the 20th century.

Nicaraguan economic history

Here we look at the economic history of Nicaragua and the underlying development theories that seem to have formed the economic policies of the different Nicaraguan governments.

Once settled after the Spanish conquest, the Nicaraguan economy was for a long time based around an agricultural sector dominated by a few large *latifundio* properties of over 500 hectares, which produced for export, and many small *minifundio* properties of under 5 hectares, which provided for subsistence farming. This structure existed in much of Latin America since the time of the Spanish conquest and continues in many places. During this phase, Nicaragua provided ample opportunities for the investment of international capital in the latifundios. Most native indigenous people were killed or sold into slavery. It meant there was an almost constant lack of laborers for the latifundios. This problem was solved by preventing agricultural laborers from leaving the property they worked on as much as possible, and by raising cattle rather than growing crops. Raising cattle required little human intervention in comparison with growing most crops. In the 17th century, cattle represented the main basis of the Nicaraguan economy. In addition to cattle, two cash crops were grown; cacao was produced for the Mexican market, and indigo was exported to Europe. The combination of the three products worked well together for a while. With time competition from other countries grew, the labor shortage extended and British pirates made transport increasingly unsafe. Thus the production of both cacao and indigo eventually lost profitability (Biderman 1983, 9–10; Tijerino 2008, 93–97; Román 1975, 13–103). This period lasted until the second half of the 19th century.

Obviously, the amount of choice that lay in following this model of development for the Nicaraguan state must have been very limited; even if they had wanted to follow a different development model, it is questionable whether they would have been able to control Nicaraguan farmers and prevented foreign intervention to protect foreign capital. It may be wrong to say Nicaragua followed any particular development theory in this period. If one were to specify a theory, it would be that of classical liberals such as Ricardo (1821), seeing a value first and foremost in international trade and the specialization on only one or a few products, and following a doctrine of little or no state intervention, as neoliberals preached much later.

The following period, the last third of the 19th century, was a short-lived phase of nationalist-bourgeoisie development (Román 1975, 106–107). Coffee-production was introduced and production techniques modernized rapidly due to favorable policies towards increasing national production levels under 30 years of Conservative government. Even more such policies were instituted under the following, nationalist government of Liberal President/dictator José Santos Zelaya López (1893–1910). Zelaya López had come to power by way of a military coup, yet the policies before and after the coup seem to have gone somewhat in the same direction. Coffee production doubled in the first few years after 1899 (Biderman 1983, 10–12; Tijerino 2008, 166–176). The changes that this phase brought consisted of, among other aspects, the forced breaking up of indigenous, communally owned land and replacing it with private individual land ownership in the form of large plantations. Laws were passed to require all indebted persons to either find work or go to jail (Mahoney 2001, 250; Biderman 1983, 11). The first professional Nicaraguan army, which Zelaya López put into place, was used to hunt fugitive workers and send them back to the estates where they had worked (Mahoney 2001, 249). Another measure under Zelaya López was the incorporation of the Atlantic coast into the state of Nicaragua with help from the United States, providing unfavorable economic terms to this area, which housed the center of US trade (Powell 1928, 45–46). The new government's policies effectively started the first developments toward a capitalist production model where both land and labor became commodities, and the first private bank was established. These were limited in scope, and wealth was largely built using massive exploitation of the workforce and lands as had been done previously (Biderman 1983, 10–12; Tijerino 2008, 166–176; Román 1975, 104–106). Zelaya López also tried to diversify trade patterns by establishing trade connections to European markets (Ortega Saavedra 1979, 46). Today, Zelaya López's uprising in 1893 and the writing of a new constitution 1894 are officially celebrated by the Liberals on July 11th, but as mentioned, I have only heard Sandinistas speak positively about him. They recognize he was a Liberal, but understand the economic policies of that time period are more in line with the current Sandinista policies than the policies of the Liberals before 2007, in that they favored national over foreign capital.

Although Zelaya López would not have known it, his policies were somewhat in line with the post-WWII development models. Part of his policies can be seen as being in line with modernization theory in that much of the population was forced into capitalist production, and other parts could have been the program of Structuralist Dependency Theorists in that he built up institutions necessary for industrial growth at home, such as a national bank. It is interesting to note that although Sandinistas identify with Zelaya López today, he did not put much emphasis on eliminating social differences within Nicaragua. He was definitely not a follower of Radical Dependency Theory.

Economic policies between Zelaya López and the Somozas

The end of Zelaya López's government was the end to the phase of nationalist-bourgeoisie development, which gave way to a yet another phase of development led by international capital. Many Nicaraguans today believe what halted the overall development of Nicaraguan production, was that Zelaya Lopez's nationalist policies did not continue after he was removed from power (Biderman 1983, 12). The United States overthrew the Zelaya López regime in 1909/10 through a coup and gave control over agriculture back to a landed coffee oligarchy. This oligarchy had no interests in modernizing the industry they controlled, as they made good profits without needing to reinvest much. According to Sandinista historian Román (1975, 106), it was mostly the fear that Zelaya López could cooperate with non-US companies in trade and possibly in the building of another canal to compete with the one the United States was building in Panama, which led the US administration to this step.

For the next three decades, private bankers from the United States took control over just about the entire Nicaraguan economy. Combined with ever recurring US military interventions to hinder popular struggles, this meant economic development was not feasible (Biderman 1983, 12). The production practices, such as the planting of low-yielding types of coffee and very limited use of pruning and pest control, were not renewed between 1900–50, and with a lack of focus on soil preservation, these factors led to a decline in total yields of 4% per year between 1925–49. As late as 1957–58, the yield/tree or yield/hectare was half that of Costa Rica and El Salvador (Biderman 1983, 10–12). In 1951–52, mechanized farming was almost nonexistent, and when it was employed it was without much access to spare parts or expertise on how the machinery was to be used

In the period between 1910 and the 1950s, Nicaraguan production practices were only moderately modernized (Biderman 1983). Although policies changed somewhat in the later Somoza years, the usage of the machete rather than machinery as a universal tool is still widespread among small agricultural producers. *Photo: UN Photo by Yutaka Nagata*

(Winters 1964, 502; Román 1975). Furthermore, the cattle industry did not modernize in those years and a dairy industry did not come into existence before 1943 and 1953 with the installation of the first and second pasteurizing plants and subsequent modernization of them (Patten 1971).

It is not difficult to see that during this period it was once again classical liberal theory which governed Nicaraguan economic policy. Different from the previous phase, at this stage it had been proven that the institution of a different type of development policy would be possible in Nicaragua – given the absence of intervention by the United States.

Economic policies under the Somozas

The Somoza period is generally treated as one single period of government during which a combination of the Somozas and the interests of the United States governed Nicaragua. In reality it included periods with different economic policies. At times the Somozas followed ideas of noninterventionist government in much the same way these ideas later were incorporated into neoliberal theory. At other times, the government's policies leaned more toward ideas about modernization theory, with some state intervention to modernize agriculture, and Structuralist Dependency Theory with import-substitution schemes.

The Somoza regimes took the first steps to move back to a phase of nationalist-bourgeoisie development with control of international capital in the late 1930s and early 1940s. Although very limited and without any great consequence to the overall demographics at first, the regime used the power of the state to encourage the development of new crops (cotton and sesame) and started the import of tractors. World War II allowed for the development of some limited mining, lumbering and rubber cultivation operated by foreign companies on the Atlantic coast (Biderman 1983, 13). The main economic policies of the Somoza regime remained the same until the 1950s, permitting reasonably free access to foreign capital and doing nothing to close the income gap between rich and poor. In the mid to late 1950s, policies used to modernize agriculture dominated to some extent where they could be successful in modernizing production and elevating the GDP, which grew significantly throughout the 1950s and 1960s with cyclical downturns in 1958–69 and 1968 (Heston, Summers, and Aten 2011). Between 1950 and 1955, the total number of tractors used in Nicaragua grew from 500 to 2500 (Biderman 1983, 13–16). At the same time, the country became increasingly dependent on foreign companies as many other Latin American countries did (Muro Rodríguez et al. 1984, 70). To counter this trend, import-substitution schemes for the manufacture of chemical sprays for agriculture, the production of footwear and textiles, and food processing were successfully set up in the early 1960s (Irvin 1982, 36).

The gross value of manufactured exports increased from $4.1 USD million ($27.1 USD05 million[2]) in 1960 to $143.1 USD million ($491.2 USD05 million) in 1976 (WB LA and Carib. Office 1978, 9). Exports and imports grew rapidly at a similar pace during the 1960s and 1970s (Banco Central de Nicaragua 2010a). At the end of the 1970s, industrial production accounted for 28% of Nicaragua's GDP, slightly more than agriculture (Pres. of IDA 1980, 1). However, a large part of the value of the main industrial export, chemical products, went to pay for the ingredients that had to be imported to manufacture them(WB LA and Carib. Office 1978, 27). Food production remained, therefore, the most important source of export earnings.

By the time of the overthrow of the Somoza dictatorship in 1979, the country had less foreign ownership of its agricultural sector than any other Central American country—helped by the advantageous position held by its agricultural and industrial products in the regional market, *Mercado Común Centroamericano* (MCCA, created in 1961) (Irvin 1982, 36). Throughout Latin America, the development of import-substitution schemes spread, and with it the buildup of stronger national capitalist interests (Pollin and Cockburn 1991, 28).

Radical criticism of Somoza's economic policies

In the first few years following WWII, the Soviet-allied *Partido Socialista Nicaragüense* (PSN) stated that pre-capitalist countries such as Nicaragua needed to develop industrial capitalism before a struggle for socialism could begin. For Carlos Fonseca Amador and other radical students who initially associated with the PSN, the economic advances under the Somoza regime in the 1960s and 1970s were not enough, and they strongly disagreed with the unequal distribution to which these advances in development would lead. Fonseca Amador (1969, 24–25) saw the politics of Central American integration, during the time of the MCCA, as a project

---

2. *USD05* are USD adjusted for inflation to 2005 levels, using the *US Urban Consumer Price Index* (USCPI-U).

The $9.2 USD million ($44.4 USD05 million) *Fabritex* cotton mill was set up in Managua shortly before the 1972 earthquake by organizations from Colombia, Nicaragua and the *Mercado Común Centroamericano* (MCCA). At full capacity it could handle 1800 tons of Nicaraguan cotton a year (UN 1971). The later Somoza years saw schemes of import-substitution and industrialization and Central American economic cooperation through the MCCA after the organization was established in 1961 (Irvin 1982). USD05 are USD adjusted for inflation to 2005 levels, using the *US Urban Consumer Price Index (USCPI-U)*. Photo: UN Photo by Yutaka Nagata

for US American companies to better drain the area of its riches and not as a help in terms of enhancing national economic development, much in line with how Dependency Theorist Baran (1957, 190–194) sees the setup of some infrastructure projects in the third world. Big companies were given rights to mine and cut lumber for very low fees (Fonseca Amador 1969, 23–25).

Although GDP grew, development remained fundamentally unequal. In 1951–52, 42% of all agricultural land was in the hands of only 1.6% of the population (Winters 1964, 501) and 55% of the total area of privately owned farms in 1952 were held by very few private proprietors (Fonseca Amador 1969, 24). The modernization in production that the state promoted starting in the late 1950s, meant that big producers—those producing for export—received preferential treatment over those producing for local consumption (Biderman 1983, 16–22; Wall 1993; Dijkstra 1999, 212). The focus on export crops led to food being grown in the worst possible areas, and in order to feed the population additional imports of food had to be made (Fonseca Amador 1969, 24). By 1969, cotton production took

In 1972 an earthquake destroyed most of Managua and with it much of the country's more advanced production facilities. Most houses that had not been completely destroyed by the earthquake were subsequently taken down. To this day, the inner city has not been rebuilt, and doing so would not be wise, as the location is prone to earthquakes. *Photos: Marcel Toruño*

up 75% of all cultivated land (Muro Rodríguez et al. 1984, 71). The number of students exiting school prematurely and the number of deaths and severally injured due to production related incidents reached record levels, even in a Central American comparison (Fonseca Amador 1969, 25). One of the consequences of the state's policies was more rapid migration to the population centers, most of all to Managua. In Managua, various capitalists with close connections to the Somocista regime built factories to take advantage of laborers flooding in (Wall 1993, 2).

Fonseca Amador and other leading Sandinistas proposed to equalize the development of the country, with a focus on equalizing economic development in the city of Managua with the rest of the country (Wall 1993, 1). While modernization led to the creation and strengthening of the bourgeoisie and a professional middle class in the cities, especially on the Pacific coast, it also meant peasants were transformed into urban wage laborers – often unemployed and destitute city dwellers (Irvin 1982, 37).

Conflict of interest between bourgeoisie Nicaraguans and Somoza

The Somoza dictatorship managed to keep up high overall growth rates throughout the 1960s, but the saturation of the Central American market for Nicaraguan products, the Managua earthquake (1972), the world oil crisis (1974), combined with cyclical economic downturns, led to a downturn at the beginning to middle of the 1970s. This downturn proved to be a huge obstacle for the Somoza regime. New investments were increasingly made by government borrowing, first through development assistance, then by borrowing in the commercial market. By the mid-1970s, debt payments made up one third of all export earnings, and the government accounted for 40% of all investments. The ratio of taxes to GDP fell in the years following the earthquake from 10.8% in 1973-74 to 10.5% in 1975-77, despite increased income and sales taxes (WB LA and Carib. Office 1978, ii) and although Nicaragua had the second lowest taxes to GDP ratio in Central America next after Guatemala (WB LA and Carib. Office 1978, 23). In 1978, the WB proposed to stabilize the economy by decreasing planned public investments 35-40%, only carrying through projects with a high socio-economic priority as well as other austerity measures, increasing taxes, and augmenting exports to pay down external debts (WB LA and Carib. Office 1978).

Control of the economy also shifted markedly during the last years of the Somoza regime. At the beginning of the 1970s, the Pellas family from Granada and the Montealegres from León together were responsible for 20% of GDP (Dijkstra 1999, 296). As late as 1975, the Somozas were still only the third richest family (Brown 1994, 212). Through ownership of various enterprises and their rule of the country, the Somozas tried to appropriate an increasing part of the total national income. By the end of the 1970s, the Somozas were the richest family, and they were responsible for 25% of GDP (Dijkstra 1999, 296).

The policies that aimed to enrich the Somozas in relation to other Nicaraguan capital owners led to an increase in dissatisfaction with the regime among the bourgeoisie (Irvin 1982, 36-37; Brown 1994, 212), and much attention at the time focused on the part of the business community that disagreed with Somoza and the part they played in the organizing efforts against the Somoza regime. Relatively little attention is given to that now, either by Liberals or Sandinistas. The Somozas were generally described as having been in control of just about everything and they are seen as the richest family of that time. A reason for this may be that the other two families have survived and the Montealegres finance a great part of the Liberal opposition.

Masaya in 1979: On the left, a street turned into war-zone, and on the right, one of the first celebrations of the revolutionary victory. The end of the dictatorship brought with it both cause for joy and the beginning of many years of economic hardship due to the war. Photos: Pedro Meyer

Economic realities and policies under the Sandinistas of the 1980s

The insurrectionist war (see also — *Under the Sandinista in the 1980s*, p. 45) left the country indebted by $1.5 USD billion ($4.0 USD05 billion), most of which Somoza had spent on arms purchased from the United States during the 18 month insurrection. In order to be eligible for any foreign loans, the governing post-insurrection junta accepted the debt of the Somoza regime, although only $3.5 USD million ($9.4 USD05 million) was left in Nicaragua's reserves (Berrios 1985, 125). It is estimated that 40,000 Nicaraguans were dead and 100,000 wounded (Irvin 1982, 37). The damage to building structures was valued at around $250 USD million ($672.5 USD05 million). Capital flight during and directly after the insurrection totaled around $500 USD million ($1.3 USD05 billion) (Pres. of IDA 1980, 2). In addition to the economic difficulties the country had inherited from the last Somoza years, these war-related issues had an enormous impact on the Sandinistas' achievable short term production levels and the type of trade the country could realistically set up.

Ideological influences on economic policies

After the successful Sandinista insurrection of 1979, the influence of Dependency Theory on the way the Sandinistas tried to set up the country's economy was strong (Velasco 2002, 42). Jaime Wheelock Román is known for his work *Imperialismo y dictadura: crisis de una formación social,* which analyzes Nicaraguan history in a Marxist Dependency Theory perspective, and for being among the nine members of the national directory of the FSLN representing the *Tendencia Proletaria* (TP) during the 1980s. He also became the Minister for Agriculture and Agrarian Reform after the insurrection. His book achieved cult status among most Sandinistas, especially those not having a background from the *Tendencia Tercerista* (TT), and several reedited editions of *Imperialismo y dictadura: crisis de una formación social*, and several other books representing much the same economic thinking, were published during his time in government.[3]

The governing junta nationalized the banking sector, the Somoza property and put foreign trade under national control. This put 20% of industry, 25% of agricultural production and more than 50% of the service sector under national control. This made out an important part of the national production. In the early 1980s, agriculture represented around 25% of GDP, employed 50% of the labor force and generated 70% of export earnings (Pres. of IDA 1980, 1–2). In the first year after the insurrection, the public sector share of GDP rose from 15% to 40% (Pres. of IDA 1980, 2). Each years in the period 1984–87, this figure was higher than 40% (Heston, Summers, and Aten 2011), while a much smaller part of the total productive sector was in public hands. This made state planning difficult. The export oriented industry which still operated was entirely in private hands (Irvin 1982, 38). In the 1980 and 1981 economic plans, the prioritization made the shift in economic policy from the Somoza years obvious. The plans tried to restore the same levels of growth and capital accumulation existing in the Somoza years, but with consumption geared toward the poor rather than the luxury sector. The idea was that while in the short term, Nicaragua would be almost entirely dependent on foreign aid, in the long-term it would be able to lower dependency on aid while diversifying its sources rather than relying on aid only from the United States (Irvin 1982, 38–39).[4]

---

3. The description of the early years of the FSLN in the 1960s and 1970s by Borge Martínez (1990) suggests the theoretical studies of most central Sandinistas had not gone beyond Marx, his friend and co-writer Friedrich Engels, Lenin, and Augusto Nicolás Calderón Sandino. It seemingly did not include much from the writers of Dependency Theory, even though their ideas were associated with Sandinismo. The knowledge horizon must have varied quite a bit among leading Sandinistas. With his central position in the government, Román did make central economic policy decisions and economic theory. In that sense, the Sandinista period represented a period of development with the stated goals of achieving more national independence and achieving more equality.

4. With the Sandinistas in power, social scientists of all types flocked to Nicaragua, and the economy was analyzed much more than before. Berrios (1985); Irvin (1982); Cuenca (1992) studied the economic reality Nicaragua faced during the first few years of the Sandinista rule with no support from the United States, limited support from Western Europe and somewhat more support from Soviet allied countries. Many figures that demonstrate economic development are only available for the years after 1979 due to this increased interest. It also means that it is not possible to compare all aspects of the

Government Consumption Share of GDP Per Capita (PPP)

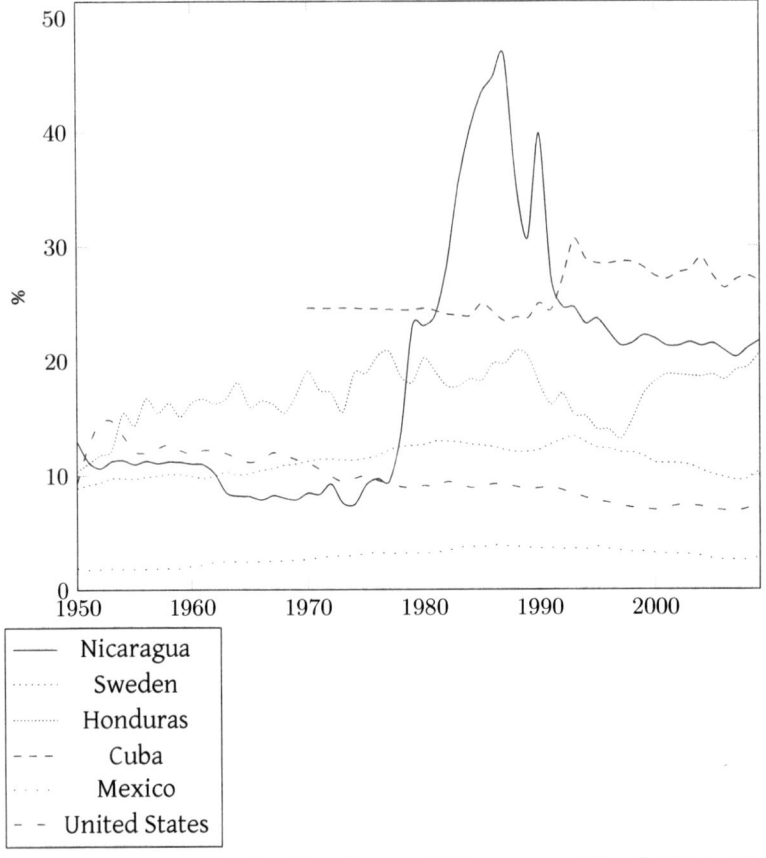

Legend:
— Nicaragua
⋯ Sweden
⋯ Honduras
- - - Cuba
⋯ Mexico
- - United States

Government spending has long been a higher percentile of GDP in Nicaragua and Honduras than in the United States and Mexico and at times even Sweden. The 1980s brought the government portion of GDP up to more than 40% – almost twice that of Cuba. In the subsequent years of Liberal governments it declined to around 20% – still more than twice what it had been in the 1970s. In the period 2006–09, it increased insignificantly by 1.4% per year. The figures are somewhat skewed. Until 1979, the businesses of the Somoza family were part of the private sector, even though the Somozas and the Nicaraguan state worked much like a single unit, and since 2007 the activity of the Sandinista owned company *ALBA de Nicaragua, S.A.* (Albanisa) has been counted as part of the private sector, even though it operates like an extension of the state. Recent figures for Honduras look similar to Nicaraguan ones, although Honduras did not go through a similar revolutionary process. *Source: Heston, Summers, and Aten (2011)*

Land reform, trade and oligarchs

The main Sandinista reform in the 1980s within the sector of production was in the area of land redistribution. The lands of the Somozas were nationalized and divided out through agrarian reforms. The titles were not always written out on paper, and oftentimes were just informally known by Sandinista authorities at the time. It was believed the first land disbursements would be followed by further steps of land reform which would include measures to further the collective usage of lands. Land reform on a large scale did not start before 1984 (Fonseca Terán 2008g). Altogether around 60,000 families received redistributed lands, either collectively or as individuals (Tijerino 2008, 313–314). The land titles given out generally had provisions in them, such as, land given to cooperatives could not be sold. The idea behind this setup was it forbid any future renewed accumulation of lands by the few.

State run businesses were also part of the Sandinista economic plan, especially in the early 1980s. Yet quite differently from other socialist experiments, the stated goal by state officials was not that all land would essentially be state-run, but rather the growth of an economy dominated by a mix of small producers and the encouragement of the formation of voluntary-based cooperatives (Borge Martínez 1980, 96). Government takeover occurred more at the level of foreign trade. Part of taking trade into state hands was done through the creation of the *Ministerio de Comercio Exterior* (MICE) in August 1979 which was to regulate everything that entered and exited the country (Berrios 1985, 119).

The remaining two super-rich families, the Pellas and the Montealegres, who had made up the oligarchy together with the Somozas, continued to function as important economic entities. Several leading activists of the FSLN had direct family connections to the companies connected to the Pellas family, the *Grupo Pellas* (GP), and some had been involved in the management of the *Ingenio San Antonio* (ISA), a sugar mill controlled by the GP, during the years of Somoza (Vilas 1992, 424–425). The head of the GP, Carlos Pellas Chamorro, stayed in Nicaragua until 1987, and not before 1988 was the ISA confiscated by the government (Everingham 2001, 71). This was only due to failing re-investments in the plants and it was agreed the state would pay the GP annual compensation payments (Everingham 2001, 71). Several Montealegre properties connected to their

---

Nicaraguan economy in the 1980s with the years before the revolution due to lack of data.

Banco Nicaragüense de Industria y Comercio (BANIC) were confiscated by the state (Everingham 2001, 71), but Eduardo Montealegre Rivas, one of the current opposition leaders, worked as vice-president of the *Banking Investment Group* of *Shearson Lehman Hutton* in the United States during the 1980s (GWU 2010).

Economic involvement of the United States

Just two weeks after the revolutionary victory, at the end of July 1979, a first inquiry was made for military aid from the US government. In August of that year, the United States decided to only give monetary aid of $75 USD million ($201.8 USD05 million) – $5 USD million ($13.5 USD million) as a grant and $70 USD million ($188.3 USD05) as a loan. In September, José Daniel Ortega Saavedra, Sergio Ramírez Mercado and Moisés Hassan Morales, the FSLN members of the governing junta, went to Washington to ask for military help once more. Military aid was denied again (Berrios 1985, 112).

In January 1980, the *US Congress* (USC) legislated that 60% of the already decided upon help of $75 USD million was to go to the private sector (Berrios 1985, 112-113). One interpretation of this move may be that this measure would fund the opposition to the Sandinistas in the private sector (Leogrande 1996, 331). In *Nicaragua* the WB called for that – this report warned that too many loans had been given to the public sector and that the private sector was lacking behind due to uncertainties in how far Sandinista reforms would go. It warned that if Nicaragua wanted to maintain a mixed economy as had been announced, more attention had to be given to the needs of the private sector and specifically entrepreneurs (WB LA and Carib. Office 1981).[5]

In February 1980, even more conditions were laid upon the aid by the *US House of Representatives* (USHR) even further restricting access to the limited funds. Altogether 16 conditions, including that the money be used to buy products from the United States and that no economic ties with Cuba were to be established, sought to restrict the options available to the Nicaraguan government (Berrios 1985, 112). Washington expressed fears that Nicaragua would develop into "another Cuba" by spring 1980 (Der Spiegel 1980, 191).

---

5. The 1981 report is the last WB economic report from the 1980s currently available publicly, but there is no reason to believe that the views of the WB changed subsequently.

By the end of 1980, the last $15 USD million ($35.6 USD05 million) still to be paid out was suspended by the US administration under President James Earl Carter, with the excuse that the Sandinistas supported insurgents in El Salvador logistically and politically. On 2 April 1981, newly elected President Reagan formally suspended the aid altogether (Berrios 1985, 112; Der Spiegel 1980, 191; Veterans Peace Action Team Pre-election Observation Delegation to Nicaragua 1989; Dijkstra 1999, 299). In its place he put a policy of trying to overthrow the Sandinista run government through economic blockade and a war which lasted for the rest of the decade.

An additional economic part of trying to overthrow the Sandinistas 1981–90, was to try to block all commercial credit from abroad. Although lines of credit were officially still open due to the acceptance of the Somoza debt by the FSLN, the US government tried openly to discourage any further credits. Often this was done by directly threatening potential lenders. From 1981, Nicaragua was on a list of countries to which United States officially tried to deny loans, and in 1983, the United States downgraded Nicaragua's creditworthiness rating from 'substandard' to 'doubtful,' which made it more difficult for the FSLN to obtain credit. This continued throughout the Reagan presidency, and institutions such as the *Inter-American Development Bank* (IDB) were used as leverage to push through the 'no loans' strategy the United States had decided upon (Leogrande 1996, 331–334).

Involvement of Western Europe / countries allied with the United States

In 1979, the *Bundesrepublik Deutschland* (BRD, Federal Republic of Germany), Belgium, Brazil and Spain turned down Sandinista requests for arms. Only France sold Nicaragua $15.8 USD million ($33.9 USD05 million) worth of military equipment in 1981, but due to pressure from Washington, all subsequent sales were halted (Berrios 1985, 113). Nevertheless, in the years 1979–82, Western Europe was actually a greater provider of aid than the state socialist countries combined. During this period 38.42% of the economic value of the total amount of aid sent to Nicaragua came from Western Europe, and only 21.16% from the Soviet allied countries (Berrios 1985, 121).

Even though the United States tried to block aid, often times Western Europe voted with the Soviet Union and the nonaligned countries, the group to which Nicaragua counted itself (Ortega Saavedra 1979). In 1983, when the IDB was to vote on a $2.2 USD million ($4.3 USD05 million) loan to finish a rural road project already 90% complete, 42 of 43 countries voted for the loan. The United States vetoed the loan. In the end it was given as part of a bilateral aid project from the Netherlands (Leogrande 1996, 334). When in 1985 the President of the United States, Reagan, announced a full trade embargo on Nicaragua without approval of the USC by invoking the *International Emergency Economic Powers Act* (IEEPA), even such close allies as the BRD and the United Kingdom openly opposed the move (Leogrande 1996, 338–339).

Involvement of Eastern Europe and other Soviet allied countries

The biggest giver of aid, in terms of health and education, during those years was Cuba, accounting for 23.37% of all help with approximately 4000 citizens on the ground in Nicaragua in 1985. The *Deutsche Demokratische Republik* (DDR, German Democratic Republic) helped with education, building a polytechnic institute in Jinotepe[6], and gave food in the form of wheat. Additionally, Nicaragua received help during extraordinary crises, such as the 1982 flood disaster, as well as $148 USD million ($290.2 USD05 million) worth of farm machines and raw material in 1983, and $24 USD million ($45.1 USD05 million) in credit in 1984 (Berrios 1985, 120–123).

Since no western countries were willing to sell arms to Nicaragua, requests were made to socialists countries, which were more willing to accommodate them (Berrios 1985, 113; Dijkstra 1999, 299). In the first year, between July 1979 and July 1980, Nicaragua doubled the number of countries it had economic and political relations with, most of which had to do with its new connections to the Soviet allied countries.

Starting in 1984, kerosene was imported from the Soviet Union, producing energy which accounted for as much as 50% of Nicaragua's total energy needs in 1985. From 1980 on, the main export to the Soviet Union was coffee, while the main imports were machinery and oil, financed by a 2.5–5% trade credit to be paid back over a period of 10–25 years. The second biggest trade partner, and in 1983 the biggest overall trade partner, was Bulgaria (Berrios 1985, 115).

The Soviet Union became Nicaragua's main supplier of oil. Until then oil was obtained from Mexico (Dijkstra 1999, 299). The Soviet Union gave

---

6. Jinotepe is a city in the departamento Carazo.

almost no economic aid in the first years, 1979–80, when Nicaragua was classified as more a friend than a close relative. In the years 1981–83, somewhat more money was given (Berrios 1985, 120). This trade with the Soviet Union and its allies created friction inside Nicaragua, principally because most production was still in private hands, and these private investors didn't particularly like the idea of trading with the Soviet Union (Berrios 1985, 117). Writing in the mid-1980s, Berrios (1985) predicted the continued existence of the private sector for many years to come. Leftist theoreticians Ernest Mandel and Oskar Lange warned third world regimes who were trying to introduce socialism, that nationalizing gradually would not work, as the remaining private sector, in fear of being exterminated, would sabotage the economy or flee the country (Harris 1988, 28), and Nicaragua seems to have been a good example of just that.

FSLN leaders argued the economy was not developed enough to be nationalized entirely. As late as 1989, Ortega Saavedra argued the speed at which socialism could advance was different for different societies, and that in Nicaragua, a speed in accordance with the special conditions of Nicaraguan society needed to be pursued (Wall 1993, 1).

Economic reality

In spite of all efforts, Nicaragua did not do very well during the 1980s in terms of economic development. The war drained the economy tremendously, and the economic policies did not help alleviate the situation. Full land reform was not to be in the immediate future. In delivering real and measurable economic growth for the masses, Nicaragua hardly improved and towards the end of the decade the situation worsened.

In 1979, $618 USD million ($1.66 USD05 billion) in debt payments were due, 70% to go to private banks (Berrios 1985, 119). Nicaraguan foreign debt rose from 107.6% of the *Gross National Income* (GNI) to 1210.1% in the period 1979–89 (WB 2011a). In 1985, the private sector still represented approximately 50% of all trade and did not reinvest significant money in Nicaragua (Dijkstra 1999, 298). In 1979, Nicaragua had a current account surplus of $220.1 USD million ($592.1 USD05 million). By 1985, it had built up a current account deficit of $726.5 USD million ($1.32 USD05 billion). This change was largely due to the increasing trade deficit and both fell simultaneously until the end of the decade (Banco Central de Nicaragua

An incinerated desk and typewriter demonstrate one of the main targets of the Contra attacks—the facilities utilized to promote the Sandinistas' social and educational programs. The goal seems to have been to ensure that the Sandinistas would fail in their attempt to develop the country. *Photo: Witness for Peace*

2010a). Nicaragua kept a trade deficit during the 1980s[7], and the growth in both exports and imports from the Somoza period was effectively halted (Banco Central de Nicaragua 2010a). In the beginning of the 1980s, the exports to other developing countries went up slightly, while imports from them went down. In relation to the CMEA a trade surplus at the beginning of the decade turned into a deficit by 1982 and it remained throughout the 1980s. Inflation rates also increased rapidly, and went beyond 1000% every year in the period of 1987–90 (IMF 2010, 2000).

Much of this arguably did not have to do with the policies of the Sandinista regime directly. Investments into Nicaragua were generally unattractive to other countries due to the initial Somoza debt, so very little new capital flowed into the country. According to the CEPAL, Nicaragua did end up doing fairly well in the economic slump of 1983, considering a collapse in exports to its neighbors of the MCCA (Berrios 1985, 129). The economic embargo by the United States and the war aimed at destroying the nation's finances, made economic planning increasingly difficult. Besides the war, the negative development in terms of trade could also have

---

7. Nicaragua's total trade deficit was $344 USD million ($815.3 USD05 million) in 1980 and declined to $241.7 USD million ($361.2 USD05 million) in 1990 (Banco Central de Nicaragua 2010a, 114).

Nicaraguan trade balance

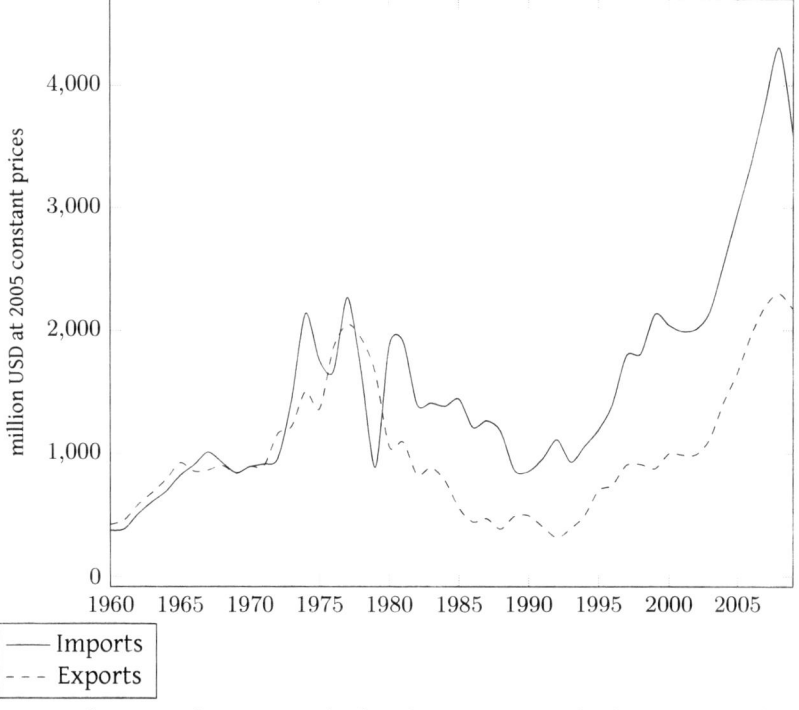

— Imports
--- Exports

During the time of Somoza and Liberal governments, both imports and exports increased. During the Sandinista years of the 1980s, imports declined, but exports declined even more, leaving the country with a permanent trade deficit. Before 1979, exports and imports balanced each other out for the most part. But since the Sandinista insurrection, imports have always been greater than exports. Instead of becoming less dependent on foreign countries, the way the Sandinistas had hoped their policies would work, ever since 1979 the country has been more more dependent on the outside world. After 1990 both imports and exports have increased once more. Yet, while exports only barely have reached the level of the 1970s, imports are almost twice as high.

Values have been adjusted for inflation to 2005 value of USD using the *US Urban Consumer Price Index* (USCPI-U). *Source: Banco Central de Nicaragua (2010a); USDL-BLS (2011)*

to do with the fact that most trade shifted from being mainly with the United States and western Europe to the Soviet Union and the countries connected to the *Council of Mutual Economic Assistance* (CMEA) (Berrios 1985, 113-114; Dijkstra 1999, 299). In the later years it was the gigantic inflation rates which made most economic planning impossible.

Due to all these problems, plans that were meant to lead to more equality and to build up national industries were abandoned or simplified. It was initially planned to set up a cotton-textile plant in northwestern Nicaragua in order to export cotton cloth rather than the raw cotton fiber. This was meant to decentralize the cotton industry. The project was abandoned, but two similar plants were installed in Managua. Several other projects that were built, were meant to increase national production in areas such as milk production and hydro-electric power. These projects, all built in the subsequent years, were financed by aid money and were highly technical to such a degree that Nicaragua and Nicaraguans were unable to maintain them (Wall 1993, 6-9).

Transition from power

Known as the *Piñata*, the FSLN used the months between February, when they lost the election, and April 1990, when power was handed over to the election winners, to redistribute ownership on a large scale. 20% of all land distributions under the FSLN were done in this period. Some of these were clearly redistributions for farmers who technically had been using the land already and been working on it for a long time. Critics claim much of the redistributing was in reality handing over property to FSLN leaders (Cupples 1992, 299-300). I have not been able to check the validity of these claims, but it is true that several Sandinistas did extraordinarily well in economic terms in subsequent years.

Liberal economic politics

The Liberal regimes after 1990 started another phase of giving access to international capital and limiting state intervention. This was clearly in line with neoliberal ideas about development. In Nicaragua, the term 'neoliberal' is also what is used to describe the economic policies of these governments. The years between 1990 and 2006 are commonly referred to as 'the 16 years of neoliberalism' due to the high rate of privatizations of major areas of economic life, such as the pension system (Téfel et al. 2000),

Undernourishment

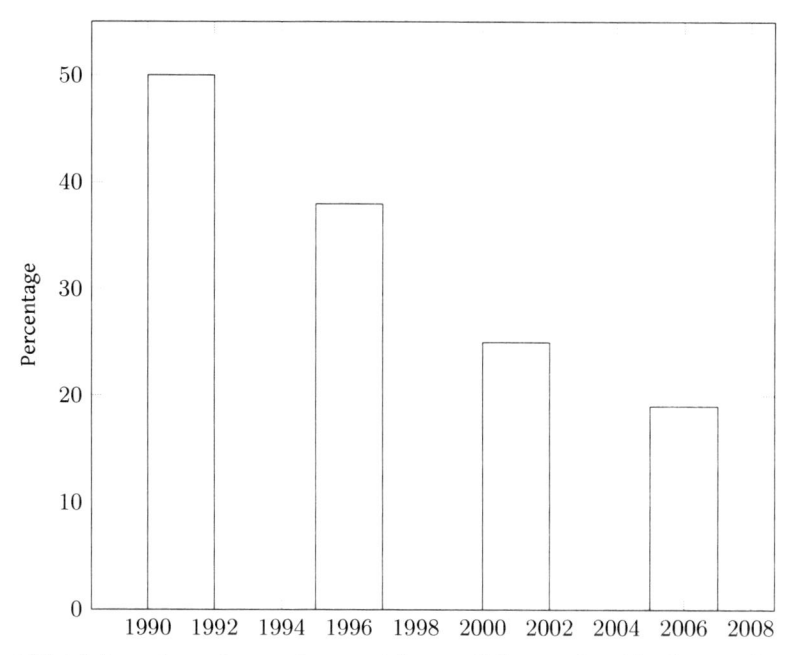

Official data show that undernourishment fell considerably during the period of Liberal governments (1990–2007). *Source: FAO (2010)*

and the principle of constantly lowering social program expenditures as instructed by the IMF (Vargas 2006, 56).

It was the first non-Sandinista president, Violeta Barrios Torres de Chamorro, who opened the country for trade with South America and the United States. The Montealegres and Pellas were returned large parts of their respective properties, and promises were made to give some properties to decommissioned members of the military and the Contras (Everingham 2001, 71–72).

International economic ties also changed fundamentally. The economic situation on a global level had changed when the Soviet allied countries fell away as trading partners. The *International Court of Justice* (ICJ) in Den Haag decided by 1986 that the United States was obliged to pay damages for the war on Nicaragua – a total of $17 USD billion ($30.29 USD05 billion). The government of 1990 forgave the United States this debt (Equipo Envío 1991), sold off most national industry, and did away with the country's train system (Grigsby 2005). Instead of sanctions from the United States, Nicaragua was integrated into a free trade zone with the United States as part of the *Dominican Republic-Central American Free Trade Agreement* (DR-CAFTA), which was ratified in 2004.

Nicaraguan Foreign Debts since 1970

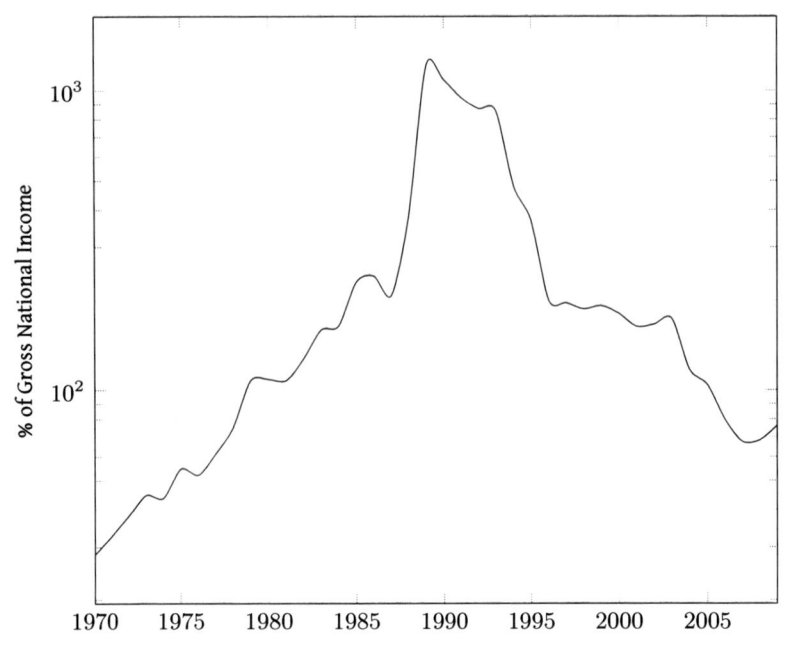

During the Sandinista years of the 1980s, dependence on foreign money lenders increased. It had been hoped that such dependence would decrease. Nicaraguan external debt as a percentage of *Gross National Income* grew from 32.6% to 74.7% following the 1972 earthquake (1971–78). Yet the biggest increase happened in the Sandinista years of the 1980s, when it increased from 107.6% to 1210.1% (1979–89). In 2007, the external debt was down at 67.4% and that was the first time it hit pre-revolution levels. In 2009, it had risen once again to 76.2%. The increase during the current Sandinista government is much less than what was the case in the 1980s. These figures do not include the $17 USD billion ($30.29 USD05 billion) in war-reparations, the *International Court of Justice* (ICJ) in Den Haag had awarded Nicaragua from the United States in 1986 (Equipo Envío 1991).

"Total external debt stocks to *Gross National Income* [(GNI)]. Total external debt is debt owed to nonresidents repayable in foreign currency, goods, or services. Total external debt is the sum of public, publicly guaranteed, and private non-guaranteed long-term debt, use of *International Monetary Fund* (IMF) credit, and short-term debt. Short-term debt includes all debt having an original maturity of 1 year or less and interest in arrears on long-term debt. GNI [...] is the sum of value added by all resident producers plus any product taxes (less subsidies) not included in the valuation of output plus net receipts of primary income (compensation of employees and property income) from abroad." *Source: WB (2011a)*

Nicaraguan Foreign Debts in recent years

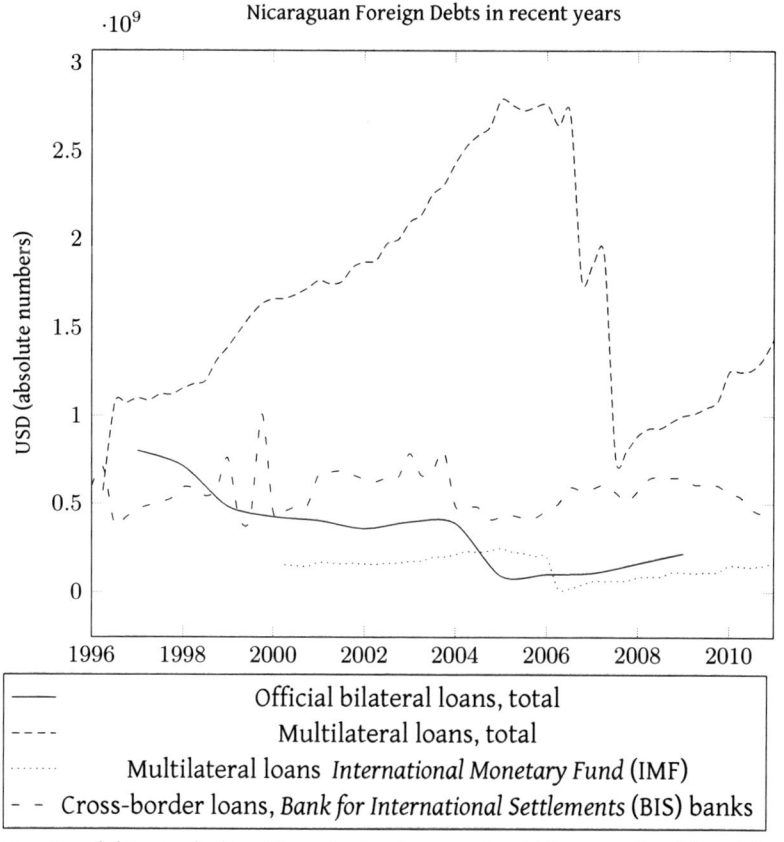

—	Official bilateral loans, total
----	Multilateral loans, total
······	Multilateral loans *International Monetary Fund* (IMF)
- -	Cross-border loans, *Bank for International Settlements* (BIS) banks

Foreign debts, including those to the *International Monetary Fund* (IMF) have grown constantly since the mid-1990s, under the Liberals and the current Sandinistas. In 2006, the IMF forgave Nicaragua its entire debt (Beachy 2006). The *Inter-American Development Bank* (IDB) agreed to forgive Nicaragua's debt in 2007 (IDB 2011). The Nicaraguan debt to the IMF and to other multilateral organizations has again grown under the current Sandinista government. In that sense, Nicaragua is not moving away from control by the IMF under the current government. *Source: WB (2011b)*

A family photo from Los Cedros, Managua taken in 2007 shows the continued existence of extreme poverty among many Nicaraguans. Official figures show an improvement in several development indicators since 1990. Most Nicaraguans seem to attribute the high amount of extreme poverty that existed in 2007 to the failed economic policies of the Liberal governments of 1990–2007. *Photo: Wikimedia Photo by Robert Picard*

Among the most prominent parts of privatized public infrastructure is electricity, which was privatized in 2000 when *Unión Fenosa, S.A.* (UF), a Spanish utility company, obtained a contract to run the Nicaraguan electricity system. In 1998, the applicable laws were changed with the votes of all parties in a way that allowed for the subsequent privatization of the electricity network. Two smaller companies, *Dissur* (DS) and *Disnorte* (DN), were set up to bid on the electricity net. There were no counteroffers. UF then bought DS and DN and has since been the sole operator of the Nicaraguan electricity network. Nicaraguans have since accused UF of trying to make a profit by not reinvesting into the Nicaraguan electricity system. This was the cause—it is oftentimes claimed—which led to the power outages of 4–12 hours in major cities by 2006 (Tortuga – Grupo anti-militarista 2006).

There are some discrepancies in the views on what counts as Nicaraguan exports. Up until 1996, all sources seem to agree Nicaragua had a negative trade balance with the United States. Nicaraguan statistics show the same for the following years, but according to figures provided by the United States, in the years after 1996 Nicaragua exported to the United States more than it imported. According to these figures, all trading between Nicaragua and the United States totaled just $612.6 USD million ($762.5 USD05 million) in 1996, with the balance being $88 USD million ($109.5 USD05 million) in favor of the United States. In 2008, it had grown to $1.7 USD billion ($1.54 USD05 billion), with $677.6 USD million ($614.6

USD05 million) in favor of Nicaragua (US Census Bureau 2009; USDL-BLS 2011). Nicaraguan sources show an increase in both imports (see also p. 95) and exports (see also p. 96), yet the balance continues to be in favor of the United States rather than Nicaragua. The difference in methodology between how Nicaragua and how the United States obtained their numbers is that the United States included the production data of free trade *Export Production Zones* (EPZ) and Nicaragua did not. The US government sees these as part of the Nicaraguan export, while the Nicaraguan government does not. Singer (1950, 475) was the first to point out, that in cases where the production is completely and only connected with foreign investment, it creates more wealth in the country from where the investment originates than in the country where the production takes place. Also Baran (1957, 190-193) made this point. In relation to all trading partners, exports and imports once again increased, but different from the time of Somoza, a constant trade deficit remained (Banco Central de Nicaragua 2010a).

Even though Liberal policies did not emphasize poverty reduction and social development, many statistical development indicators for this period point to an overall improvement of the economic situation for the majority of Nicaraguans. Infant mortality fell (UNIGCME 2010), the rate of undernourished Nicaraguans also declined (FAO 2010), and the unemployment rate remained stable (BCN 2007, 2009, 2011). Since the late 1990s, even the economic gap between rich and poor Nicaraguan families seems to have diminished (CIA 2011b; FIDEG 2010).[8]

Nicaraguan economics during the second Sandinista government

Ortega Saavedra was sworn in as president of Nicaragua in January 2007, shortly before a global financial crisis hit. Unemployment figures have increased since (BCN 2011, 2009), and most other economic development indicators continue in the same positive direction as before. There are

---

8. Although I have tried to find statistics that are verified by international organizations and parts of the Nicaraguan government, after having worked with Nicaraguan statistics and Nicaraguans who have handled such statistics for decades, who have very little confidence in any statistical figures obtained in Nicaragua, I am not overly confident that not at least part of these numbers were made up somewhere along the line. In particular, several of my informants were highly doubtful to statistics that showed that the Gini-index had fallen during the time of Liberal governments.

Infant mortality and public health spendings

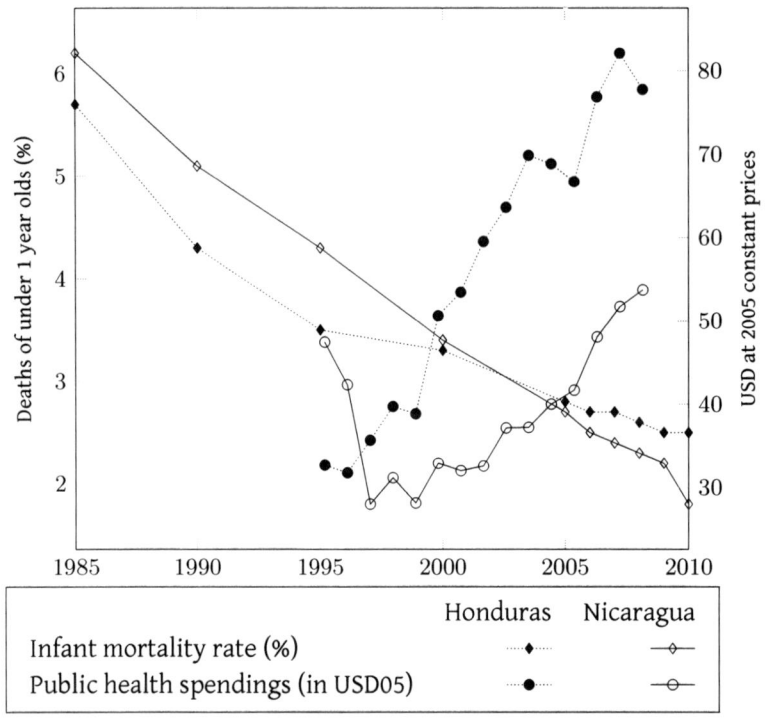

	Honduras	Nicaragua
Infant mortality rate (%)	◆	◇
Public health spendings (in USD05)	●	○

The infant mortality rate of Nicaragua has sunk faster than that of neighboring Honduras, although government spending on health has been larger in Honduras 1997–2008. Liberal and Sandinista governments in Nicaragua have not shown remarkably different results nor have Nicaraguan government investments in public health during the Sandinista government developed remarkably different than those of Liberal controlled Honduras. Exceptions are found in the most recent years: In 2009, when Honduras cut spending markedly following the military coup, and in 2010, when Nicaraguan infant mortality rate fell from 2.2% to 1.8% within just 1 year.

Values have been adjusted for inflation to 2005 value of USD using the *US Urban Consumer Price Index* (USCPI-U). *Source: WHO (2011); UNSTATS (2010); UNIGCME (2010); USDL-BLS (2011)*

not yet statistics available for all indicators up to the present, but among almost all of those available, no radical shift in any direction can be noticed. There are some social programs and major economic development projects in place that may affect future statistics positively. In a sense, the current situation is somewhat similar to the 1980s, in that positive change is promised for the future, yet in many areas has not been achieved yet.

The social programs *Hambre Cero* (HC) and *Usura Cero* (UC), which the Ortega Saavedra government started, are aimed at changing production patterns, although with much lower expectations than some projects of the 1980s. These are two profiled programs that make up part of a series of programs. HC is a program which provides a few livestock (one pig, one cow, five chicken), shelter for the animals, food and seed to grow more food and training and monitoring by the *Ministerio Agropecuario y Forestal* (MAGFOR) to women in the countryside who control between 0.7 and 2.1 hectares of land. The woman then pays a total of $300 USD of the money recovered from the sale of piglets, eggs, and other products that originate in the livestock back into a fund for her neighborhood. This money is then accessible for future collective investments, and is supposed to encourage collective decision making and the creation of cooperatives. The program is meant to benefit 75000 families during the period 2007–11 (Kester 2010). UC is a program that gives out micro-credit loans to women with small businesses, such as small shops in the cities. For 2010, the goal was to benefit 42000 women and at least a fair share of the money comes directly from donations from countries such as Taiwan (Navas 2010). The nationally owned bank 'Banco Produzcamos' started in 2010. It is supposed to handle the money for the two programs and all similar programs and give credits to small and medium producers in the agricultural production sector. The creation was for a long time blocked and dragged out by opposition politicians in the national assembly.

While land redistribution is not a policy of Ortega Saavedra, it can be seen in some places. The common practice that is used seems to be to put in doubt land claims of rich landowners through the legal system which is dominated by Sandinistas, and thereby unofficially redistributing some lands (see also — *Power through combining parliamentary and activist work*, p. 170). Presumably such actions only affect a small number of families.

Ortega Saavedra has partially retaken control of some of the privatized infrastructure. The UF was forced into selling 16% of the local company in Nicaragua to the government in a deal which gave the government a seat on the board of UF in Nicaragua in 2009 (Reuters 2009). Energy prices are politically controlled in Nicaragua and do not entirely follow fluctuations in world markets. For Nicaraguan consumers prices rose around 9% in 2007 during a global energy crisis. During this time, government subsidies were given to public transport. General power outages due to incapable infrastructure happened also in 2007 but were about to end (Fonseca Terán 2007).

When it was clear that Ortega Saavedra was elected and would assume power, Venezuela invited Nicaragua to participate in the *Alternativa Bolivariana para los pueblos de nuestra América* (ALBA) network of countries opposed to current global trade structures. It included Cuba and Bolivia at the time, and has since grown to also include Antigua and Barbuda, the Commonwealth of Dominica, Ecuador and Saint Vincent and the Grenadines. The ALBA was initiated in 2006 with a stated goal of organizing trade between its members. Unlike other trade networks, the ALBA aims not to liberalize trade, but rather to work as an economic mutual aid network. The ALBA is meant to evolve into more and more of a controlled economy in common among countries with a similar economic level of development. This seems to be much in line with Radical Dependency Theory. Since 2006, the ALBA has grown to include a project of a common virtual currency for trade between the countries and is also linked to numerous cultural and educational exchanges (AlianzaBolivariana.org 2011). ALBA negotiations in December 2007 ended with a decision to create a telecommunications company to be set up by the ALBA members by 2008 and the making of "huge advances" in talks to set up a common bank for the ALBA countries to gain more independence from changes in the economies of western countries (END 2007). Ortega Saavedra signed Nicaragua onto the ALBA immediately after assuming position (Rodríguez 2007b). The ALBA network was used to bring oil from Venezuela to the Central American republic starting immediately in January 2007. By November 2007, a total of 1.55 million petroleum products had been imported through the ALBA (N. García 2007).

Even though the trade pattern of Nicaragua is in the process of change, a strong connection to the United States is still present both in terms of imports and exports. Imports have been diversified somewhat in recent years, with the share from Asia and Venezuela growing significantly. The share of Central American imports has been even with that of the United States since 1990 (see also p. 95). Exports look somewhat different. The

Origin of Nicaraguan imports

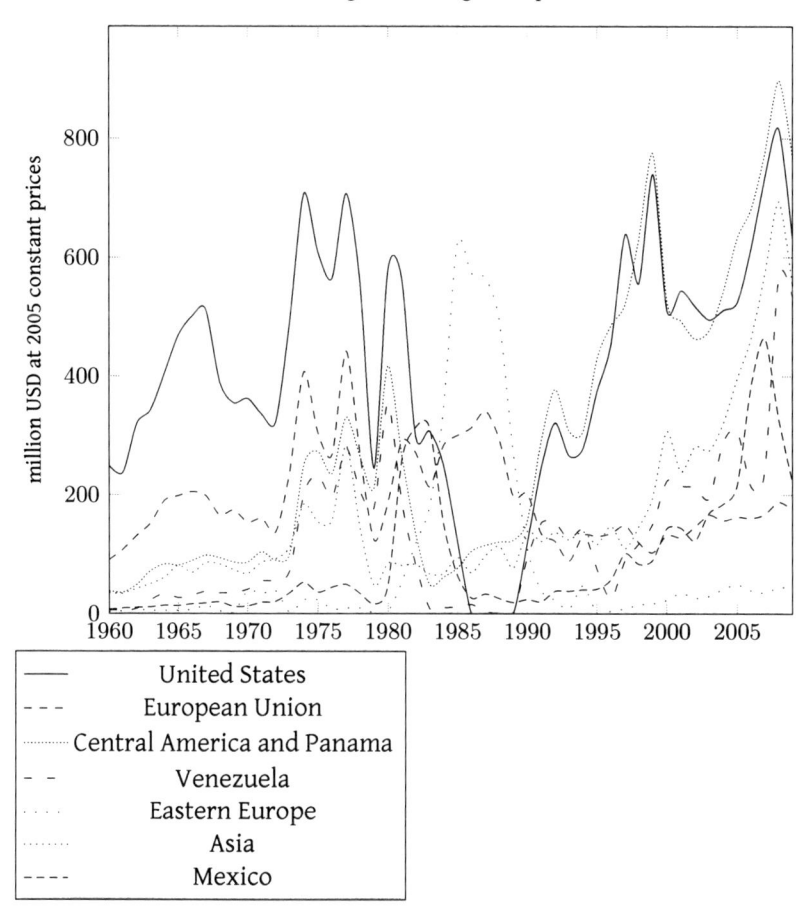

——	United States
- - -	European Union
········	Central America and Panama
- -	Venezuela
· · · ·	Eastern Europe
....	Asia
- - - -	Mexico

During the time of Somoza, imports came primarily from the United States, with the European Union in second place. During the 1980s, Eastern Europe temporarily took the place of the United States as the leader in . During the Liberal years, imports from other Central American countries became ever more important. Mexico became a major source of imports in 2006–07. In very recent years, imports from Venezuela and Asia have become almost as important as imports from Central America and the United States. Despite the political talks about renewed links to Russia during the current government, imports from Eastern Europe have not increased significantly since 2007. While in the 1970s Nicaragua imported from only one major trading partner, imports are now much more diversified. *Source: Banco Central de Nicaragua (2010b)*

Destinations of Nicaraguan exports

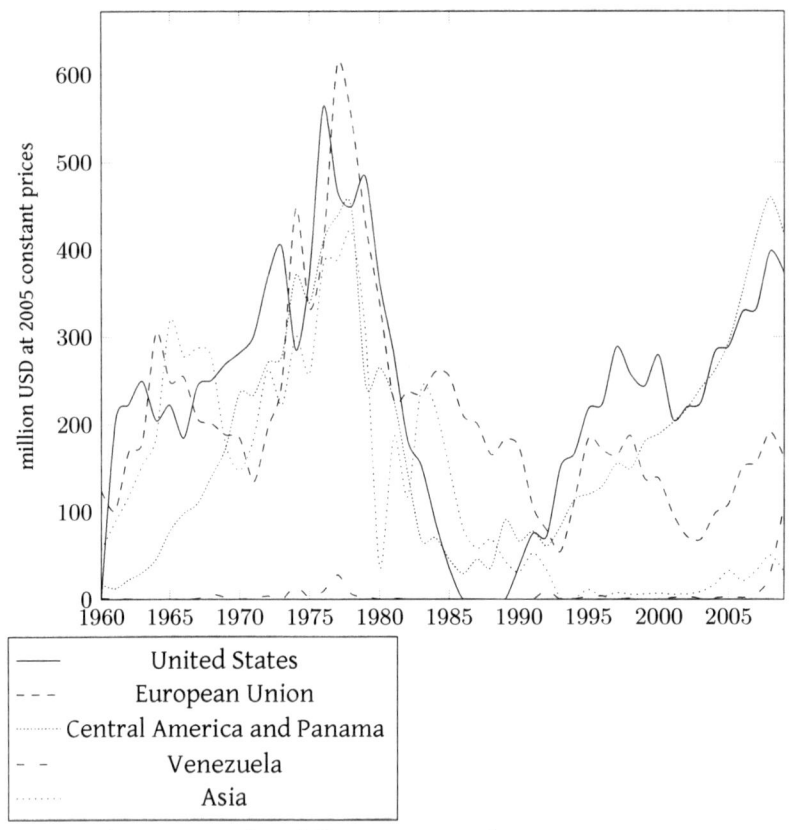

- —— United States
- --- European Union
- ······ Central America and Panama
- – – Venezuela
- ········ Asia

Exports show a somewhat different picture than imports: exports to most markets topped in the late Somoza years and have since been much lower. Only exports to Venezuela are greater now than ever before, and the amount of that is still much smaller than exports to the United States, the Central American neighboring countries and the European Union. Exports to Eastern Europe were never significantly large.

The data does not include productions in *Export Production Zones* (EPZ). *Source: Banco Central de Nicaragua (2010b)*

shares going to the United States and Central America are the largest, with the European Union share at about half that and Venezuela at about a third, but growing rapidly (see also p. 96). For all the talk there is of the renewal of relations to Russia and the negative view the current government has of the United States, trade relations at this point do not (yet) reflect that.

For Nicaragua, private ownership still stands quite central, more so than in some other ALBA member countries, reflecting in the way the Nicaraguan part of the agreement was set up. Through a layer of two subcompanies, revenues from oil sales in Nicaragua are paid to the company *ALBA de Nicaragua, S.A.* (Albanisa), which is 60% owned by Venezuelan state oil company *Petróleos de Venezuela, S.A.* (PDVSA) and 40% by 'unknown partners' in Nicaragua. Albanisa then splits the revenues, sending 50% to the Venezuelan state, 25% to a social development fund controlled by ALBA and it is not quite clear where the remaining 25% goes. José Francisco López Centeno is at the time simultaneously secretary of finances of the FSLN and vice-president of Albanisa (N. García 2007).

The role of the FSLN in relation to private capitalists is at times unclear. At the celebrations on 19 July 2009, Ortega Saavedra officially thanked the Pellas, for staying in Nicaragua throughout the 1980s, and Sandinista controlled labor unions held celebrations in honor of the company, for the stated reason of the company having helped Nicaragua. At the same time, during much of 2009, protesters against the Pellas installed themselves at the Rotonda Metrocentro, claiming they are former workers of the ISA who now suffer from chronic renal insufficiency. According to them, up to 3000 workers died due to renal insufficiency they believe is caused by the usage of pesticides. Those organizing these workers seem to at least unofficially be directly connected to the FSLN. The official line of the FSLN leadership is to recognize the continued importance of the oligarchy, which consists of the same families that were rich in the time of Somoza (Cuadra Núñez and Fonseca Terán 2010a, 2). There seems not to be universal agreement on this issue among FSLN Sandinistas.

The Sandinista policies of today seem a bit contradictory at this stage. There seems to be more of a willingness to cooperate with private capital and much less ambitious plans for fundamental economic changes than was the case in the 1980s. At the same time, grassroot organization against big capital continues, and the state is taking some control back and helping some poorer sectors in becoming more independent. If the official data is to be believed, class differences among Nicaraguans are in rapid decline.

Some of these data may be easier to understand in a few years, when one knows where the current development leads.

Popular ideas about economic realities and models of the past

The difference in economic policies between the different governments over the past decades is a major point of political controversy in today's Nicaragua. Very few seem to believe it possible to return to the economic policies of Zelaya López, but the late Somoza years, the Sandinismo of the 1980s, and the policies of the subsequent Liberal governments, all seem to be seen as offering possible policies for future governments in the view of most Nicaraguans. Simultaneously, most of my informants judged the economic policies of a given historic period rather independently of their own political affiliation. The criteria used to judge the Somozas and the Liberal governments is very different from the criteria by which most Nicaraguans judge the Sandinista government of the 1980s. I think it is important to look at some common judgments about the last one or two decades of Somoza government and the years since, in order to understand how Nicaraguans evaluate the economic realities and policies of these times.

The 1970s

Today, a surprising number of Nicaraguans want to go back to how things were in the 1970s. I found this opinion mainly, but not only, among urban elites. These Nicaraguans generally want someone to be put in charge as president who tries to re-implement all the economic policies and follow the same plans of development the Somoza regime of the time used. Their argument is that economically everybody was better off before the revolution. "Back then, everybody who wanted to work to make money did make money," my second host in León explained to me once. She owns a large downtown house and her family operated several buses during the times of Somoza. The defense of the Somoza times does not focus on political freedoms or the amount of capital created by foreign companies due to their economic activities in Nicaragua, but rather on the total amount of money accessible at the time. Somocistas seem not to focus upon the fact that opportunities to create wealth were extremely unevenly distributed.[9] Another aspect they tend to leave out is the earthquake in Managua in 1972, the bombarding of cities at the time of the Sandinista insurrection, and the Contra-war which all greatly contributed to the loss of wealth, and for which the Sandinistas cannot be held responsible.

Those today in favor of the revolutionary insurrection of 1979 focus on Fonseca Amador's plans change Nicaragua as well as the exploitative aspects of the Somoza era and end the unequal distribution of wealth of that time. They do not talk about how the overall amount of wealth present in Nicaragua at that time may have been greater than now. None of the groups seem to see how Somoza's economic plans would have developed, had they been allowed to continue. When talking about the economics of Somoza, Nicaraguans describe what concrete economic realities were like at the time of Somoza. I have never heard anyone claiming Somoza's policies, had they been extended for another few decades, would have led to better welfare and prosperity for a greater share of the population or that they would have let Nicaraguan business owners enjoy increasingly greater returns.

The 1980s

The 1980s economic history is largely simplified by both Sandinistas and Liberals. Liberals often claim that the land reforms of Sandinistas scared away all owners of capital. Sandinistas claim that all lands were redistributed to the land workers. The various political acts which still left three quarters of agricultural production under private control might, at first, not seem particularly communist/socialist. As noted, transition periods of nationalizations are generally seen as necessary when socialists come to power. The FSLN believed more time would be needed for Nicaragua and a mixed economy would be necessary for the foreseeable future.

A few professional Sandinistas, who realize that socialism in much of Eastern Europe is less popular than Sandinismo in Nicaragua, portray this as a virtue of Sandinismo. The Sandinista Fernando Fonseca explained how he believed Nicaragua in the 1980s was different from its East European

---

9. Whether opportunities in reality were less evenly distributed, is something I have arrived at purely by letting myself be convinced by the majority of my informants. To my knowledge the Somozas recorded no data on economic inequality.

allies as part of an explanation why it made sense to work for the return to power during the 1990s, when the 'real socialism' of Eastern Europe had disappeared:

> Yes, we did use Marxism, but we used it as a method to analyze reality. [...] We never gave up on Christianity. We took that in. Here, we never did away with private business. On the contrary, we said that Nicaragua would be a mixed economy.

According to most theories by Sandinistas I have come across, in the 1980s Nicaragua followed a development path which eventually would lead to a more prosperous society for all. The complete nationalization of all oligarchy property may have been planned at a later stage, when the country would be ready for it. On the other hand, several Sandinistas tell me things such as: "It has to be recognized that the GP stayed during the entire period." This seems to show they are unaware of the nationalizations of the late 1980s. Such statements are generally made by those Sandinistas who emphasize the nationalist aspect of Sandinismo. Most Sandinistas see the economic involvement of the United States and the meddling in Nicaraguan politics of the US government as through-and-through evil and directly opposed to the plans of the Sandinistas and the interests of the Nicaraguan people. The little economic aid the Carter regime gave in the very beginning is also not considered. The differences between Carter and Reagan are not considered, and the actions of the United States are seen as mechanically linked to its role as an empire and not as the result of any decisions by individual people. The fact that the worsening of terms for loans to the third world happened globally to allies of both the Soviet Union and the United States, does not seem to be an important factor for most Sandinistas or Liberals. One side blames the Sandinista government of the time, while the other side blames the blockade and war perpetrated by the United States. Sandinistas generally like to speculate how their policies would have continued, and they believe eventually all the problems the government faced would have been resolved had the same politics been continued. Most Sandinistas point out that the Contras destroyed crops and infrastructure, and that this was a major detrimental factor for the economy. They believe it would have been much easier to turn the economy around without the war and that the economic problems would eventually have vanished.

Inflation rate for consumer goods

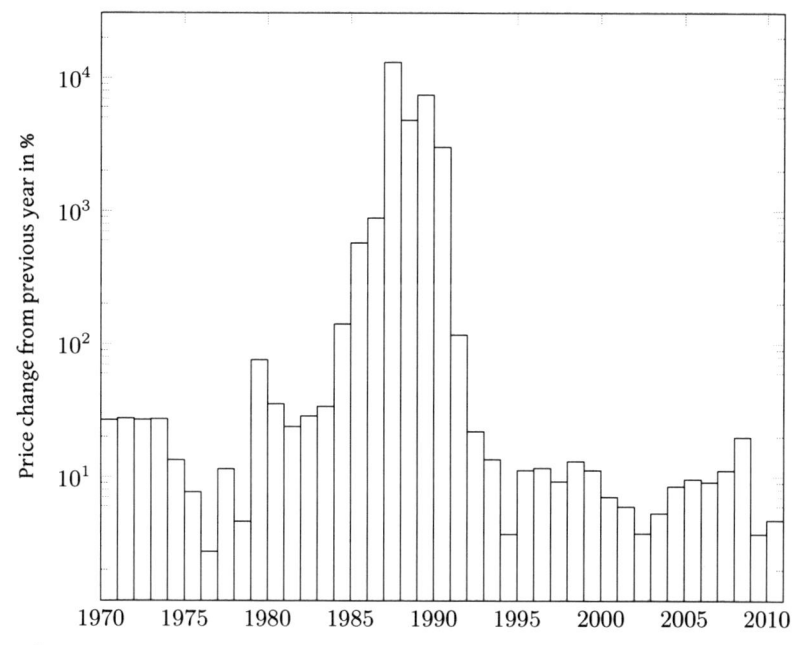

Inflation rates were more stable in the Somoza and Liberal years than in the Sandinista years in the 1980s, reaching 13109.5% in 1987. Also during the second Sandinista period, the years 2007 (11.127%) and 2008 (19.826%) showed the highest inflation rates within a decade.
"Due to political and economic events (civil war and hyperinflation), data [after 1979 and] prior to 1995 are less reliable." (IMF 2010). The two databases of the *International Monetary Fund* (IMF) do not agree on inflation rates for several of the years in this period. Data from the 2010 database has been given preference over those from 2000. *Source: IMF (2000, 2010); CIA (2011c)*

Due to the CW, some Nicaraguans from both political camps argue the radical policies eventually adopted were mostly due to external pressure from trading partners in Eastern Europe, rather than any internal ideology. In that sense, it is difficult to determine whether the use of Dependency Theory was central due to the will of the Sandinistas, or because this was expected by the Eastern European governments they dealt with. Most Sandinista informants who speak about their own involvement and experiences since the time of Somoza leave out the late 1980s or just mention them in general terms, stating what happened to the country rather than to themselves. Carolina Icabalceta Garay was one of very few Sandistas willing to mention the economic problems of the late 1980s and how these were felt at the time:

> ...It was quite hard. It was not only a war, but also an economic embargo which meant that certain measures were taken, such as the condensing of the state apparatus, which meant letting thousands of people go. If there was a source of employment in Nicaragua, it was the state. It was always the state who maintained the people and kept them busy. Obviously when they let people go that means that there are things happening in the economic sphere that are very serious.
>
> Now we from the popular classes and those with some... let's just say: level of culture, didn't feel that the 3000% inflation hurt us much. We felt, that we were always reimbursed every week and it was only hard to manage so many bills. Other than that, however... Maybe it's because we didn't have a culture of economics, knowledge of economics – it had been negated: about how a budget works or that what was happening wasn't good.
>
> We didn't feel alarmed by it. There were so many things to do – the health campaign, the vaccination campaign, campaign for cleaning up, the campaign to plant trees... All that we liked and were very animated to do. We were many who just didn't feel like getting into the structure [of state or party], because we felt there were certain people who wanted their position of power there. Many of us simply wanted to do things.

Serafín García Torres is a friend of Bayardo José Fonseca Galo, the brother-in-law of Icabalceta Garay, from the days of the revolution. When I interviewed him, he described it as one of the initial tasks of his group before the revolution to go out into the countryside of Nandaime[10] and explain to the population, that they were fighting for an agrarian reform to empower the poor. García Torres then went on to explain:

> It is a historic conquest. And it continues to be a struggle today, because the revolution did not manage to achieve this goal and for other reasons – the economic situation, and the war – it didn't permit us to develop an agricultural reform

---

10. Nandaime is a small village situated in the departamento Granada.

Serafín García Torres explains that the initial goals of the revolution were economic reforms to benefit the poor majority of the population, but that these were never achieved during the 1980s, due to the circumstances the revolutionaries faced, and that these reforms, therefore, still need to take place.

> that would permit the Nicaraguan citizen, the poor, to be a fundamental part of the economic and social development of the country.

No matter whether the story is told by Sandinista or Liberal, the problems that did exist do not seem to count against the Sandinistas. The Sandinistas seem to be judged more by what they eventually would have done, rather than the reality of their accomplishments. In a sense, this has a certain similarity to the form of Rostow's phase model (see also — *Mainstream modernization development theories*, p. 60) and several other non-socialist theories of development: The economic welfare of the masses is seemingly the focus of economic policies. Yet, it is assumed by these theories that improvements in overall living standards are not achievable in the short term and a phase of economic hardship which temporarily may even worsens the individual's position is necessary before an improvement will be possible.

It must be said, that the land redistributions and social policies were meant to benefit the populace immediately, and that it was due to factors outside the control of the Sandinista government, especially the war, that made this impossible. The difference between dreams and reality in the 1980s is considered by many Sandinistas today. "See, in the first phase of the revolution we had war," one informant told me, "In wartime you cannot plan anything. Now in this second phase, the war is gone, and we finally get a chance to do something." This sentiment seems to be shared by many Sandinistas. This is truer at a higher organizational level than among the common people.

The transition from power

One can interpret the Piñata as the government trying to bring at least parts of the dream of the future into the present. No one discusses what would have happened if the incoming non-Sandinista government had decided to reverse the Piñata. It does not sound as though anyone felt this would be an option for the new government.

The 1990s–2007

Some look back at the period between 1990 and 2007 as a period of economic opportunities. This is a small group which was able to build up business during this period. It is easier to find Nicaraguans with a positive opinion of the economic policies of Somoza than of the Liberal regimes after the Sandinistas, even though it was a formally democratic period with positive economic development according to several indicators.

When one boards a taxi, it is very common for the driver to ask one what opinion one has of Nicaraguan politics. Many times when I cannot guess the driver's ideology I have tried to speak about aspects of Nicaragua that just about everybody agrees upon. One such subject is how the UF operates the Nicaraguan electricity net. Just about all Nicaraguans seem to agree that the privatization of 2000 was wrong and that Ortega Saavedra did not go far enough in his re-nationalization. I have been amazed about how flexible many Nicaraguans are in combining a negative view of the economic policies of the time of Liberal governments or Somoza with a positive view of the political leaders – when a Nicaraguan starts out by accusing Ortega Saavedra of being a communist and a thief, only then to switch the theme of the discussion to why Ortega Saavedra should immediately nationalize the UF. This also works in other combinations of defending the political leaders of one period and the economic ideology of another. At one point, a taxi driver who had just outed himself as a Somocista and indicated that another Contra war should be initiated against the current 'dictatorial' Sandinista government, switched to discuss the

Gross Domestic Product per Capita

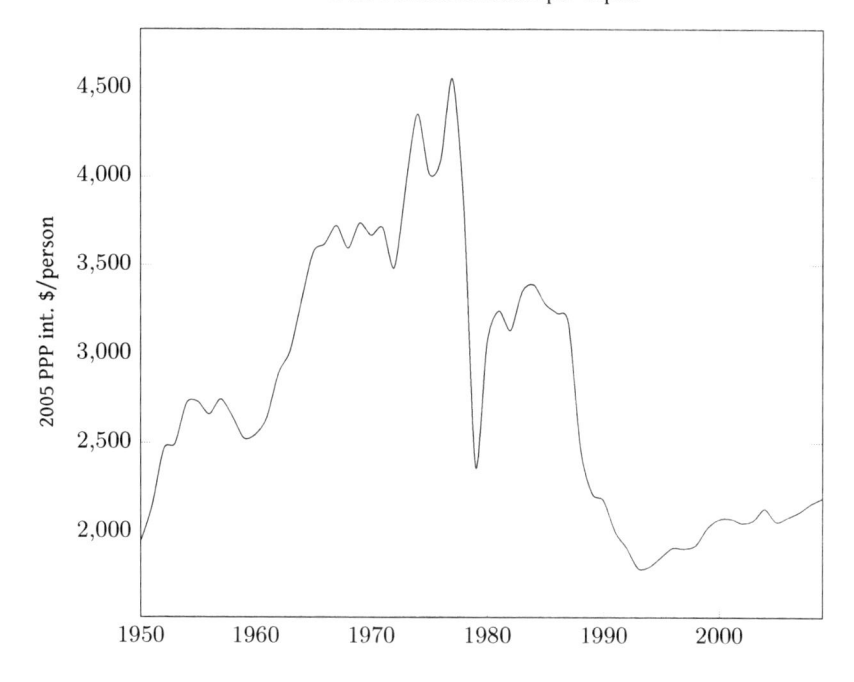

The *Gross Domestic Product* (GDP) per Capita rose for most of the period from 1950 until the revolutionary insurrection of 1979, with cyclical downturns in 1958-59 and 1968 and drastic downturns in 1975-76 and 1978-79 which likely were caused at least in part by the fights between *Guardia Nacional* and Sandinistas. In the period 1950-77, GDP grew at an average of 5.0% a year. GDP rose again 1979-84, although it only reached 3/4 of the 1977 level. 1985-90 it fell again drastically until it had reached just 48% of the 1977 level. The Liberal governments stabilized GDP with a moderate increase of 1993-2004 of 1.7%, but did not manage to increase it overall as GDP fell in 1990-93 and 2004-06. In 2006, GDP was under the 1951 level. GDP has been rising again during the current Sandinista government again at an average 1.7% a year. The *Gross National Income* (GNI) per Capita which is used by many newer data sources closely follows the development of the GDP in the case of Nicaragua (WB 2011c).

The figures presented here do not seem to be accepted universally. Large discrepancies were noticed in comparison with other data sources, some of which showed up to a 300% overall increase in GDP in the period 1960-2009. The data source chosen here is the only data source that includes the full data range from 1950 to 2009. *Source: Heston, Summers, and Aten (2011)*

UF and explained not only that he believes that Ortega Saavedra was perfectly capable of running a nationalized electricity system, but also that the representatives of UF should immediately be hung on their own cables for stealing from the Nicaraguan people. He saw no contradiction in his two views.

No Nicaraguan I met fantasized about some better future that may have come if only the economic plans of the Liberals had they been allowed to continue without interruption. This again has to do with a very different way of judging this period in comparison to how the period of Sandinismo in the 1980s is judged. It seems that while some Nicaraguans wish to revive the Liberal party as a stronger political force, the economic part hardly finds any proponents, even though economically this period may have been more prosperous than the war-torn 1980s.

The current Sandinista government

When the second Ortega Saavedra government took office, many Sandinistas hoped for the return of some of the economic policies of the 1980s. When the position of mayor of Managua was won by the Sandinista candidate Herty Lewites in 2000, it did not bring with it leftist economic reforms. As some see it, neoliberalism was made compatible with Sandinismo (Vargas 2006, 85-86). This again may have somewhat limited expectations of a Sandinista presidency even before the 2006 elections.

"See, we have already had an agrarian reform," one Sandinista told me, explaining why it is not possible to once more redistribute lands. In addition, it is generally believed that conventions with the IMF prohibit any further land redistributions. Those Sandinistas who speak about it, mostly hope for the state to buy portions of lands that can then be redistributed. Most FSLN Sandinistas realize some type of wider land distribution is needed, if the goal is for the poorest sectors of society to benefit from HC, because the minimum requirement for participation in HC is owning 0.7 hectares of land. Without this land ownership, they would never be eligible to participate and advance.

Most FSLN Sandinistas see the programs HC and UC as positive measures. Even though poverty levels have not changed much since they were put in place, many FSLN Sandinistas expect this to change in the future. "Nicaragua will be a very different country," I was told more than once. It is emphasized by Sandinista officials that the socialism about to be created

Gini coefficient for families

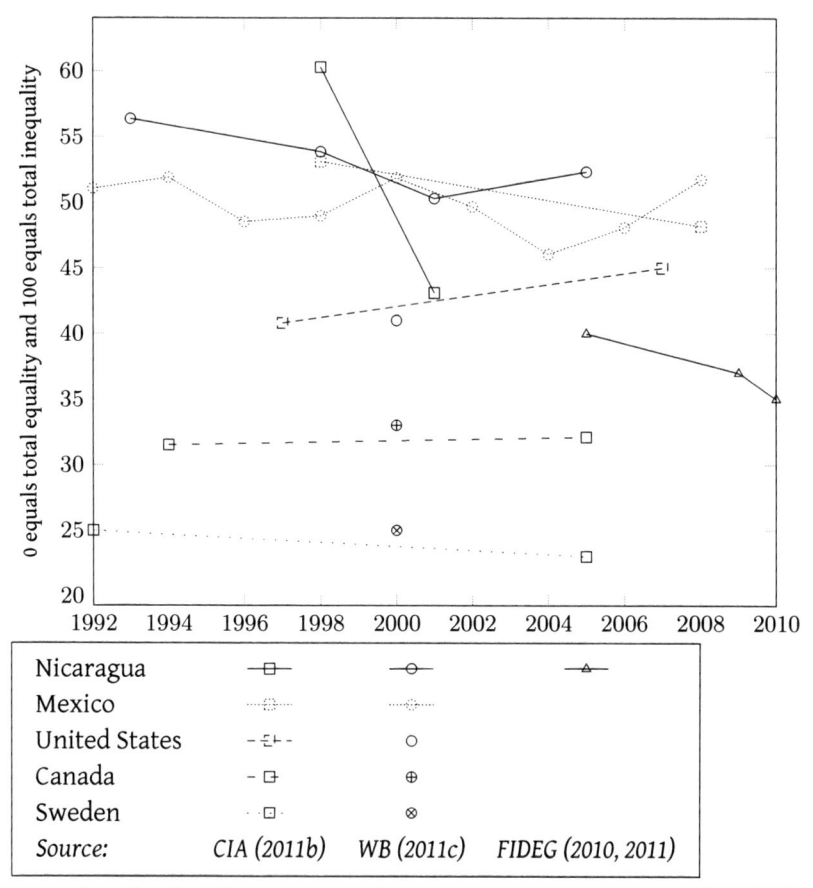

Nicaragua	—□—	—○—	—△—
Mexico	⋯◌⋯	⋯◌⋯	
United States	- Ɛ⊦ -	○	
Canada	- ⊡ -	⊕	
Sweden	⋅⋅□⋅⋅	⊗	
Source:	CIA (2011b)	WB (2011c)	FIDEG (2010, 2011)

Even though Liberal economic policies are seen as unconcerned with the poor, figures from the CIA show that economic differences between rich and poor have been diminishing, similar to Mexico and opposite to what has happened in the United States. The figures from the FIDEG also show an improvement during the current government. One explanation for this could be that the government is successful in promoting the cause of the poorest. Other plausible explanations could be that the figures have been manipulated before publication, that the rich have discovered more ways of hiding their money efficiently, or that Nicaraguan capital has lost in the struggle with multinational, foreign-owned companies. None of those Nicaraguans knowledgeable about Gini coefficients who I consulted were confident in their explanations of the numbers. The figures from the WB show somewhat more negative developments for Mexico and Nicaragua, while their only figures for the US, Canada and Sweden, all from the year 2000, are close to those of the CIA.

Unemployment rate

— Nicaragua
---- United States
.... Mexico

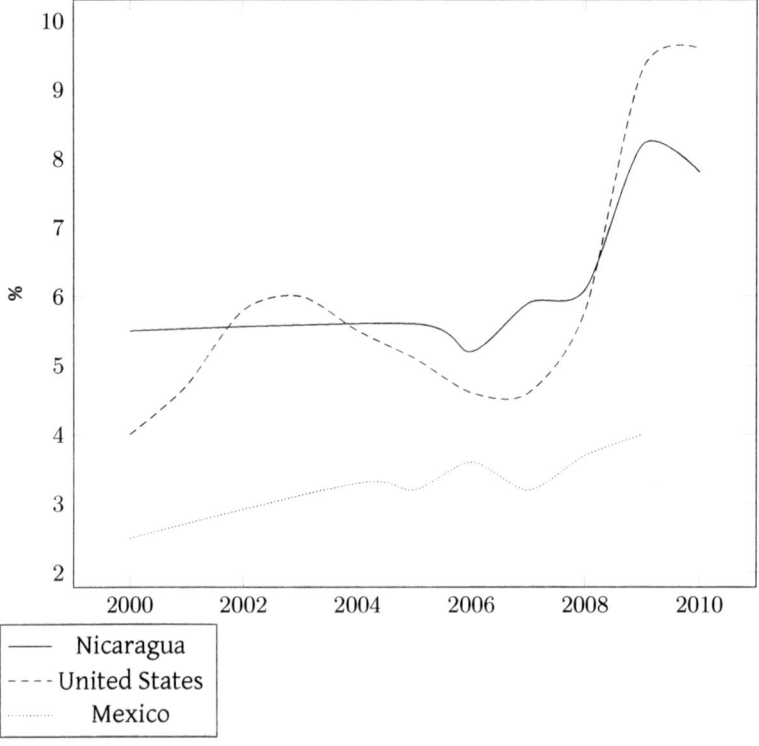

The government of José Daniel Ortega Saavedra has to deal with higher official unemployment figures than its predecessors. The problem is global. It touches countries such as Mexico and the United States during these years. The 2010 figure for Nicaragua is based on the average of a new monthly survey, whereas the older figures where based on annual more general surveys. The figures are, therefore, not necessarily comparable. Both in the case of Mexico and Nicaragua and to some extent also in the United States, underemployment rates are large. Therefore, unemployment rates say little about whether most people are working or not and cannot necessarily be compared meaningfully between countries. Nevertheless, the curves of these graphs are similar when including various types of underemployment and, therefore, give a somewhat accurate picture of developments within each country. *Source: BCN (2007, 2009, 2011); BLS (2011); IM (2010)*

Registered Crimes per Capita since 1980

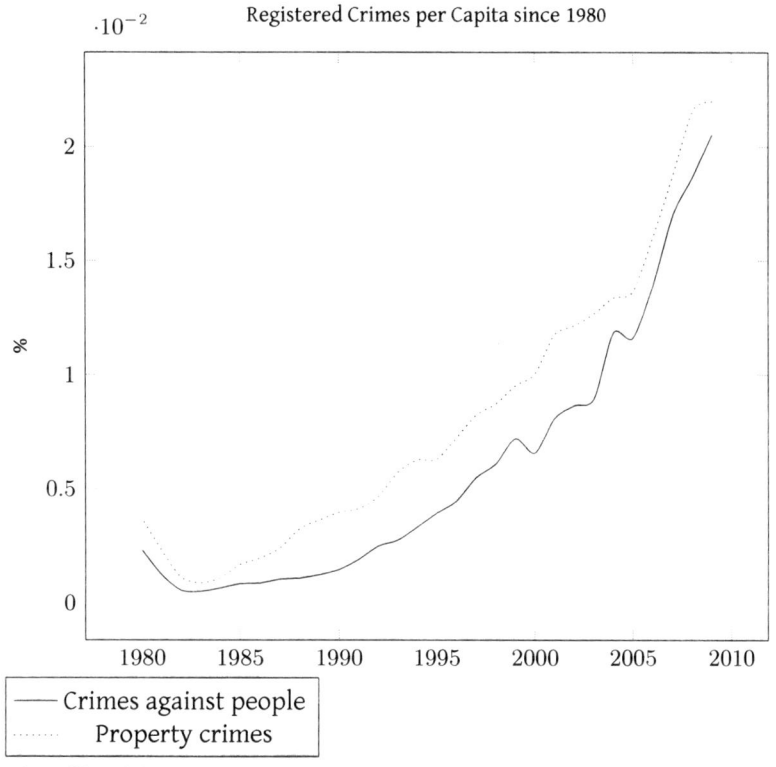

— Crimes against people
...... Property crimes

The official figures measuring crime rates show a negative development since the mid-1980s. These have increased rather dramatically since the 1980s. The current government does not seem to have been able to decrease crime levels significantly through its measures. The Nicaraguan police nevertheless believes that Nicaraguan crime statistics are still much lower than in most of Central America, although the Nicaraguan police force is much smaller than that of its neighboring countries. *Source: Policía Nacional (2010); WB (2011c)*

will focus not only on the material well-being, but equally on spiritual satisfaction without any loss of freedom of expression (Fonseca Terán 2009a). It can be assumed that allowing the political right with its media attack the government constantly will make the process more time consuming, but also that the focus away from material well-being will mean that economic reforms will be limited.

Some of Ortega Saavedra's policies which seem to have no immediate visible effect in terms of dramatically increasing living standards of any group, are seen by Sandinistas as preventing a worse scenario. The exact effect cannot be measured because it is impossible to know how bad a crisis otherwise would have been. According to Fonseca Terán (2007) the subsidies given for public transport in 2007 would have been unsustainable if not for the arrival of Venezuelan oil and according to Albanisa officials, the price hike in 2007 would have been around 16–18%, instead of 9%, if prices were not subsidized (Rogers 2007). I hear that same story often when using public transport in the Sandinista strong parts of the Pacific coastal areas.

Almost no Liberals consider any of the programs positively. For them, everything the government does is corruption. A few *Movimiento Renovador Sandinista* (MRS) followers had some positive things to say about the programs when I asked them, but immediately pointed out that while "socially this government is doing great, in terms of democracy it's much worse [than during the Liberal governments]."

Criticism (hidden) also comes from the side of Sandinistas who expect more radical reforms. Some party officials, such as Fonseca Terán (2008a), continue to argue for the replacement of capitalism with a Cuban style socialist economy. Such a system is specifically distinguished by Fonseca Terán (2008f) from a social-democracy where capitalism continues to exist and in which only gains are redistributed at a higher rate, and he sees the ALBA as a stepping stone in that direction. There are two main interpretations among Nicaraguans of what the complex setup with the ALBA-related businesses means. Those critical of the government claim the FSLN uses aid money for private financial gain. They say that the usage of the state for private gains is not the first time in the history of the FSLN. Whereas those in support of the government claim it is just an accounting trick to get around the regulations the IMF has on caps of employment in the public sector, and to get the money around the national assembly, where the opposition has a majority. These are the same people who claim the Piñata was first and foremost a rush to make land deals official, and had already been put into practice but for which the corresponding paper work had not been filled out. The two, Alba and Piñata, are oftentimes connected by these claims.

The socialism that Sandinismo stands, at least for some sections of the party, always is a project of the future. At times this project stands in contradiction with current policies. This shows in an underlying debate on what to do with the ultra rich. Even though Ortega Saavedra officially pronounces support for the Pellas family, 'the oligarchy' is a term frequently used by Sandinistas today to describe their enemy. At the celebrations on 19 July 2008, banners with slogans such as "Our enemy is the oligarchy" were evident. Such banners may at the time mainly be targeted at the Montealegre family and Eduardo Montealegre's bid for the presidency or any other political office. No Sandinista I found said openly that the properties of the Pellas should be nationalized immediately. The Sandinistas seem in some way for now to accept such a contradiction which lies in the proclamation of socialism in combination with the continued existence of such oligarchy groups.

In economic relations with other countries, there is a discrepancy between currently existing trade flow and what Sandinistas talk about, which is what is to happen in the future. While the importance of the United States clearly has not faded in real economic terms, the way it is often discussed is as if the connection to the United States already is closed off and Venezuela already is the main economic force in Nicaragua. Besides Venezuela, a few other countries are often mentioned as delivering economic help and being future trading partners. Among these are Taiwan (Ma highlights Taiwan-Nicaragua ties 2009), Russia (see also — *The Georgia conflict*, p. 127), Libya (Castro 2007) and Iran (Morrissey 2007). These countries are mentioned as a secondary level, with their support seen as less significant when compared to the support provided by Venezuela.

As in the case of the first Sandinista government, the current Sandinistas are in charge of a country which is not doing well, with future plans for a completely different economic system that will not be implemented fully for a long time to come. Nevertheless, Sandinistas are not judged by this in the same way as Liberals are judged by the economic reality of Nicaraguans in their period of government. FSLN Sandinistas expect economic success some time in the future, given that Sandinista policies are continued.

Concluding remarks

As we have seen, over the past century, Nicaragua lived through at least two phases of nationally controlled technical modernization connected with centralization, during the times of Zelaya López and the later part of the Somozas, and some phases of stagnation in which virtually no technological advances were made, but international capital was permitted free access. In contrast to both types of phases, stand the two periods of Sandinismo. During both of these, advances in the living standards of the masses are coupled with higher levels of equality and national control of development, which also includes elements of popular control of the economy through the establishment of cooperatives. The last chapter showed that the political outlook is highly informed by the past. Yet in this chapter we have seen that the ideas of the economy are for a great part concentrated on the future. The measure of success for most seems never to be the current economy as much as the future economy if the developments started during Sandinista governments are continued indefinitely. In this sense, there is a marked difference in how the groups are seen in comparison with the last chapter, in which it was presented that largely two groups (Liberals and Sandinistas) have two equally valid versions of history upon which they hope the future will be based.

Fourth Chapter

Shaping politics

I here want to present some of the main political events during my time in Nicaragua. Several for me surprising events took place during this period, but having followed the country closely before and after I think that overall it was fairly average for the current presidency (2007-11). This following presentation should, therefore, give an overall insight into the political life of Nicaragua since 2007.

Most significant political events in Nicaragua have an element of popular participation. In each of these events, Nicaraguans interpret them as being in line with well-known historical events. Since then, several of those events that happened during my time have turned into historical events of their own, and Nicaraguans refer to them as such. These events demonstrated to me how Sandinista politics are influenced by a combination of events on the world scale and the organization efforts of the popular masses within the country. Similar to how Nicaraguans portray their national history, also when describing current events it is common that they place agency in Nicaraguan hands, even when they relate the actions taking place in Nicaragua to international movements. Complicating matters even more, different groups believe they speak in the name of Sandinismo as much as the government does and try actively to shape the politics of the José Daniel Ortega Saavedra government. These factors jointly make up a dynamic which means popular participation and interpretation of international events is an essential part in shaping the country's policies. This, coupled with popular participation in Nicaragua, is at times used to try to achieve gains internationally. I hope this chapter demonstrates that Nicaragua is not as centrally controlled by President

Ortega Saavedra as the Nicaraguan right tries to make the international media believe. For me, following the daily politics also made me realize that the Ortega Saavedra government and the Sandinista part of the population can be creative in their portrayal of international politics, in order to achieve gains at a national level. To gather material for this chapter, it was vital for me to be present when politically relevant events happened. Subsequently interviewing people who heard about the event while being unrelated to it, gave me another side of the what transpired.

Transport worker strike (May 2008)

This strike showed me how an international event (a rise in oil prices) influenced the premises for inner-Nicaraguan conflicts, although this was not recognized by most of the Nicaraguans I discussed with. One of the first events of political significance I witnessed during my stay in Nicaragua was a transport workers' strike. It lasted for 12 days, during which transport in-between cities in theory came to a complete standstill. In the city of León, where I was at the time, all transport did stop, and transport workers stood at the entrance road to the city from Managua to hinder anyone from entering the city. From other parts of the country, I heard that the situation was not as serious. León is known as the most Sandinista of cities, and most of the transport workers I spoke to used that as the explanation for why the protests were the largest there.

The issue they fought over was gas prices. The government had obtained petroleum at favorable prices from Venezuela, in a scheme in which Venezuela sold oil to the *Frente Sandinista de Liberación Nacional* (FSLN) party at market prices. Only 50% had to be paid within 90 days, and the remaining 50% were to be paid 23 years later, with a favorable interest rate of 1–2%. Nevertheless, the FSLN decided to sell gas at market prices to consumers, and allegedly spent the money they see as a loan for 23 years, to finance social projects.

Before and during the protests, the right-wing media tried to prove that gas prices in Nicaragua were higher than anywhere else in Central America, despite the favorable terms with Venezuela, and hinted that the money was going into the personal pocket of Ortega Saavedra. At the time, oil prices peaked, and because the government regulated the fare price for the intercity transport, profits and wages of the transport workers shrank.

During the days of the protest, I ran back and forth between strikers

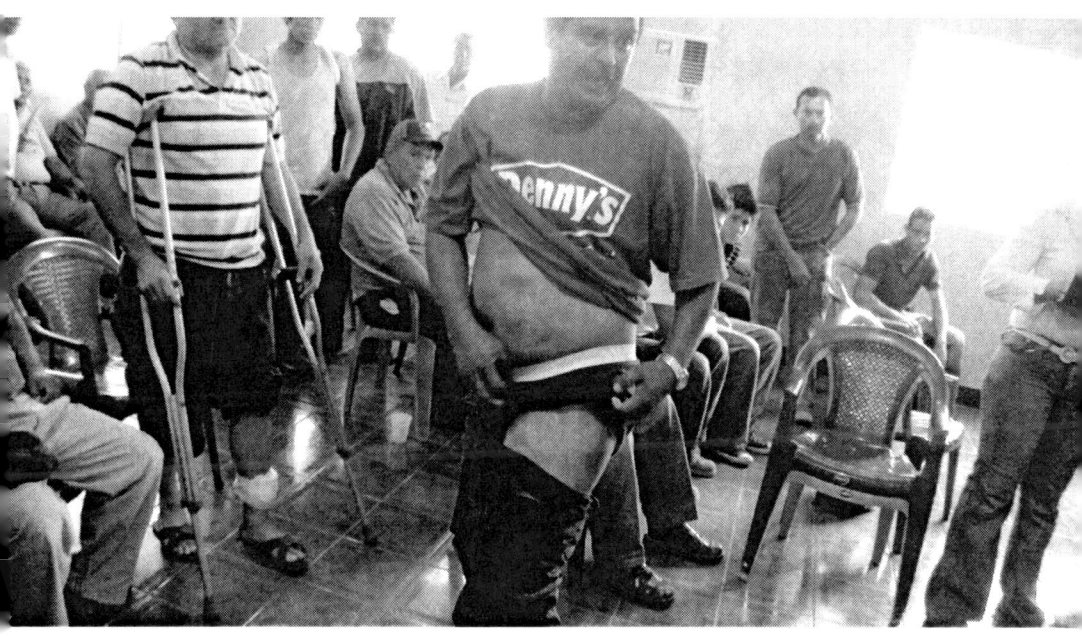

Sandinista transport workers show the wounds inflicted upon them by police during what they refer to as a 'massacre' organized by President José Daniel Ortega Saavedra.

and FSLN headquarters. Until then, transport workers were one of the strongest bases for the FSLN. Also, it is a common rumor that the police is heavily infiltrated by Sandinistas. Now the police were sent to stop the transport workers from blocking the road. The city of León was where the biggest clash between demonstrators and police occurred, and at the press conference, the transport workers held after the clash, the spokespeople of the transport workers publicly stated: "We have not seen a massacre of this magnitude since the time of [dictator] Somoza". The newspaper *La Prensa* announced that one of the transport workers had died in the clash. They did not retract this statement when FSLN officials pointed out that this had not, in fact, taken place, but they acknowledged it quietly by not reporting on it any further. The León police and local party officials showed some sympathy for the demands of the transport workers in their public announcements. When speaking to me, the party officials highlighted that the money recovered from the Venezuela oil deal was not only meant to benefit the transport sector, but also other areas, therefore, the transport workers should not win the conflict.

At first, I believed I witnessed the end of the FSLN as a united political force; It seemed logical the party would split into various factions. At one time, I sat on the curb while the transport workers blocked the road, and next to me sat the La Prensa reporter covering the confrontations. La Prensa had been positive towards the strikers, and I wondered why, given that the La Prensa normally is a newspaper of the right. "This is a battle in-between 'them.'" the reporter explained to me. This 'them' is the certain Sandinista part of the population. Both the Sandinistas and those not belonging to the them, all seemed to believe that 40% of all Nicaraguans identify with FSLN Sandinismo. Most transport workers I spoke to whom I asked about the Sandinista connection saw themselves as part of said 40%, but explained they felt cheated by Ortega Saavedra. One of them stated:

> For all those years we have been helping them in all the campaigns, so of course we expected them to give us something [once in power].

As the strike drew to an end, Ortega Saavedra went on TV and showed how the government spent the money they obtained from the oil deal. The explanation seemed to satisfy most Sandinistas, but some of my informants remained skeptical. The cynicism did not seem to have reference to any concrete point in Ortega Saavedra's explanation, but was a general skepticism as to whether any information originating from any Nicaraguan government could be accepted as truth. The government promised the transport workers to give them a discount on gas prices at certain gas stations, and it seemed the transport workers forgot about the alleged 'massacre.' Half a year later Liberals and FSLN Sandinistas clashed under entirely different circumstances, and the transport workers once again held with the FSLN. I learned through this, that the Sandinista part of the population uses such physical manifestations as part of their repertoire of internal negotiations. Although all the involved use strong words, it seems to be clear to all involved that they can retract these at a later stage without any permanent damage. When the arch enemies, the Liberals, show up in the political arena, the Sandinistas forget all about their internal disagreements.

At the end of the same year, the government withdrew the transport subsidy. At this time, prices had fallen considerably, and the transport workers did not complain much about the re-institution of market gas prices. Although made into a Nicaraguan event, the transport worker strike was ultimately caused by fluctuations in the international oil markets. The focus by all parties involved in the conflict is the part that played out in Nicaragua. Protests did not launch against international oil companies, but against the Sandinista government.

The MRS protests (May – November 2008)

The following episode showed me how an inner-Nicaraguan conflict could be manipulated by the parliamentary opposition to Ortega Saavedra, in a way that could turn it into an event with international consequences and how the FSLN is a more fractured and uncoordinated group when it comes to political action than the opposition portrays them.

The next wave of protests was the alliance *Movimiento Renovador Sandinista* (MRS) which started in late Spring 2008. The MRS had recently lost its license to run in elections for the next few of years, because they did not fulfill all the requirements of registering as a party laid down by the Nicaraguan constitution and laws. Specifically, the rules require each party to have a registered leadership in each of the 153 municipalities of the country. The MRS was not able to do this. While the constitution adopted during Sandinista-rule in the 1980s permitted the creation of new parties, subsequent changes during the years of Liberal rule made it harder for smaller parties to survive. The MRS previously lost its license to run due to the same regulations; therefore, between 2000 and 2004, they ran in an electoral union with the FSLN. In the presidential elections of 2006, the MRS once again ran by itself. In 2008, the authorities audited the party again, a move which the media portrayed as being directed by the FSLN with the aim to eliminate a competitor before the municipal elections of November 2008. At the time, I taught English at the *Universidad Nacional Autónoma de Nicaragua-León* (UNAN–León), and one of my students, Douglas Augusto Varela Vilchez, was one of the main youth activists of the MRS in the town. I went to Managua to a demonstration once with him and another time with other MRS activists. Only a handful of the MRS activists showed up at the MRS headquarters in León during the time of the protests. Varela Vilchez was among those who did most of their activities through other organizations, which were, according to him, more or less directly paid for by the US embassy.

Part of the MRS internal split had to do with another group, the *Movimiento por el Rescate del Sandinismo* (MpRS), a breakaway group from the FSLN that joined the MRS as late as the presidential elections of 2006, having taken over the León party offices to a degree which made other León MRS members feel uncomfortable going there. "They just want to go back and take over the FSLN, whereas we want nothing to do with that party," one of the original MRS activists explained to me.

Former comandante Dora María Téllez (sitting in a hammock) of the *Frente Sandinista de Liberación Nacional* (FSLN) stays in a tent at the Rotonda Metrocentro in June 2008 during her hunger strike against the decision not to let her current party, the *Movimiento Renovador Sandinista* (MRS), participate in the local elections of 2008.

During the protests, 4–6 June 2008, one high standing member, the former FSLN comandante Dora María Téllez, went on a hunger strike during which time she stayed in a tent at the Rotonda Metrocentro in Managua. This initiated protests marches throughout Managua for the next few months. To understand why the event at the Rotonda Metrocentro was so significant, one needs to look at the physical structure of Managua. The rotondas, of which Managua only has about a dozen, were essential in the resistance by Sandinistas against the Liberal governments in the last years of Liberal governments. It began with the 1996 presidential campaign of José Arnoldo Alemán Lacayo of the *Partido Liberal Constitucionalista* (PLC), President of Nicaragua 1997 to 2002, when he focused the campaign on the first rotonda he ordered to be constructed while mayor of Managua in the preceding years. Since that time, a few more rotondas were built, and positioned so when the Sandinistas occupied them, they could stop traffic through all major thruways of Managua.

When the MRS took control of the rotondas, Liberal and MRS forces could march during the summer of 2008. The FSLN had no means to prevent them from doing so. The most severe clash between FSLN Sandinistas and the other groups took place in León, and not Managua, on 29 June 2008. The MRS planned to have Téllez speak in a certain room of the university, and that same day students decided to occupy that part of the

Sandinistas connected to the *Frente Sandinista de Liberación Nacional* (FSLN) frequently occupy the Managua rotondas, thereby virtually controlling the capital physically.

university. They allegedly protested for the payout of student scholarships. I investigated more during the following weeks, and I concluded that the students had staged the event in order to prohibit Téllez from entering the university. On the day of the confrontation, students threw dirty water on Téllez and a Conservative who had lost his seat as a member of the national assembly when it was proven that he is a US citizen, and their ideological followers. I was present and filmed the event.

The officials of the *Centro Universitario de la Universidad Nacional-León* (CUUN-León) had officially organized the student protest that day. While officially declaring they were not Sandinistas, my investigation revealed they described themselves as Sandinistas in all other connections. I asked one of their leaders why there were so many pictures of Augusto Nicolás Calderón Sandino in their headquarters, if they were not Sandinistas. The explanation I received from the student sent as a representative of the organization was:

> Well, yes personally I am a Sandinista, but we as an organization represent all the students. [Calderón] Sandino was a Liberal, right? So it's their problem, if the Liberals don't identify with him.

Internally the members of this group from the CUUN clearly saw themselves as acting on behalf of the FSLN. Given the Nicaraguan context, it does not follow that they were controlled by the FSLN. When I went to

When Dora María Téllez comes to León to speak at the university, students throw dirty water at her. In this photo she accuses President José Daniel Ortega Saavedra of being behind the action.

FSLN headquarters and asked about their opinion of the conflict, they said that the students likely had gotten a bit "too excited" and "very creative" when throwing the water. Much as with the transport worker strike, they did not condemn the actions of such Sandinista groups, yet they made sure not to endorse them either. The representatives of the CUUN, when I talked to them a few days later, claimed their representatives rushed over to the demonstration when it happened to stop the water throwing. My video tapes showed that once the CUUN President was present at the scene, the water throwing stopped.

More revealing were events about a week after this confrontation. Another group of students occupied the preparatory school of the UNAN-León. There had been student elections, and the occupying students had formed a group that ran against the representatives endorsed by the CUUN. According to the occupiers, it ended with the CUUN taking the ballot boxes by force and moving them to their own offices and then proclaiming themselves the winners. The occupiers claimed they won. They made a point of being against the water throwing action that happened a week earlier. In spite of their differences, they also saw themselves as FSLN Sandinistas. Different from the CUUN, they claimed themselves to be Sandinistas openly. One of them told me: "Look, we are all Sandinistas – both them and us – but we just don't agree with the form of what they did last week." They claimed it was ridiculous that formerly the Conservative member of the national assembly wanted to enter the university, when under Liberal

The MRS protests (May - November 2008) 121

rule he had tried to cut funding for universities. They were certain the student action was not planned by, nor carried out by adults of the FSLN.

Téllez spoke to the media while standing covered in dirt outside the UNAN–León right after she had been attacked. She claimed that Ortega Saavedra and Alemán Lacayo were behind the action and that it was meant to suppress democracy. All the MRS activists I associated with at the time claimed the students who attacked them were more or less directly controlled by Ortega Saavedra.

'The horseman,' an MRS activist whom I told about what CUUN and the second group of Sandinistas had told me, said he believed the second group of students to be set up by the FSLN just to hide their traces in the doings on the 29th. I believe this to be highly unlikely, as they occupied a university building for several days, and I was the only journalist around they could have impressed with their action.

Another person who showed up at many events in León, including the attack, was Francisco Alegría, the only Nicaraguan owner of a hostel in León. His family has historic ties to the Somoza regime, while he often explains that he is in favor of seeing things from 'all perspectives.' Whenever clashes occur, somehow he manages to be present. This time he stood around watching the confrontation from a few meters distance. According to him, the actions this day were most likely directly controlled by the FSLN and was done to try to hinder 'free speech.' Afterwards, his physical presence was enough for the MRS to count him as one of their supporters.

In this case one again can see how the FSLN party does not act as one block controlled by one entity, but how it expresses more of a general ideology. Those who portray the FSLN as being built clear around hierarchical command structures are those who are not members of the party. Although FSLN party leaders most like were not responsible for the actions, they shied away from criticizing some of 'their own.' And although the MRS ran in elections together with the FSLN for several years after the year 2000, now all commonality was suddenly forgotten and emphasis was put on the alleged shear limitlessness of Ortega Saavedra's power to control each and every arm of the Sandinista movement.

Although the MRS at other times had labeled itself as the 'truly Sandinista party,' they chose to let the FSLN have that label and joined Liberals and Conservatives under the banner of 'democracy' in the 2008 elections. Starting in September 2008, the MRS decided to participate in the election

Eduardo Montealegre Rivas speaks to the students of the *Universidad Thomas More* in Managua in 2008 (left). Montealegre Rivas belongs to one of two Nicaraguan oligarch families, accused of fraud by Sandinistas, and one of the Nicaraguan opposition's main figures. He lost the presidential elections in 2006 and the elections for mayor of Managua of 2008. He often changes party membership—allegedly because President José Daniel Ortega Saavedra gains control of all the parties he joins. His goal is unification against Ortega Saavedra. Instead of running in the 2011 presidential elections, Montealegre Rivas supports the candidacy of the radio show host Fabio Gadea Mantilla (b. 1931) (right). In opinion polls half a year before the election, Gadea Mantilla has the second-most support after Ortega Saavedra, though with only slim chances of winning. *Photos: Silvio Tercero and Jorge Mejía Peralta*

campaign of the PLC. In the spring of the same year, the MRS still had claimed that the PLC with its leader Alemán Lacayo had a pact with the FSLN to split all state positions of power between them (see also — *El pacto*, p. 149).

Instead of endorsing any of the other parties running against the FSLN, they decided to endorse the PLC and especially the candidate for mayor of Managua, Eduardo Montealegre Rivas. Montealegre Rivas was the presidential candidate for the *Alianza Liberal Nicaragüense* (ALN) in 2006, but subsequently lost the support of the ALN leadership. Since then, he worked for a candidature of his own, forming a group known as '*Vamos con Eduardo*' ('Let's go with Eduardo,' VcE) and at the time of the 2008 elections, Alemán Lacayo offered to let him be the candidate for mayor of Managua.

The contradiction between the accusations against the FSLN and PLC of pacting and then allying oneself with one of the parts of that pact, was a move the MRS also performed around 2000, when the party ended up pacting with the FSLN for 6 years after having accused PLC and FSLN of

The 2008 Sandinista candidate for mayor of León, Manuel Calderón (white shirt), is out in the streets both on the day the results are announced and a few weeks later when Liberals and Sandinistas march simultaneously. He is never more than a few hundred meters from where clashes with Liberals occur.

forming an anti-democratic alliance (Fonseca Terán 2008e). International newspapers did not take notice, and most FSLN Sandinistas I spoke to did not seem surprised of the rhetorical u-turn either. With time, I understood there was a level of dynamism in political discourse I had not been familiar with in Europe.

The MRS and PLC tried to put on protest marches in Managua up until the elections, while their trial of marching in León ended with FSLN activists closing all entrances to the city in guerrilla war style. The FSLN candidate for mayor of León, Manuel Calderón was previously chief of police and apparently thought the police would respect his orders and not intervene. When the police did put themselves in-between Sandinistas and Liberals, the photographer of La Prensa managed to take a picture with Calderón attacking a policeman with a stick. The MRS then attacked the ALN for being controlled by the FSLN. This argument was also reflected by both Alegría and Varela Vilchez. I confronted them with the fact that just a few months earlier the MRS claimed something similar about the PLC. They saw no contradiction in this. Alegría said: "Yes, well, but Montealegre [Rivas] lost that party."

This event once more shows an advanced and at times contradictory level of organizing in the FSLN in a conflict seemingly wholly internal to Nicaragua. The overall picture of the fractiousness of FSLN Sandinismo must be known to at least a sizable part of the Nicaraguan media and all those journalists who interviewed different representatives of this group. The alliance of the MRS with the FSLN of the last few years prior to the 2006 elections could also hardly have been forgotten by all Nicaraguans in 2008.

All this points to the real target group for the protests, the international media, who it is much more reasonable to assume have had no clue of the local circumstances and do not grasp the contradictory aspects of the various statements of the MRS. The MRS activists knew that their party did not stand a chance in the Nicaraguan debate or against the various groups of FSLN Sandinistas. In reality, the MRS seems to have tried to put international pressure on the Ortega Saavedra government to change the country's course the direction favorable to themselves.

Award given to last Minister of Education of East Germany and alliance with Honduras (19 July 2008)

The following showed me how Sandinistas invoke international relations symbolically, even though this may make little sense in gaining any foreign aid or cooperation. 19 July 2008 was the date of the celebration of the 29th anniversary of the Sandinista revolution. The day is usually celebrated in Managua by the FSLN supporters who gather in the John Paul the Second plaza near Lake Managua. This year the celebrations were planned with more international guests than usual.

The MRS also planned celebrations. They had for the past years held their celebrations in alternating places around western Nicaragua. This year they held them in León, in the part of the city called Subtiava, a somewhat poorer neighborhood with a partly indigenous population. The celebrations were to take place in León because the MRS allegedly had a lot of support there. I loitered around the MRS office at the time. I knew the MRS did not trust their local chapter in León with the preparations, and that they had sent people from Managua to take care of all planning efforts. For them, the celebration of the 19th of July was just as much a protest against Ortega Saavedra and the loss of their license to run in elections, as it was a commemoration of the revolution they fought together with the FSLN and which they now (at times) believe only themselves to be the true representatives of.

Most international FSLN guests came from allied South American countries. The two exceptions were José Manuel Zelaya Rosales, President of Honduras, the neighboring country to the north and traditionally not an ally, and Margot Honecker, last minister of education and wife of

Left to right: First Lady Rosario Murillo, President José Daniel Ortega Saavedra, Venezuelan President Hugo Chavez, and Honduran President José Manuel Zelaya Rosales at the celebrations of the 29th anniversary of the Sandinista revolution victory on 19 July 2008.

the late general secretary of the central committee of the *Sozialistische Einheitspartei Deutschlands* (SED, Socialist Unity Party of Germany) of the *Deutsche Demokratische Republik* (DDR, German Democratic Republic).

Zelaya Rosales declared that day the Honduran people had "always" followed the social struggles of their neighbors to the south, since the time of Calderón Sandino. Honecker was present to receive the Ruben Dario medal for the help of the DDR in the literacy campaign of the 1980s. Zelaya Rosales was not yet ready to sign any concrete agreement with Nicaragua, but his mere presence and what he said was enough to be the talk of the town. The concrete signing of various treaties came between that date and 28 June 2009, when he was deposed through a military coup.

The fact Honecker received the medal, a somewhat minor event no Nicaraguans I met saw as controversial, caused headline news in Germany. Honecker had been absent from public life since her escape to Chile together with her husband in the early 1990s, and it came as somewhat of a surprise that she reappeared in this way. German media highlighted her nickname in East Germany was the 'purple witch' (a reference to her hair-color) and what horrible policies the media believed she was responsible for in East Germany. In Nicaragua, not everybody knew who she was. To find qualified opinions, I went to the FSLN headquarters in León and asked about what the significance of the visit was a few days after the ceremony had taken place. Instead of putting me in contact with those giving the official party line, the secretary asked everybody waiting in line to explain the matter to me directly. She had by now seen me many times,

The last socialist minister of education of East Germany, Margot Honecker (right), receives the Ruben Dario medal from President José Daniel Ortega Saavedra (center) on 19 July 2008.

and seemingly was not worried about what those waiting would tell me. I told them, that in Germany reactions were rather negative. The secretary looked somewhat angry at me and then said: "The entire German working class should be proud of this prize!" Everybody cheered.

The Sandinistas I met all had rather positive views of East Germany in comparison to West Germany. In terms of terminology, it is common in Nicaragua to shorten the official term for East Germany, 'The German Democratic Republic,' to 'The Democratic Germany,' and to shorten the official term for West Germany, ' The Federal Republic of Germany,' to 'The Capitalist Germany.' 'Capitalist' has for them a clearly negative connotation, so the terms they use clearly position the value they place on the two countries.

Openly allying oneself with the former minister of education of a nonexistent, and in some parts of the world almost hated, country can hardly have been done in order to receive more economic assistance or other political support. This was in effect a move highly influenced by the historical past of Nicaragua and an understanding of international relations originating from it. The relation to Honduras may to a higher degree be relevant to Nicaragua today, yet the reinterpretation of Honduran history by Zelaya Rosales hardly helped him gain any support in Honduras. This must have been aimed at the Nicaraguan audience. Both appearances seem to have caused problems for the Nicaraguan government and its allies at an international level. The popular support from sectors of Nicaraguan society for these appearances must have been the most crucial factor when the government decided to invite them. Although the MRS was able to organize an event in León in spite of their undisciplined local planning, it ended up being the FSLN that drew the largest crowd.

The Georgia conflict

The following showed me how the Sandinista understanding of the importance of what happens in Nicaragua has an impact in an international context, at times can impact on the country's politics. The next major conflict focused upon in Nicaragua was the conflict between Georgia and Russia of August 2008. Two territories of Georgia, South Ossetia and Abkhazia, had not been under Georgian government control since the end of the *Cold War* (CW), and the majority of those living there were Russian citizens. Georgia attacked South Ossetia immediately after a joint Georgian-US military training exercise (Wikileaks 2008; Centre for Research on Globalization 2008). The conflict quickly spread to Abkhazia (Harding and Tran 2008). After the initial Georgian attacks, Russia retaliated and after securing the area, continued to send its ground troops far into Georgian territory (Agence France-Presse 2008). In the end, the two territories declared themselves independent from Georgia, but no country other than Russia accepted their independence (Levy 2008).

In Nicaragua I initially followed the Georgia conflict through European Internet sources. Nicaraguan papers certainly did not make this their main theme at the start of the conflict. I wrongly assumed this mater would not have any importance for Nicaraguans. Some days into the conflict, at the UNAN–León, I followed a lecture about Nicaraguan history for Nicaraguans – part of a series heavily controlled by Sandinistas who tried to give their students a revolutionary perspective. The issue of Georgia was discussed there. One of the lecturers, representing the party line, used part of his lecture to criticize the United States and its role in the conflict of supporting Georgia. Russia was described as merely being responsible for keeping the peace in the area. Nobody seemed to disagree. Shortly thereafter, Nicaragua was the second country in the world officially to recognize the independence of these two territories (NYT 2008). When I discussed this with Sandinista informants, they all seemed to think this is the most natural step for Nicaragua to take.

Russia is seen uncommonly positively, and any foreign intervention the United States is involved in is seen as negative by most FSLN Sandinistas. Initially, Nicaragua had no stake in this event, and none of Russia's allies initially recognized the independence of the territories from Georgia. Thus, it is only logical to assume the most important reason for the Nicaraguan government's actions was their own political opinion and that of the majority Sandinista part of the population. The event led to Nicaragua renewing relations with Russia. This included several visits by the Russian Vice-President, a visit of the Russian navy and the signing of various aid packages. One of these included a donation of 130 buses (RIA Novisti 2010). Russia donated these buses directly to the FSLN party (Potosme 2009), who then sold them to Managua cooperatives for $25,000 USD each (Morales A. 2009).

It is noticeable the help was sent to the FSLN instead of the Nicaraguan state. I can only speculate, that this setup was arranged to prevent the Liberals from having access to the money. Ortega Saavedra said as part of a speech during those days that Russia was "illuminating the planet" by struggling for "peace and social justice," and that the United States "turns its military force against these in an attempt to shatter them" (Silva 2008). These words seem exceptionally sharp and as if Ortega Saavedra would be speaking of the Soviet Union of the 1980s rather than Russia in 2008. In my experience, Nicaraguans use 'Russia' and 'Soviet Union' interchangeably and Russia is not seen as something fundamentally different from what the Soviet Union used to be. Ortega Saavedra's statement reflects that. The entire incident shows two points of understanding of the world on the part of the Sandinistas. They see Nicaragua as significant enough to play a role in incidents that take part in Eastern Europe, and the country can have a policy independent of the United States, Western Europe and all the regional Latin American powers. Furthermore, an understanding of the continuance of Soviet Union and Russia is unique to Nicaragua.

It can not be disregarded that the situation shows through this understanding, the international communication of this Nicaraguan perspective on the events, did allow for a shift in the international positioning of the Nicaraguan state in relation to Russia and the United States. While I initially viewed the Nicaraguan intervention in the conflict as a product of an ill-informed picture of the world in which Russia would help Nicaragua and other countries in similar situations escape the domination of the United States, I came to recognize the application of this view in the forming of Nicaraguan state policy led to geopolitical realities moving closer to the initial Sandinista perspective.

León FSLN candidate for mayor clashed with police (September 2008)

To me, this showed how not only the actions of the government, but also grassroot activism is believed to be a reflection of worldwide events on the part of the Sandinistas. A much talked-about 'clash' between police and FSLN supporters took place as part of the election campaign in fall of 2008. I was not in León on that day, but the next day I saw a number of pickup trucks with Sandinista flags drive up and down some of the main streets. I asked if I could join them and was allowed to sit on the back of one. A girl sitting next to me explained:

> See, the political right at a world level is trying to halt the revolutionary process by arranging these marches. Here in Nicaragua, it is the Liberals who try to take León, because it was the first capital of the revolution.[1]

As we drove around, it turned out to be a victory parade with Calderón, on the day of the clashes photographed hitting a policeman, and Gladys Báez, a local FSLN member of the national assembly, mounted on the back of pick up trucks. The trucks went through some of the poorer parts of León, cheered on by the masses. The episode of the day before apparently did not hurt Calderón's imagine as much in León as in Managua and other places.

In León, this was one of several such events during the next few months with many forceful FSLN marches, which looked as though the liberation from Somoza's forces were re-lived by those participating. It is the only logical explanation why the FSLN, while in control of the government, the police and the military, took the step of digging trenches

---

1. A reference to the fact León was liberated by the Sandinistas before Managua, and that it has always had FSLN city governments since.

and chasing small groups of Liberals when these wanted to march in a city where the FSLN had a clear majority.

The incident of the clashes between Calderón and the policeman was noticed nationwide, and most other places it was not seen as positive. Calderón since then had a reputation for not being equipped for the job of mayor. Outside of León, it was mainly the scene of that day to which people referred when talking about him over the next year or so. In León, other rumors about him seemed more prominent in giving him an image, such as the rumor according to which he allegedly ate at a fish restaurant without showing the proper manners of cleaning his hands at a time when he was mayor.

The matter of Calderón's clash seemed relevant to many Sandinistas, especially in Managua. While there may have been a certain class difference between those approving and those going against the actions of the candidate for mayor with middle-class Nicaraguans less likely to support his attack on the police, an undeniable difference existed between León and Managua in what events were taken as fundamental. My informants in Managua talked about the incident as an isolated act by Calderón. For the Leónese participants of the marches, the Calderón incident seemed to be part of the marches against the Liberals and was not attributed much importance.

No-one I met questioned whether the clashes between Liberals and Sandinistas represented an international tendency. The difference in understanding between León and Managua, and many other places, must be something of which many Sandinistas are aware. From that they should have been able to deduct that the perspective from outside of Nicaragua would be even more different, yet somehow this seemed not to have been done.

FSLN won local elections (November 2008)

Nicaraguan elections are events which take on significance for both Liberals and Sandinistas that go beyond electoral politics and are seen not only as a formal process, but as a part of popular organization. This was apparent during the preparations for the 2008 municipal elections, and in the reactions to the results. Also, the elections showed how central international relations are for Nicaragua, while Nicaraguans again place agency on the Nicaraguan side.

International observers from European Union and United States were not allowed to observe the elections but various Latin American countries did receive observer credentials. This was somewhat new and reflected the fact Sandinistas were in charge. It also caused the election results to be questioned by those excluded from observing. It seemed just about everybody remotely related to politics was somehow involved in the electoral process. On the days before the election, I circulated with Javier Díaz, a former student of mine in his late 40s who lived in Ciudad Sandino, just outside of Managua on the road to León. On the night before the elections, we visited his mother-in-law. The family of his mother in law was preparing food for the FSLN fraction which sat at the election stations in a certain sector of Managua the next day. Instead of organizing food for members of all parties who sit at an election booth together, the food preparation is done party by party. It is just one of several election related activities which involve the public, and it reinforces the personal alliance of the food preparer with the party.

Díaz was involved in the *Juventud Sandinista* (JS) in the 1980s and studied in Cuba in the late 1980s to early 1990s. Now he said he was disappointed by the movement, without specifying the overall reason. Nevertheless, he still voted for the FSLN. He explained his vote was part of what is popularly known as the 'voto duro' (hard vote) which refers to those who will always vote FSLN, no matter how much they disagree with the day-to-day politics of the party. No equivalent term exists for voters of other parties. Manuel Corea, one of those who went to the cadre school Wilhelm-Pieck in East Germany at another time presented to me a category of Sandinistas which seems to cover the same group, and he explained the distinction between them and other Sandinistas this way:

> There are those Sandinistas who are Sandinistas because it is where they receive something. They will dance to the tune of whoever feeds them. And then there are those of us who are Sandinistas out of conviction. We will always be Sandinistas, even though we recognize that the Frente... the upper leadership of the Frente, commits errors.

During election day, Managua remained calm, and in the early afternoon, I stood at the Rotonda Metrocentro. FSLN Sandinistas were already present before polls closed, waving Nicaraguan flags. Once election booths closed, they exchanged their flags for red-and-black Sandinista flags. At this time,

I joined one of the JS gatherings a few blocks away and encountered a friend, Ninfa Patricia Ramos. Ramos was involved in the student section of the Sandinista movement for a prolonged period, and she had worked at exit polls on election day and already knew the FSLN had won in Managua before the official results were in. She introduced me to another type of voter, the 'voto oculto' (hidden vote). These are people who do not tell pollsters how they vote. Nicaraguan pollsters count them as likely voting in favor of one of the Liberal parties.

The four types of voters pollsters operate with are: FSLN voters who vote due to the politics of the FSLN, FSLN voters who vote in spite of the politics of the FSLN ('voto duro'), open Liberal votes, and hidden Liberal votes ('voto oculto'). This indicates a vote in favor of the FSLN seems 'more correct' morally or otherwise, than casting a Liberal vote for Nicaraguans.

The FSLN won the elections of November 9th 2008 overwhelmingly. The FSLN won 105 mayors, while the PLC won 37 and the ALN 4 mayors (Hurtado 2008). Immediately after the preliminary result became known, the opposition cried foul and called for marches. I listened to all sides of the story. In the end, I must admit that Fonseca Terán (2008c) was right in his analysis that, at least at a formal level, the elections were legally and correctly won by the FSLN, as allegations of electoral fraud could not be substantiated. Even though this seemed to be recognized by most Liberals, it was of little practical importance to them. A protest against a Sandinista victory for them seemed only normal. The Latin American election observers approved the election results. The *Consejo Supremo Electoral* (CSE) leadership, and the two Liberal representatives within it approved the results of most major cities where the FSLN won according to their data. The two Liberal representatives were then consequently expelled from the PLC.

The next days the Liberals in Managua tried to cause havoc by physically attacking Sandinista positions. They managed to capture a few of the rotondas, but as soon as Montealegre Rivas called one of the rotondas 'liberated territory,' the Sandinista activists took it back immediately. Fights broke out all over the city with several dead Sandinistas, and for the next few weeks, Ortega Saavedra disappeared from the public scene. He was replaced by the members of the CSE who seemed to lead the country during this period. Marches broke out everywhere. The statements of the CSE members spread through mass media and mouth-to-mouth propaganda in a highly politicized atmosphere.

The Sandinista victory in the 2008 municipal elections is celebrated as if it were part of another revolutionary insurrection.

In many cities like León, the PLC and MRS claimed to be the real winners and only electoral fraud kept them from taking over the city government. On the day of their first announced march in which Montealegre Rivas was to participate, FSLN activists blocked the roads from Managua, and a few thousand Sandinistas chased about 200 Liberals, who managed to arrive in León. Among others, I met Sandinista farm workers from the countryside who had come to León to 'defend' the city against the Liberals. When I asked what was taking place between Liberals and Sandinistas, Liberals claimed strongly they had been robbed of their victory, while the Sandinistas claimed their march was a demonstration of 'yet another victory' and the Liberals were to blame for all violence which may still occur.

Young and old Sandinistas were in the streets that day, and both groups seemed mostly interested in the physical manifestation of political differences. Even the police looked very happy and did not actually try to stop the Sandinistas from chasing the Liberals. Some blocks from the front line between the two groups, one could see groups of young Sandinistas shoot homemade firecracker-arms at police lines, who 'defended' themselves with shields as if they were in a war. Yet, behind the police there were no Liberal marchers. One policeman filmed the confrontation with the young Sandinistas with his mobile phone. No attempts at arrests were made. It just seemed like a part of an action-filled happening for both police and activists which both sides seemed to enjoy.

At first, I was amazed the Liberals dared march in León. The number

While a few thousand Sandinistas chase up to 200 Liberals through the streets of León, some Sandinista students launch mortars at the overwhelmingly Sandinista police nearby. Neither police nor students seem to take such physical clashes seriously. None of the students involved in the street fights that day are arrested.

of people they managed to assemble showed quite clearly it was highly unlikely they could have won in León, whereas other cities, such as Masaya, where the FSLN also won but has much less support historically speaking, would have been easier targets for claiming voter fraud. After talking with the Liberal candidate Ariel Terán and some of the MRS people, I became aware of why their confrontation with the Sandinistas in León was so crucial for them. The reason for their march seemed to lie outside of Nicaragua. Many representatives of western countries made comments during those days to the effect that cheating and fraud had occurred in the elections, even though none of their countries' observers had been observing the elections. Had the Sandinistas additionally attacked the Liberals, not with demonstrators, but using the police or military, both firmly in their control, it would have received headlines throughout the United States and Europe, and could have ended in the funding of another Contra war. The opposition tried to involve international pressure, and attempted using the tactics of popular organizing to take control the way the Sandinistas had. Ultimately, they were unsuccessful in their attempt.

For the Sandinistas, the day held a different significance. Calderón explained it well, when he spontaneously tried to connect the events with its history as a Sandinista stronghold when I asked him what he thought about the events of the day:

Ariel Terán, the Liberal candidate in the 2008 elections for mayor of León, takes even greater risks than his Sandinista counterpart by running around León with the Liberals – placing himself directly in the middle of the stone throwing on the day when both groups march. On another occasion, Terán shows up at a Sandinista march with a poster saying "To steal from the people is to steal from God" – a reference to the Sandinista slogan "To serve the people is to serve God." Terán is chased into the León cathedral, where he hides until the Sandinistas have gone.

> Well, today was a momentous victory for the people of León, and I would say for the people of Nicaragua. León has shown always to be able to bring victory to Nicaragua. Because in 1956, the execution of the tyrant Somoza meant the beginning of the end of the dictatorship. And the taking of the fort [of León] on 7 July [1979], finished the dictatorship and made the establishment of the government of Nicaragua—here in León—possible. Today, with this victory over the [political] right, over the modern-day Somocismo, León gives Nicaragua the chance to recover the level of stability that is needed to fight and overcome poverty.

I did not hear Calderón's specific way of connecting the event with history again from others, but the same event was explained to me in several other ways in the next few days by various León Sandinistas. And every time it was put in a historic context, somehow connecting it to 1979. For the younger Sandinistas who were not alive in 1979 and had not experienced the 1980s, the event seemed to be the closest they got to having participated in the revolutionary struggle.

In municipal elections, it is essential that either 'they' or 'we' win, and not so much which particular candidate wins. This became appar-

After the Sandinista victory in the 2008 municipal elections in Managua, riots break out. When 3/4 of a year later the Sandinista mayor of Managua, boxing champion Alexis Argüello commits suicide, he is replaced by Daisy Torres. The change-over is universally accepted. Torres tells me that she believes God has a plan for everybody, and that his plan for her was to put her into this position.

ent to me a few months later. In theory, the candidacies for most top posts are individual, in that the elections are set up like elections in the United States which are more about individual candidates rather than a party. Yet, Nicaraguans typically see the importance of the candidate as secondary to his or her party affiliation. When in Managua Alexis Argüello (FSLN) was elected and the opposition fought it, there was a great uproar. When Argüello was replaced by the FSLN with Daisy Torres (FSLN) the following summer, after he committed suicide on 1 July 2009, hardly any grumbling was heard, even though many conspiracy theories would have it that Ortega Saavedra was behind the death. No-one suggested that new elections should be held which Liberals would have a chance of winning. Some of the other FSLN mayors were exchanged before their term ended in the following years, and while, at times, it ended with two different factions within the FSLN supporting different candidates, at no time was it suggested having an open vote with participation of all parties to decide who should take over.

Parliament stopped working (November 2008 – February 2009)

For 4 months, between the elections in November until February 2009, the country was ruled by presidential decree. The Liberals initially decided they would declare the municipal election results invalid through the use of their parliamentary majority. Ortega Saavedra explained that this was unconstitutional, and that he would write a presidential decree against it. For the next few months, a standoff ensued between Liberals and the FSLN in which neither was able to form a majority in parliament and nothing was passed through parliament, which, according to both sides, led to foreign help to be canceled due to lack of decisions by parliament. A few marches by Liberals against what they claimed to be electoral fraud were organized, and the FSLN countered them with marches and celebrations in connection with the 30 year anniversary of the 1979 triumph of the Sandinista revolution. None of these later marches reached the size of the earlier marches at the end of 2008.

The crisis was resolved when Liberals voted for the Sandinista proposal of parliamentary leadership and a group of judges lifted the house arrest of their leader Alemán Lacayo. The MRS people were quick to point out this proofed the existence of the pact between Alemán Lacayo's PLC and the FSLN. In the mean time, Montealegre Rivas left the PLC again, and tried to establish his own group, the *Banca Democratica* (BD), to which several of the Managua city council members followed him. Then Montealegre Rivas changed his mind and asked his followers to join the *Partido Liberal Independiente* (PLI)[2], until that party decided they did not want Montealegre Rivas because he had too many connections to the Somozas. The Liberals then started to subdivide themselves into various groups, to the joy of the FSLN Sandinistas.

The episode showed that after not being able to make advances in the popular arena, the opposition was for once able to unite and pressure the government at parliament level. Also the FSLN was unable to counter this with any form of popular organizing to force the opposition into accepting the result. At a general level, one can say at times the FSLN is willing to give in to a more or less corrupt deals that give them most positions of power. Different from most other actions, which included popular organizing in

---

2. The PLI was a party believed dead by most Nicaraguans I talked to.

some way or other, the deal with Alemán Lacayo was almost universally criticized by all Sandinistas. Yet, few of them saw any other solution to the crisis in the country, and ultimately they accepted the actions of Ortega Saavedra as necessary. The issue they seemed to have with it, was mainly that a critical decision was made without involving events of mass popular participation, as that is what usually gives legitimacy to Sandinista initiated projects.

Military coup in Honduras (June 2009)

The most direct way, Nicaragua politics were influenced by the international scene during this period, besides the cutting of aid, was when the military coup in the northern neighbor of Honduras took place. Since the appearance of President Zelaya Rosales on 19 July 2008 in Managua, Honduras joined two alliance agreements to which Nicaragua also subscribed, the political alliance/trade network *Alternativa Bolivariana para los pueblos de nuestra Américas* (ALBA) and the Caribbean alliance to buy oil from Venezuela called *Petrocaribe*. Honduras then experienced a military coup on 28 June 2009, the day when President Zelaya Rosales planned on holding a referendum on whether the people wanted to hold a constitution assembly, to change some of the land rights and open up for institutions of direct democracy, such as the *Consejos de Poder Ciudadano* (CPC) in Nicaragua.

In Nicaragua, the reactions to the coup followed the classic divide FSLN vs. the Liberal parties. On one side, the Liberals decided that they want to march in favor of the coup. The MRS parliamentary group had at this time split, with two of four members leaving. Most importantly the *Movimiento por el Rescate del Sandinismo* (MpRS) and their one member of the national assembly left, criticized the MRS for helping an electoral campaign in El Salvador against the *Frente Farabundo Martí para la Liberación Nacional* (FMLN). The MRS left-leaning elements exited, and the rest of the party did not object to the protests in favor of the coup in Honduras.

At the time, I associated with younger FSLN party activists in Nicaragua. Erick Saul Rios Juarez, a 20 year old Sandinista radio show host and activist, spent many days occupying the rotondas, to prevent the political right from showing their solidarity with the Honduran coup makers. Sandinistas in the border region with Honduras wrote protest songs and housed some of the Honduran exiles following the coup. I visited the Sandinistas in the border town of Ocotal in early August 2009. They made the point that they did not help the Hondurans organize a revolution against the coup. "That has to be the work of the Hondurans themselves," the guy in charge of the FSLN office explained to me, "Our help is humanitarian more than anything." The theme of Nicaraguans planning a revolution in Honduras was extremely common in conversation during those days. All the Sandinistas I met agreed, that a revolution was the solution for Honduras now, and many of them were interested in helping Honduras to do so. One of the Honduran youth organizers showed up in Nicaragua and went on Rios Juarez's show. "This guy suddenly said that 'Zelaya [Rosales] is not the right person to lead this,'" Rios Juarez told me after I came back from a trip to Honduras where I met the same youngster. Rios Juarez was hesitant in giving me the contact details and the party ultimately decided against providing them. It was by coincidence I met the same fellow. Also this episode demonstrated the Nicaraguan understanding that popular mobilization is essential in day-to-day politics. Even the Liberals, who by then had managed to build up some respect internationally through the elections they supposedly won, believed they needed to march, even though no government in the world officially was in favor of the coup. If international media were to focus on their marches, they would lose all credibility they had built. For Sandinistas, the coup marked a difficult time, and from some of the comments I heard, there seemed to be a fear higher up in the party that individual Sandinista groups would try to organize a revolutionary effort in Honduras in disregard of the understanding of the events of Honduran activists who fought in the resistance against the coup.

30 years of revolution and some advances (summer 2009)

On 19 July 2009, the 30th anniversary of the revolution was celebrated. Yet instead of saying '30 years since the insurrection,' my Sandinista informants insisted on calling it 'the 30th year of the revolution.' The director of the *Oficina de Ética Pública* (OEP) explained: "Well, during those 16 years, we did not stop. We just prepared ourselves for this phase of the revolution." Her life seems to confirm that. It is remarkably similar to the life stories of many other Sandinistas I interviewed: during the early years of Liberal governments she studied for a higher degree as a lawyer and then

Adult illiteracy rate

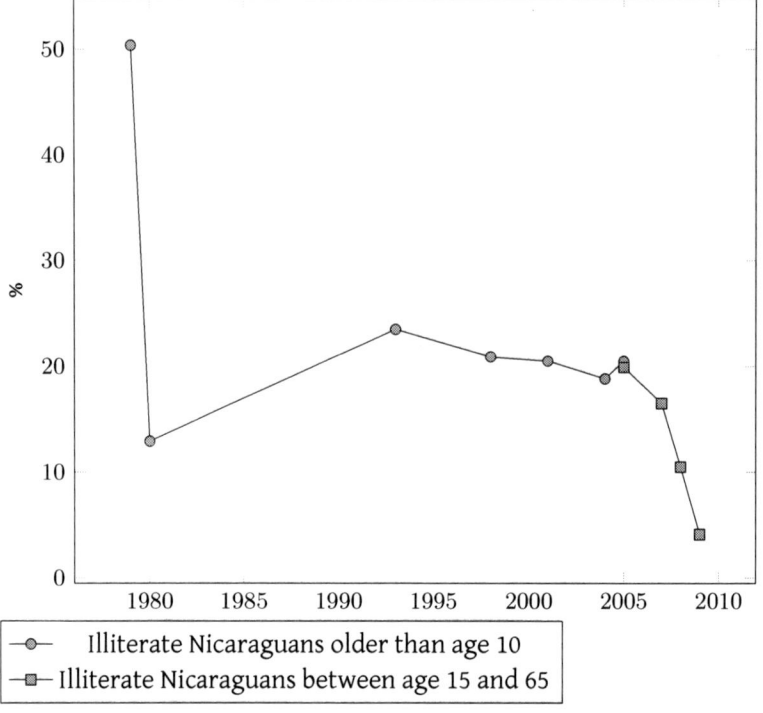

— ◦ — Illiterate Nicaraguans older than age 10
— ▪ — Illiterate Nicaraguans between age 15 and 65

The literacy campaign is one area in which a marked difference can be seen between Sandinista and non-Sandinista governments. The latest campaign had already started in 2005 at a regional level in municipalities where Sandinistas were in charge. In 2007–09, it was carried out at a national level. *The 2007 figure is an estimate by the Nicaraguan government. The 2008 figure is based on survey results, and the 2009 figure was calculated by taking the 2008 figure and subtracting the amount of people who had gone through the literacy program in that year. The exact meaning of 'illiterate' is not specified for any of the figures. Source: Arrien (2006); Paguaga (2006); MINED (2009); Hanemann (2005)*

spent the last few years working on the NGO-level.

In August 2009, in the middle of the financial crisis, the FSLN declared a success in reducing illiteracy from 20.7%[3] to 3.56%[4] with the literacy campaign it started in 2007. The figure is approved by the *United Nations*

---

3. The figure 20.7% is quoted in all news stories about the event. In my own calculation using the base numbers from Paguaga (2006), I arrive at 19.9%, which is the figure used in the graph.

4. The figure 3.56% is disseminated widely. Asking Sandinistas at the time, it is explained to me that the UNESCO certified an illiteracy rate of 4.1% and that subsequently the figure fell to 3.56% during the same year.

Education, Science and Culture Organization (UNESCO) (Nicaragua Network 2009a). The government also celebrated the start of a hydro-electric energy program, that supposedly some day will generate 40% of all electricity produced by the *Tumarin Hydroelectric Project* on the *Rio Grande de Matagalpa*. With cooperation from the international company *Eolo, S.A.* and the international consortium *Amayo, S.A.*, the government built wind farms scheduled to produce another 12.5% of Nicaraguan energy needs (Nicaragua Network 2009b).

The government made several similar points at this time. Some of them, such as the literacy program, involved large amounts of popular participation, while others were highly technical and would most likely require more than anything the collaboration of highly skilled professionals. All these projects have as a stated goal the improvement of the standard of living of the general population and eventually to make the country more self-sufficient. The approval for such programs is almost always looked for in international organizations. Instead of using the numbers of the *Ministerio de Educación* (MINED), the government mostly refers to the numbers produced by the UNESCO. For all the talk of independence from the empire and the unique national discussion, multinational companies and organizations were strongly involved in these Sandinista projects.

Concluding remarks

We have seen how a diverse range of political challenges is handled by Sandinistas on various levels. This includes how internal Nicaraguan conflicts oftentimes originate from developments at a world level which are not much referred to in the country. At times, actors on an international stage are called for by various Nicaraguan groups and this can mean the Nicaraguan reality changes quite concretely. Through all their actions, the Sandinistas seek to make Nicaragua a more independent country. Sandinista leaders also seek approval for the success of their programs in international organizations and work on programs together with international companies. Various events have shown popular organization is a central element in Nicaraguan political life, and some events such as elections, have a distinctively parliamentary connotation, and are in Nicaragua cause for popular organization. At times, mass gatherings are staged in order to provoke a reaction internationally, and at times the international political scene is invoked in order to appease the Nicaraguan masses. Altogether, the whole structure of international influences, and uncertainty in the command hierarchy of the FSLN and the relationship between various groups all believing to represent Sandinismo presents a picture of a vibrant, but chaotic, political landscape. This is truly representative of Nicaraguan politics.

Fifth Chapter

Sandinista projects of change

In the aftermath of the 1980s version of Sandinismo and a succession of different right-wing governments, the return of José Daniel Ortega Saavedra/Sandinismo in 2006 was cast against a much more variegated backdrop of sub-versions of Sandinista ideology. These different versions are not so much reflected in different fractional versions of Sandinismo, although there are such diffuse tendencies.

The current situation of the country is mostly portrayed in foreign media as being extremely centered around President Ortega Saavedra and the decisions he makes. In reality, the Sandinistas are in power (2007-12) in more than just the sense that the Nicaraguan President happens to be a follower of the Sandinista ideology. The last chapter looked at age as a major factor in terms of what it means to be a Sandinista. This chapter looks at different types of Sandinistas and how they act politically. We take a look at the historic structure of the *Frente Sandinista de Liberación Nacional* (FSLN), and how the party now works differently and has changed to a model in line with what is known as the 'Socialism for the 21st Century.' Then the significance Sandinistas attribute to political alliances and the different ways one can be a Sandinista activist are viewed.

The historic structure of the FSLN

When the FSLN first started in 1961 it consisted of only one ideological tendency with one national directory. In the 1970s, two other tendencies came into existence, and, for a few years, the party operated with three rather independent leaderships. In early 1979, the party held a unification conference in Honduras where it decided a group of nine Sandinistas, three from each tendency, would make up the national leadership. This organized division of power remained the same throughout the 1980s. The party was not one unified bloc, and the divisions were institutionalized (see also — *The FSLN divided into three tendencies*, p. 7). In addition to participation in the ideological tendencies and work inside the party, a number of activities were offered to engage the general population so they could see themselves as part of the Sandinismo project. So-called 'mass organizations' were created to facilitate this. They were given formal representation at various levels. Party membership was not acquired by most people involved in these activities, yet they soon referred to themselves as Sandinistas (see also — *The FSLN structure*, p. 14). During the 1980s and into the 1990s the party controlled TV stations and the newspaper '*La Barricada.*' Opposition newspapers were allowed during Sandinista rule, but complained about being censored frequently by Sandinista authorities. Working in the Sandinista media outlets was nevertheless one way to become somewhat creative and independently involved in the Sandinista project. Most involvement with the politics and the FSLN party in the 1980s was rather hierarchically organized, most of my informants claim. In short: Many different ways existed of being a Sandinista in those years.

In the post-Sandinista years, around the time when the *Movimiento Renovador Sandinista* (MRS) split off from the FSLN in the 1990s, the national leadership of nine dissolved. After that, Ortega Saavedra has served as the General Secretary of the party. Several other individuals hold high party posts and are known for it. The names I heard people mention are the Organizational Secretary Reinaldo Gregorio Lenín Cerna Juárez,[1] Communication Secretary Rosario Murillo, the International Secretary Jacinto Juárez, and his media-savvy vice Carlos Fonseca Terán.

The formal structure of the party that decides how the individual leaders arrived at their posts are conducted is of little concern to most Sandinistas. No-one I met outside the FSLN offices was quite able to explain how it worked, and no documents or charts existed on the web pages of the FSLN which explained what offices existed and who was elected to what position. After visiting the department of organization of the FSLN León to ask specifically about this issue and searching for the statutes of the party on other websites, I discovered that the national leadership of nine in the

---

1. The post of organizational secretary of the FSLN was suspended in May 2011. (Arévalo Alemán 2011)

Although Sandinistas have control of many aspects of the state, including military and police and various law-making bodies, individual groups of Sandinistas oftentimes prefer to work in a clandestine manner. These students have taken hostages inside a building because they disagree with the budget proposal of the largely Sandinista university leadership of León. Whether they need to cover their faces is questionable, as the strongly Sandinista police shows no signs of wanting to arrest them or use photographic or filmed evidence to prosecute them.

1980s was replaced by a national Sandinista council of 40–50 members, which is appointed by national congresses of around 1300 Sandinistas every 5 years and additionally includes the FSLN mayors of departamento capitals and political secretaries of the party at the departmental level. It appoints all the heads of the party that I had heard about already, and additionally secretaries and vice secretaries for the areas of women, youth, political education, and finances, as well as two committees: one that organizes party-internal elections and one that insures that all structures of the party stick to the statutes of the party. At a level in-between the national congress and national council is the national assembly of around 300 members. The national assembly includes the political secretaries and mayors at the municipio level. The assemblies make all decisions of major importance that come up in-between national congresses. The structure of the the party at a national level is largely copied at the departamento and municipio levels. At a neighborhood level, the party consists of general assemblies and *Consejos de Liderazgo Sandinista* (Sandinista Leadership Councils, CLSs) (FSLN 2002).

While the fact that hardly anyone knows about the formal structure of

President José Daniel Ortega Saavedra's inauguration ceremony in January 2006 hosted international leaders such as Hugo Chavez and Evo Morales and was well visited by the public. When Ortega Saavedra started speaking about which aspects of the 1980s policy agenda he would not be reinstituting, many Nicaraguans left the ceremony.

the party may at first glance indicate an extremely closed leadership model, upon closer inspection it is only so in the limited sense of determining who the presidential candidate is to be. Power differences among Sandinistas exist, but the party does not function as hierarchically as one may initially think. When I visited Nicaragua for the first time (December/January 2006/2007), and was in Managua for the inauguration ceremony of Ortega Saavedra, I was amazed to discover only one party/group with one set of symbols making up the Left of Nicaragua. Compared to Mexico with its wealth of social organizations and parties, it was noticeable how in Nicaragua everything was centered around the FSLN and the symbolism connected to Augusto Nicolás Calderón Sandino. This gave me an initial picture that the FSLN had not changed much since the 1980s.

With time, I noticed marked differences among various parts of the Sandinista movement, involving many different activities. When Ortega Saavedra called the FSLN an 'anarchist party' (Gaynor 1999), he seemed to use that term to mean the party was not as centrally controlled as was the case with many soviet aligned parties. Similarly, with the FSLN in power, the party control of the country is not as tight as one might think. This is evident given the media coverage of Ortega Saavedra's administration. At the same time, it cannot be denied the FSLN connected part of the Sandinista movement was exerting power. A good example of how the party functions decentralized, yet exerted limited power, could be seen in the current structure of the media. Currently the only three daily papers of Nicaragua are *La Prensa, Hoy* and *El Nuevo Diario*. All three of these are Conservative or center-Conservative. This would under other circumstances seem like a media scene controlled by Conservative forces. The papers only print 100,000 copies daily altogether – in a country with a population of 5.3 million. Radio is much more influential – 95% of households have radios and 180 FM and 65 AM radio stations broadcast. The state, much of which during Sandinista governments is an extension of the party apparatus, only owns one station – Radio Nicaragua. The FSLN owns one news program and holds shares in the national station Canal 4 and nine of the many local radio stations[2]. In addition, another 20 stations call themselves 'Sandinista,' but they are outside the party's direct control. Around 80% of all Nicaraguans are reached by the Sandinista news program and around 30% by their other programs. William Grigsby Vado, current director of the Sandinista radio station La Primera, explained the relationship between the various stations this way as part of an interview to a German newspaper:

> The various stations partially also pursue different political interests. We are all children of the revolution, but these days every radio fights on its own. [...] We are Sandinista and we are autonomous. (Berger 2008, 3, own translation)

The independent Sandinista radio stations are still bound to the state, partially sponsored through government advertisements. The media are clearly not wholly controlled by the Sandinistas, although Sandinista media make out a crucial part of the media landscape. The Sandinista media are not entirely controlled by Ortega Saavedra, but have a number of different Sandinista groups controlling each of the various outlets. This structure of the Sandinista media is similar to the structure of the party overall. The rest of the chapter shows this.

The principle of alliances

While the party is not quite united and decision making structures oftentimes unclear, in many instances, alliances are sought with other groups

---

2. The FSLN ownership of media outlets is changing rapidly. The data are from 2008-9; Canal 8 and 13 were also Sandinista stations by 2011, and are directed by the sons of Ortega Saavedra.

outside the Sandinista camp to achieve single advances on certain issues. Tricks, such as passing laws to please one alliance partner, only to subsequently subvert it by not enforcing it or using other laws or judicial practices to counteract the initial law, and advanced schemes of short-lived alliances with various groups to achieve a certain goal by some Sandinista subgroup, I find to be typical of Sandinista rule. We now look at some of the most well-known examples of this in recent years.

Therapeutic abortion

One of the two most known examples of Nicaraguan politics outside of Nicaragua is how Ortega Saavedra apparently finds Jesus just in time before the 2006 presidential elections and marries his partner of over 20 years, Rosario Murillo, in a Catholic ceremony in 2005 (Gooren 2010). That same fall, the Catholic church mobilized against women's right of abortion even in certain limited cases when the woman's life is in danger and only the life of the woman or the fetus can be saved. This right had been part of the constitution for about a century. The right was first removed in 2006, and officially outlawed by 2008 – all with the approval of the FSLN and all the right-wing parties. In exchange for that, some Catholic priests supported the FSLN in the elections (Gooren 2010). "In the 1980s, the Catholic church was against us, and now they are with us," an elderly person at a León center for old revolutionaries tried to convince me as to why the step (on abortion) was needed tactically in December 2006. It gradually became clearer during my time in Nicaragua, that 'forbidding' abortion did not mean and was not meant to mean stopping its practice or even to stop the state from organizing it.

It took another investigator, Rakel Helgheim of the University of Bergen, Norway, to conduct a series of interviews with members of civilian society to find out what exact legal situation existed after therapeutic abortion had been made illegal. We stayed at the same place in León during the first months of my stay. She was furious about this change to the law. One day she came home and explained she had just found out, that around the time abortion was made entirely illegal, a change publicized in both national and international press, the code of conduct of hospitals had changed. According to the new code, hospitals had to prioritize the survival of the patient higher than any other law. This was not published anywhere at the time. It was not before the summer of 2009

Women's rights groups have protested against José Daniel Ortega Saavedra's compromise with the Catholic church on abortion. Nevertheless, a lot of his support comes from disenfranchised groups.

that the *El Nuevo Diario* carried a story attacking the FSLN for the *Ministerio de Salud* (MINSA) having conducted abortions after it was officially forbidden (Aguilera 2009b, 2009a). I received some private talking points from Fonseca Terán (2010c) in July 2010. He used them in conferences with international participants who heard about the MRS version of events. Most of his points mirrored the conclusions I had arrived at after investigating the matter for months. In the end, both MRS and FSLN favor abortion in case of the mother's life being in danger, even though the FSLN does it in a more hidden manner. In this case, I fell into the trap of taking remarks of a tactical nature to be representative of what my informants actually believed.

El pacto

The second feature of Nicaraguan politics that people outside the country have heard about, is that an alliance to splits all powerful positions in the state between two powerful groups or two powerful individuals exists. The reality is many shifting alliances appear in Nicaraguan politics, especially between different parties. The FSLN seems to seek a political majority in parliament with whomever they can on any given issue at any point in time. One such alliance is focused upon more than any of the others. This particular alliance carries with it a negative undertone both in the foreign press and in Nicaraguan society that other alliances do not. This alliance, known as *el pacto*, concerns at times the FSLN and the *Partido Liberal Constitucionalista* (PLC), and other times just their leaders Ortega Saavedra and José Arnoldo Alemán Lacayo. Alemán Lacayo and Ortega Saavedra are said to have made a pact in the late 1990s to divide all positions of state power between them, in return for the FSLN permitting Alemán Lacayo to govern more or less uninterrupted during his presidential term.

It is true that when parliament stopped working for several months after the municipal elections of November 2008, a solution was found in which certain charges of fraud were dropped against Alemán Lacayo. This happened most likely through government intervention, and the FSLN was simultaneously given control of most of parliament (see also — Parliament stopped working (November 2008 - February 2009), p. 137). El pacto may not have been the favored choice by the FSLN leadership in this situation. Cuadra Núñez and Fonseca Terán (2010b) point out the constitution was changed in 1995 in a way which obligated even the larger parties to seek approval of other groups in parliament in order to be able to appoint a wide range of officials. At the time, neither PLC nor FSLN held many seats in parliament, whereas the MRS did and was part of the group which approved this change. Cuadra Núñez and Fonseca Terán claim the idea behind the change was to obligate the FSLN and PLC to negotiate with smaller parties such as the MRS in connection with handing out positions.

In the case of the international press, it becomes easy to understand how el pacto is seen as evil: misinformation and half-information lead to strange conclusions being reached. Yet, this type of maneuvering is not all that uncommon for Nicaraguan politics. The FSLN specifically is much involved in such tactics, and it seems the result has been fantastic for them. Therefore, I have difficulties understanding the controversy this generates for Sandinistas who are angry about el pacto. When I first found out about all the individual circumstances and understood that the foreign press was mainly just spreading anti-FSLN propaganda, I started asking more Nicaraguans about the circumstances and what made el pacto for them personally worse than other alliances. Most were not able to explain it to me or chose not to try. Some explained it like Jorge Madriz, who is active in the small party *Alternativa por el Cambio* (AC), which some other informants said is filled with Sandinista-spies and which ran in the 2011 national elections together with the FSLN:

> It's quite straightforward. When other parties do it, it's called

> 'an alliance' and it's normal, but when then FSLN does the same, it's called 'el pacto' and it's terribly hurtful.

This is the same conclusion I arrive at. Yet, it gives no further information of what it is that makes such an alliance negative for a Sandinista. Carolina Icabalceta Garay said something which points in the direction of what may be the background for Sandinista skeptics of cooperation with Alemán Lacayo and his party. She explained it this way:

> I have studied the history of Nicaragua and the history of many other places, and the pactos are never acceptable; it's always the ruling class pacting in order to stay in power.

If Icabalceta Garay's analysis is the opinion of the average Nicaraguan, then that would certainly not be strange, given the high importance given to history and historical examples by Nicaraguans. I never hear the historic comparison made by others. Later Icabalceta Garay specified what her issues with el pacto were:

> I would like for you to write down two issues I strongly dislike about el pacto:
> The first has to do with the [law on] therapeutic abortion. This concession to the church I find embarrassing, unjust and inhumane.[3] [...]
> The other has to do with popular participation. Before, you could create a new party with the signatures of I don't know how many people. [...]

The first of the issues Icabalceta Garay mentioned seems to be related to the cooperation with the Catholic church. It is not strictly covered by the term el pacto between PLC and FSLN as the media and opposition parties use it, but the conflation of el pacto with other questionable deals the FSLN leadership has made with other groups is not uncommon. The explanations I received from other Nicaraguans were similar. This may explain why many Sandinistas exclaim that they are strongly against el pacto. The second of Icabalceta Garay's issues relates to some changes made to the Constitution in the 1990s, which made it harder to form new parties than under the original constitution created during the Sandinista

---

3. At the time of the interview, the media had not yet reported the fact that Nicaraguan hospitals continued to conduct abortions.

government of the 1980s. This may arguably be seen as part of el pacto. I heard this issue mentioned several times by academic Sandinistas, as one of their main criticisms of el pacto.

The new FSLN as part of a Socialism for the 21st Century

The term 'Socialism for the 21st Century' is used in much of Latin America due to the book *El socialismo del siglo xxi* (Dieterich 2007). Venezuelan President Hugo Chavez and his followers promote this book heavily. Dieterich (2007) mentions four main principles included in the new type of socialism:

1. Equal pay for things that take the same amount of time to do.
2. Incorporation of direct, participative democracy.
3. Democratic state institutions that legitimately represent citizens at a local level.
4. Self-determination and criticism by the citizens.

According to a private project file by Fonseca Terán and his wife Cuadra Núñez, Logros de la Revolución Sandinista en su segunda etapa. the parts on direct democracy planned and set up by the Sandinista government include Nicaraguan government's plan to implement the project of a 'Socialism for the 21st Century' in Nicaragua. They claim this type of socialism is compatible with some of the policies of the Ortega Saavedra government (Cuadra Núñez and Fonseca Terán 2010a).

It is noticeable I never heard any of my Sandinista informants refer to either the book or the term. The term 'socialism' was only used by some Nicaraguans who identified positively with the Sandinista experience of the 1980s in the first few years after 2006. Many of the younger Sandinistas had never even heard of it. Once, in the back of a pickup filled with Sandinistas in León following other cars celebrating the Sandinista defense of the city some days earlier against a planned march by the Liberals, I was asked by teenagers, "What are you?" I answered: "I am a socialist." They asked somewhat perplexed: "Does that mean you are right or left?"[4]

---

4. By 2011, this had changed, and *'socialista'* was now one of three words used to describe Sandinismo as part of the next election campaign, together with *Cristiano* and *Solidario*.

In spite of all the projects currently running in the name of Sandinismo, many of those identifying strongly with the socialist project of the 1980s doubt the revolutionary character of the current phase. Icabalceta Garay expressed it this way:

> Look, I'd like for this to be a revolution, but it just isn't. I will not let myself be fooled by that.

Even top FSLN officials, such as Fonseca Terán, see the current process and specifically the part of popular participation critically:

> Due to a series of historic circumstances, the political culture of Nicaragua does not include the possibility for changes through nonviolent struggles nor through social struggles. The average Nicaraguan citizen can only understand changes as a product of wars or elections. This constitutes an obstacle for the establishment of direct democracy and for Citizen Power to be installed from below; in the subjective reality of Nicaragua '[taking] power' is not a demand of the people; what they expect is not to exercise power themselves but that it be exercised to one's benefit. Therefore, change in the political system can at this point only be promoted from above through the formal installation of Citizen Power(Cuadra Núñez and Fonseca Terán 2010a, 4–5, my translation).

When I first came across this quote, I was rather astonished, as my personal experience of Nicaragua was that there was a comparatively high amount of popular participation in political decision making, especially among the Sandinista part of the population. I will try to show how diverse and complex the process of exerting power is for the Sandinistas, and that they generally lie outside the scope of what a single individual can control. I will also demonstrate that the process of exerting power for the Sandinistas is a fundamentally collective process. I believe this sets the Sandinista example apart from many other socialist movements and permits a broad-reaching identification with what Nicaraguans see as a revolutionary process.

Ways of exerting power by individuals and groups

While the alliances between Sandinistas and non-Sandinista groups takes up a lot of public discussion, the differences among and relations between

Sandinistas are just as numerous and complex. With the different types of Sandinistas come different ways of trying to exert power. Just about all Sandinistas I met agreed, that the second presidency of Ortega Saavedra is the right time for them to collectively exert power, and they have a responsibility to do that. The ways of going about this differ. Some use the party hierarchy to obtain a high level job. Others use less traditional ways. In the following, I show a number of ways I noticed Sandinistas try to exert power. I do not assume this list is complete, but it gives an insight into the range of different ways of trying to accomplish a change in society.

Power through government positions

The most obvious and painless way of exerting power and trying to move society according to one's own ideals, is as an elected representative, implementing new laws and putting into effect laws forgotten about by the authorities, when this is convenient for their party. The FSLN won the elections in 2006 and 2008. A substantial part of their personal resources goes into the work connected with holding the official positions they hold. As part of a Sandinista parliamentary group, one is generally expected to vote according to party lines, but individual elected officials can influence how or if their vote is counted. The national FSLN member of parliament from León Gladys Báez is said not to have shown up and not have sent her substitute on the day the vote of the new abortion law took place, thereby, slightly changing the outcome of the vote.

Several younger Sandinistas I spoke with would likely not reject a position as an elected representative, but different from my experience with party youths in Europe, there is generally remarkably little focus on arriving at this position in their daily discourse. That is, because, different from much of the European Left, parliamentary work is not universally seen as being the highest level of revolutionary work. An excellent example is María Antonieta Blandón Montenegro, the Executive Director of the *Oficina de Etica Pública* (OEP) during the current government, a position roughly equivalent to a minister (see also — *Views on the current government*, p. 206). Before she started in this position, she worked in the legal system on behalf of landless farmers. This she now only does during weekends. After explaining this to me, she immediately apologized for not working more on it. In contrast, in Europe it would be highly unusual for leftist politicians to continue to work as activists while holding parliamentary

María Antonieta Blandón Montenegro (second from left) is the Executive Director of the *Oficina de Etica Pública* (OEP), a position equivalent to a minister. She thinks the job is not particularly awarding for an activist like herself. Here she represents the OEP in a presentation given by government representatives to Managua students about why it is indispensable for the government not to favor Sandinistas when giving out social services.

or government office. I found it even more intriguing to hear Blandón Montenegro's plans for her future after finishing her career as a politician: To create a school for cooperatives in Matagalpa and teach them how to organize themselves. "This work here [in Managua] is not really giving [...] For someone who is an activist this is not a very good job," she explained. The way of talking about their work for government officials, and to claim there is a 'real world' outside of it to which one truly belongs, is something I found to be typical among Sandinistas holding higher positions. It is such statements, which make me realize, that at least for them, their work is not the highest form of exerting political power, and other forms have to be taken into consideration when talking about Sandinista rule.

The work of Sandinista office holders is valued so little among some Sandinistas that those who do see at least some value in it seem to feel the need to explain this. The cobbler and Sandinista Armando Martínez in the village of La Esperanza, El Rama, felt the need to say, Ortega Saavedra was necessary for Sandinismo. I did not ask him how he valued the work of those in high government offices or anything related, when he said:

> I have [...] something which makes me stay with the Frente Sandinista. I am convinced for the Frente Sandinista to be able to give something, it needs to have power in its hands. It

> can not give anything without holding power. [...] I know the role of our leader, Daniel Ortega [Saavedra], is fundamental. [...] In the sense of being a leader. We can have a ton of people, intelligent, with all capacities, but they don't have the experience or charisma of Daniel Ortega [Saavedra]. We have seen it over time – during winter and spring of the process of our struggle.

In other countries and/or contexts, it is unlikely this statement would have been made, as it contains little beyond what is a fundamental part of government systems: one needs to have a high-ranking position within the state leadership in order to exert power or 'give something' as Martínez called it.

Power through formal organizations in civil society

Another attractive way of exerting power is working through organizations of civil society. Civil society consists mainly of a vast range of NGOs and some labor unions mostly directly connected with the FSLN. NGOs and labor unions usually try not to portray themselves as Sandinistas, yet it is not tremendously difficult to find out when talking to members individually. The clearest example for me of trying to exert power on the part of Sandinista labor unions/workers was the transport worker strike of 2008. In order to receive government help in times of a spike in petrol prices, Sandinista transport workers largely shut down all main transportation, until the government accepted a compromise (see also — *Transport worker strike (May 2008)*, p. 114).

Several of the NGOs have foreign participation and funding. In some cases, this may be a factor in why they may be reluctant to show their party affiliation openly. A large percentage has a majority or exclusively Sandinistas working for them. Depending on the degree the participants are honest to one-another about their true affiliation and the lack of fear of being labeled as Sandinista agents, they try to push for programs they see as being in line with the Sandinista ideology. The origin of the party-political background of many NGOs lies in the events surrounding the change of power in 1990. Many Sandinistas tried to continue their work in the NGO-sector. 'Governing from below,' (see also — *The FSLN as an opposition force*, p. 23) in this way is not only a strategy used in the past, when Sandinistas were not in power. In organizations such as the *Fundación para la Autonomía y el Desarollo de la Costa Atlántica de Nicaragua* (FADCANIC) or the *Servicio de Información Mesoamericano sobre Agricultura Sostenible* (SIMAS) there are to this day people who are in line with the party and who through it try to influence civil society according to party ideals. Very seldom do they actively present themselves as Sandinistas. Similar to my surprise about Blandón Montenegro's continued involvement with grassroot activism, I was astonished to discover, that many of those who had reached high level positions within or close to the government, decided they liked to continue influencing society through the NGO-level. Such a case is Guimar Aminta Arias, a Sandinista who moved between different high-level government offices during my time in Nicaragua. She emphasized she continued to work in the community radio station even after she took on a position in the town government (see also — *Guimar Aminta Arias*, p. 193).

Power through the CPCs

Another new option, which did not exist during the 16 years of Sandinistas in opposition, is the participation in *Consejos de Poder Ciudadano* (CPCs). Since its inception in 2007, the CPCs promote government programs in their local area. Official spokespeople of the FSLN, such as Fonseca Terán (2009b), claim that while inspired by the direct democracy existing in Cuba, the Nicaraguan model of democracy will always be different due to its different history. According to Cuadra Núñez and Fonseca Terán (2010a), the CPCs are meant to fall under part 2 of the project of a Socialism for the 21st Century. The creation of the CPCs was one of the most talked about issues in the first year of Ortega Saavedra's presidency.

It started with the passing of a law on citizen participation in the parliament in January 2007. This was approved by both opposition parties and the FSLN. The Liberal PLC at the time went back and forth between allying with the FSLN and the *Alianza Liberal Nicaragüense* (ALN), even going as far as considering the creation of a common new Liberal party (Pantoja and Marenco 2007). Everyone initially saw the idea of citizen participation as the FSLN reaching out to other groups and parties. When the CPCs were announced a few months later, with reference to the law already passed by parliament, it was seen by leading opposition politicians as trying to merge state and party. The FSLN claims the installation of the CPCs is only one of several steps to establish direct democracy to replace the current representative democracy. Other steps include the establishment of plebiscites in matters of strategic importance, and eventually when the opposition loses the majority in parliament, making the CPCs part of the legislative branch (Cuadra Núñez and Fonseca Terán 2010a).

The CPCs were started in spite of the opposition, and have ever since been accused by the parliamentary opposition as being nothing but Sandinista councils and remarkably similar in their structure to *Comités de Defensa Sandinista* (CDSs) of the 1980s (see also — *Popular participation and direct democracy*, p. 17). In the view of opposition parties, the CPCs are the same as the CDS – which they believe were only created to control citizens. Additionally, they think they are to exert power by the presidency in a way which circumvents parliament. Rosario Murillo, Ortega Saavedra's wife and national coordinator of the Communication Council of the CPCs, described the CPCs in July 2007 in this way:

> The *Consejos de Poder Ciudadano* are in reality the enlargement and putting into practice of a policy, of a proposal, of a commitment […] of national reconciliation and unity among Nicaraguans, who can make use of this organizational form in order to participate in and to make use of their right to decide upon the programs of the government (Sandoval 2007, own translation).

In order to prevent the opposition doing away with the CPCs by passing new laws, Ortega Saavedra ordered by presidential decree that the CPCs were to be incorporated into the *Consejo Nacional de Planificación Económica y Social* (CONPES), part of the executive branch (Diario Granma 2007). After some re-scheduling, the CPCs were initially planned to be confirmed on November 30th 2007, but the parliamentary opposition voted in mid November for a law that prevented the establishment of CPCs as part of the state-structure, forced the CPCs to become part of the FSLN structure, cut them off state funding, and prevented state secretaries from taking orders from the CPCs. The Sandinista delegates said the CPCs would be established, no matter what the law said "Because the public has the right to participate in government decisions in whatever way they want" (Pantoja 2007, own translation). In January 2008, the *Corte Suprema de Justicia* (CSJ) finally ruled Ortega Saavedra did have the power to establish the CPCs and to define the limits of their power, and that parliament had no right to overrule him on that issue (La Prensa 2008).

The view of top opposition politicians is also reflected by some Liber-

A local headquarters of the *Frente Sandinista de Liberación Nacional* (FSLN) in a suburb of León shows the slogan of "[national] reconciliation, peace and work welfare" used in the 2006 campaign.

The gardener and Sandinista Félix Gómez Morales says that his *Consejo de Poder Ciudadano* (CPC) is open to opposition members, but also that the Sandinista members hope this will eventually lead to a strengthening of Sandinismo.

als on a grassroots level. My experience shows that views on the nature of the CPCs go across party lines: Liberals are involved in some CPCs and some Sandinistas are against CPCs. The CPCs at a local level work cross-politically in some places. Félix Gómez Morales, a gardener originally from Chinandega who now works in downtown León, was a Sandinista fighter during the revolutionary insurrection of 1979, and is well connected to the FSLN leadership in León. Over an extended period, we discussed why many opposition Nicaraguans had not been convinced by the government to join them, even though the main argument against the FSLN, the possible restart of the war, had been proven not to be an issue. He was quite negative about the subject and believed it must simply be in the Nicaraguan character: "The Nicaraguan is quite hard. You see, the government does all this! And still – they don't join us!" At another time, he tried to convince me the CPCs also were open to the opposition. He explained to me how his CPC in consisted of 12 people, of which five were non-Sandinistas and how the idea was to convert the opposition members to be supporters of the government bit by bit – but not through force:

> See, she [pointing at name of one of the CPC members in his book] has been with party X and party Y. And we don't say anything, but, of course, we hope that some day she realizes that it is the Frente that represents her true interests.

While Gómez Morales seemed to at least in part admit that the CPCs are connected more to the FSLN than to other parties, that is not common. Gloria María Fonseca, sister-in-law of Icabalceta Garay, is general coordinator of the CPC in her neighborhood in Managua. When I met her the first time and asked her rather provocatively whether the CPCs were part of the FSLN, she explained the connection like this:

> No, the CPCs is an organization born out of the necessity of the people to better their living conditions. Everyone is welcome, whether coming from the party or not. We don't ask what party they come from nor does it interest us what they do. All we are interested in, is that they want to work [within the CPC], that's all. […] What happens is the parties of the political right are molested by the fact that the poor people organize themselves, to express themselves and demand better conditions for their lives.

In other areas of the country, there is less non-Sandinista participation. Pedro Cerna, barber and Sandinista from El Rama explained why the political right did not want to participate:

Gloria María Fonseca, general coordinator of one *Consejo de Poder Ciudadano* (CPC) in Managua, says that the CPCs were born out of necessities of the Nicaraguan poor, rather than party-political motivations.

Pedro Cerna, barber and Sandinista from El Rama, believes the political Right is boycotting instruments of direct democracy in order to destabilize the country.

See, they don't want to participate in anything. All they want,

Blanca María Nella has organized her local *Consejo de Poder Ciudadano* (CPC) in a small part of Moyogalpa, Ometepe. She is happy to let right-wingers help in the CPC, but is not willing to give up power to them after they already have been in charge during "the 16 years of neoliberalism." She has also been in conflict with the government over the availability of pigs to those CPCs that do not have land, such as hers.

> is to destabilize this country, [...] because what they truly are out for, is power. They already lost it, but in some municipios they still have power because they have the mayor.

Those non-Sandinistas who chose to join a CPC, do not seem to focus on their own political party, as relates to their CPC-related activities. The places with almost exclusively FSLN Sandinista dominated CPCs seem to be the majority. By 2010, the FSLN leadership accepted it as a strategic error that too many FSLN leaders had taken positions in local CPCs with the exception of some areas where an effort had been made to avoid this (Cuadra Núñez and Fonseca Terán 2010a, 5).

Those Sandinistas participating in CPCs I talked to, seemed to think it necessary to have control on the part of the FSLN. In Moyogalpa, I spoke to Blanca María Nella, at the time a heavily involved Sandinista CPC member. She, like several other grassroot FSLN Sandinistas, saw the problem from the other side:

> Of course, they can all come and participate and work with us... To rule, however, that's what we do. We haven't been waiting 16 years until finally winning only to let them con-

tinue to rule.

Many of those Sandinistas who participate in the CPCs previously participated in the CDSs, yet most CPS-members deny they are the same. Pedro Cerna participated in both and gave a fairly average explanation of the difference:

> The objective before [of the CDSs] was to fight the armed enemy. Today, the CPCs are about how to share work... to work, to help, to organize a piece of social work, like [when one notices] "This street here doesn't work anymore, lets write a proposal to the national assembly [to have it fixed]. Before it was different, we had to look out block by block, because the enemy was around, and he was armed. Today that's not the case. Now it's different. It's more democratic. [...] One of the things the CPCs do here now is to build rural schools, together with the Juventud Sandinista, but as the mayor here always is Liberal, we do not have good access. That's why we want the mayor, to give it more thrust. Right now we do not have water here, just [a few] wells. That would be a project for the CPCs to take up, for the government.

It is extremely common that the explanation of difference between the two deals mainly with the historic circumstances rather than a difference in organizational structure. Many FSLN Sandinistas are not involved in the CPC of their neighborhood. Neither Carolina Fonseca Icabalzeta's nor her parents or her uncle Bayardo José Fonseca Galo participate in their local CPC meetings although they all are seriously interested in engaging in politics locally, and although none have achieved this through the party hierarchy. Fonseca Galo disagrees with members of the local CPC on political grounds. He explained, that most of those participating only did so because the FSLN was in power. One main criticism Sandinistas seem to have of the CPCs is how they function at a higher level. The local CPCs elect representatives for increasingly higher levels, until at the departmental level it becomes the departmental secretary of the FSLN who is in charge of passing on information to and from the highest level, Rosario Murillo.

I was present at a few CPC meetings in León, and many times I just came by the meeting place to hear whether anything new had happened. My initial impression was the power of the CPCs was limited to the local, and beyond that, they were just receiving orders from higher up. The CPCs members mentioned above also seemed to distinguish between participating in a CPC and exerting power as two separate processes. My understanding of the importance of the CPCs changed somewhat over time. As part of the election campaign 2008, many FSLN candidates for city council members signed a paper stating they would respect the decisions of the CPCs. Half a year later, the newly elected mayor of León, Manuel Calderón, ended up in an open dispute with the CPCs of León, trying to retract some of the powers given to them. The conflict was eventually settled, but the CPCs showed they were independent decision making bodies. Several Sandinistas I spoke with predicted that eventually the CPCs would take over as the new representatives of civil society, the part NGOs have represented. "What we will see is a different civil society. This is the new civil society that is emerging," Falguni Guharay explained.

The installation of the CPCs is not unproblematic as the FSLN officially recognizes. According to them, two reasons are to blame. One reason is the history of Nicaragua in which this institution has never existed before. The other reason given, is the little importance that FSLN militants attribute to the establishment of the CPCs as true representations of neighborhood opinions and they are used as tools for political maneuvering (Cuadra Núñez and Fonseca Terán 2010a, 5). This is also what I heard from those people close to the Sandinista cause who did not form part of their CPC. Icabalceta Garay stated:

> Well, see, this local CPC here is one that consists of party militants who worked with the party during the 16 years. They are people they feel they can trust.
>
> [...] Now, I don't know if they do it for free or whether they are paid or get some substitute for their work. Of course, I know it would be only fair to receive a little.
>
> At one time, we had a problem with the water [flow] and we started collecting signatures and the water company asked us "Are you a CPC?" and we answered "Ehm, yeah, of course. We are citizens making up a committee to gain power in that sense we are a CPC" Then they told us: "You should have the signature of so and so." She is of the official CPC here. We went, and asked her and explained what we were doing and she gave us the OK and said: "Ah, that's good."

Manuel Corea believes he continues his work as a Sandinista revolutionary by helping to organize a soccer match for youngsters in his neighborhood.

>These people use it for their political career. It is so they can show: "I have been working in the CPC of so and so."

It seems that, for Icabalceta Garay, it was not so much a problem who made up the local CPC or that she had concrete problems with those involved, as much as she was bothered that her campaign to better the flow of the drinking water in the neighborhood could help someone's political career.

Power through informal groups in civil society

Whereas the former two groups, labor unions and NGOs, offer opportunities for Sandinistas to exert power while hiding their party affiliation or at least not doing it in the name of the party, the opposite: cases exist in which the name of the party is invoked without the party officials having anything to do with the activity done in its name.

I interviewed Manuel Corea, one of the former students of the Wilhelm-Pieck cadre school in East Germany (see also — *Connections to a former center*, p. 189). He lives in a poor neighborhood of Managua. It is so poor, that the taxi driver who took me there did not dare to drop me off outside the door by myself. I was asked to call ahead to make sure Corea waited outside the copy shop he operates. It is clearly a dangerous area of Managua. One of the first things he explained, was, that he and the other Sandinistas in the area started an organized soccer match in order to get children off the streets who otherwise would be warring street gangs. Initially, I understood it as a program officially run by the government, but I gradually came to understand it was in fact activists who decided to put the soccer match together, and had chosen to do it in the name of 'Sandinismo' as a reflection of their ideals. Later on he changed the story and emphasized the games were also open to non-Sandinistas. It became obvious, that he wondered if he should have disclosed all these facts.

Fonseca Galo also worked in similar ways when I met him. He organized Sandinistas who had been active during the revolutionary insurrection and who now were 'not quite with' the current government in an organization called 'Amigos.' Ideologically, these people were still or once again are in line with the FSLN. Fonseca Galo's project specifically included some revolutionary fighters who had joined other parties. I understood that in these cases, the idea behind organizing the person was that such people would come back to the party, if only there was a viable path to do so. With time, I learned that 'not being with' the party just meant they were not employed or otherwise involved in the decision making processes of the current government or the CPCs. Fonseca Galo and some friends of 'Amigos' had many plans on how to help Sandinismo along. One of them involved building a children's center. This would be done in the name of Sandinismo in order to help the party indirectly, earning credibility among the youngsters who would make use of the center.

At first I believed people simply were formed by their personal experience of the 1980s and their loyalties from those years could not change now. I discovered among those not connected to the inner circles of the FSLN, the common practice is to reinvent oneself as Sandinista rather than portraying oneself as a Liberal in favor of Sandinista programs. For many, such a shift represents a second change in their political affiliation.

William Leiva Cardoza, the neighbor of Bayardo Fonseca and one of those Fonseca Galo had recruited to his project, was one of few Sandinistas I met who admitted how this reinvention happens. After he explained how he had fought on the Sandinista side in the revolutionary insurrection, he went on to talk about the time after 1990:

> I ended up in 1990 with absolutely no benefits. It was particularly hard for us Sandinistas to find work in some business. [...] So then [in the 2000s] I worked for the *Alianza Liberal Nicaragüense*. [...] I imagine many other Sandinistas did the same. In the end it worked; we split the Liberal vote... Many of us have said it was part of a tactic. But honestly... it was out of necessity. [...] But I have always been Sandinista. And

William Leiva Cardoza fought as a Sandinista during the revolutionary insurrection. He joined a Liberal party during the years of neoliberalism, and now again calls himself a Sandinista.

> I always will be Sandinista.

And for those Sandinistas who still had not seen a way to come back, he said:

> I think Ortega [Saavedra] should call for a meeting of all those Sandinistas in the other parties and tell them: I know why you went there [to the Liberals], but now come back.

I saw several similar projects to 'Amigos' although I did not investigate them as much as this group. Most such groups are led by people intensely involved in the party previously but who are now either out of the inner circles or left the party for another group during the years when the FSLN was in parliamentary opposition. At one point in León, when there was talk in the news on whether there would be armed contra groups in the mountains who were preparing to attack the government, I witnessed various groups of fighters from the revolution gather and prepare to fight with them in the name of Sandinismo. The government in the meantime tried to calm everybody and claimed the reports of rebels in the mountains were highly exaggerated. What all these groups have in common is they are composed of people previously active in the formal parts of the Sandinista movements, and more often than not during the 1979 insurrection.

Left to right: Carlos Alberto Rocha Castro, Adolfo Fitoria, Byron Corrales Rivas and Falguni Guharay – members of the team at *Servicio de Información Mesoamericano sobre Agricultura Sostenible* (SIMAS) I was working with to create software for the Nicaraguan state under Sandinista control using foreign aid money. *Photo: SIMAS*

Power through organizations influencing governments

Another group of organizations consists of those strongly Sandinista (FSLN and MRS), that try to influence the policies of the government. For me, these currently come closest to representations of ideological tendencies within Sandinismo. The two most prominent examples I encountered are SIMAS and the free software movement. Although their agendas relate to two different areas, in terms of personnel, they are closely linked. Denis Cáceres works for SIMAS and heads one of the Linux groups. During my time in Nicaragua, three of the most advanced programmers in the country were hired by SIMAS. In addition, SIMAS sponsors several of the events organized by the free software movement. The free software movement's core agenda is to convert the state apparatus, private businesses and the universities to use only open source software. Just about all of those participating see themselves as Sandinistas on some level (see also – *Professionals and Sandinismo*, p. 235). They originally organized in a handful of smaller groups, each promoting and using one certain version of Linux, but during my time in Nicaragua they joined forces to push their common agenda in Managua. A few people work with free software in other locations – I taught classes in León. The groups in Managua did not often coordinate with these other groups.

During a day of strategy talks for this movement that I attended, I only heard the Costa Rican participant suggest trying to push their agenda through use of the CPCs. Most others seemed to prefer direct connections to bureaucrats and politicians to push their agenda. In their view, one of their main enemies are those FSLN technicians who are not convinced of the advantages of free software. The members of the free software movement frequently accuse FSLN technicians of corruption or not having the necessary educational level to understand a free software solution would work better for them.

SIMAS tries to promote sustainable agriculture with little or no use of pesticides. SIMAS has its offices right next door to the presidential house in the Parque El Carmen, Managua and tries to play a central role in country development through the use of development funds. Head of SIMAS, Guharay, is not a member of the FSLN and is at times highly critical, but overall he is a strong supporter of the current government. Guharay explained the party internal conflict he had seen since the 1980s. One of the first things he said, was, that he set up the first agricultural information system in the late 1980s in northern Nicaragua, but that he was then ordered to delete all the data, because the project he was involved in represented the sustainable agriculture tendency which SIMAS represents today, which was and is controversial within the FSLN. Those opposed to sustainable agriculture in the FSLN, claim that it is only a trick by the United States and other industrialized countries to convince third world countries to use inefficient agricultural methods in order to keep them from ever achieving the same results as first world countries.

In the summer of 2009, the disagreement between the two tendencies manifested itself in the question of what corn processing plant Nicaragua should build. Ortega Saavedra and Rosario Murillo had allegedly already visited an industrial plant in Venezuela and Murillo was said to have exclaimed: "We need one of these in Nicaragua" as Guharay explained. SIMAS helped write an application for a grant to build a plant that would be set up without using trans-genetic corn and be environmentally sustainable.

I am not sure how many other organizations of professionals with Sandinista leaning exist. I came across the free software groups and SIMAS in other connections in where I did not expect to find them. There may only exist a small number of such organizations total. One organization which looks similar because it works in the same sector, is the *Centro para la Promoción, la Investigación y el Desarollo Rural y Social* (CIPRES). Founded in 1990, this NGO is mainly compromised of Sandinista workers of the Ministry of Agriculture of the 1980s. They came up with the model of the current Sandinista government program 'Hambre Cero' and those working there are mostly professionals. When I asked Fonseca Icabalzeta's father Fernando Fonseca, who works there, what he thought about the current government, he answered he looked at it favorably, and then immediately started to talk about the contribution of CIPRES:

> The organization I work for, CIPRES, is who invented 'Hambre Cero' – except we called it the 'Productive Food Program'... It was a battle about the analysis of the sociological reality of society in 1991. It was after [hurricane] Mitch we figured out what was key to make sure people would not sell the things we brought to them. [...] We used to give aid to the male, as the head of the family, but they oftentimes sold what we gave them.

According to Fernando Fonseca, CIPRES in a certain sense prepared the current government with studies and field tests several years before they could take power. When he said 'we' it sometimes seemed to refer to the Sandinista movement at large and at other times to refer only to those working at CIPRES. It did not seem terribly relevant for him to make a distinction. What all these organizations are defined by is that they work directly with government bureaucratic institutions. Another feature they make use of, is their knowledge as professional to convince the government of policy in certain areas. They also operate in an environment where party affiliation with the FSLN is not directly expressed.

Power through combining parliamentary and activist work

Political affiliations are a popular theme of conversations in Nicaragua much more so than elsewhere. A lot of activities are carried out through party-related networks, but they are not openly declared as such. My observations in this area stand in contrast with those of the anthropologist Babb (2004), who claimed to have encountered a Nicaragua in the post-Sandinista years that had left party politics behind (see also — *Post-Sandinista studies*, p. xxix).

I first encountered this phenomenon of combining activism with parliamentary work when visiting the city of Granada in April 2008. I ran

'Professor' Benjamín Garay (second from left) spontaneously jumps up on the scene and announces to the *Teleton 2008* in Granada that he will now take the young European anthropologist with the camera along to visit the land occupation and that these images likely will make it to Europe.

into Benjamín Garay, an older gentleman known popularly as 'professor Benji,' at the city square. When I told him of my purpose in Nicaragua, he invited me to an area outside the city recently occupied by what called itself a 'group of concerned citizens.' I went along with him to the land occupation, and was presented to some of the organizers. One girl wore a t-shirt of Calderón Sandino. She explained the setup to me and that there were areas for former members of the military, police, women and everybody else. Garay commented:

> See, these people are not grateful! The Frente does everything for them, yet when you ask what they'll vote, they'll tell you they don't know.

Another one of them said: "See, it's better this way [that it's not only open to Sandinista supporters] if we are to grow." When I formally interviewed the woman with the Calderón Sandino t-shirt and asked about their party affiliations, she said: "Oh no, we are not affiliated with any party. We are people united from all backgrounds here."

A few weeks later I wanted to interview some of the FSLN members in the Granada city council about this issue. When entering the building, I immediately ran into the second organizer from the occupied areas. He clearly worked in the city council for the FSLN group. He immediately ran over to me, and I told him what I was looking for. He explained: "Yes,

Although José Daniel Ortega Saavedra promised it would not happen, several land grabbings have occurred since he took office. Sandinistas are often instrumental in their organization.

there is one [city council member] here who has been working a lot on that case. He knows everything about it."

He guided me over to the office of said city council member. I waited there with some other Sandinistas, while the council member, as far as what I was being told, still was out in the occupied territory. Once he returned I made it clear to him that I wanted to interview him about that project. He answered:

> What land grabbing exactly? Because there is one down south there which is illegal, and we as the FSLN are of course against that.

It was clear, that he talked about the area I had visited, and it was equally clear that although he claimed to be against it, it was organized both by him and his personal city council workers. As it turned out through his explanations, the FSLN initially voted for a note condemning this grabbing of land. Before I turned the camera on to record his statement, I felt he wanted to make sure we had an implicit understanding that he would not be able to defend the land grabbing publicly. The FSLN strategy in the city council was to condemn the action, while simultaneously declaring there was no way to remove the land grabbers at this time and one needed to focus on the humanitarian aspects of the situation. This meant one had to understand the people who sat on the land, were in immediate need of an affordable place to live.

José Santos Aguirre Pérez (left) and Aracely Guillén (right) claim to be connected with the *Partido Resistencia Nicaragüense* (PRN), the party of the former Contras. They organized a land occupation in Ciudad Sandino in 2008 and claimed title to the land based on promises to Contras who put their arms down in 1990. These promises had hitherto not been fulfilled. Aguierre Pérez expresses gratitude to the *Frente Sandinista de Liberación Nacional* (FSLN) government for being the first to give them land. Later I learned that the two had indiscriminately invited poor people to join, many of whom did not know that the land occupation had any connection to the Contras. I also discovered that the PRN denies that Aguirre and Guillén are members.

I witnessed another land occupation in Ciudad Sandino. It was instructive, because it showed how groups not belonging to the Sandinismo tradition are at times permitted to be part of the popular organizing efforts within the overall Sandinista state. I reached the occupiers through my former student Javier Díaz. When I came by to visit him, he drove us to see them, as he believed it could interest me. The next few times that I went back, I did so by myself. The setup of this land-occupation seemed similar to Granada with a few activists leading the effort who were not in need of land, and the ownership of the land being in doubt with a nearby land-owner claiming that it was his and the occupiers claiming it was the property of the government.

The local political forces at play are different. Instead of Sandinistas organizing the occupation, the two main organizers of the land grabbing in Ciudad Sandino, José Santos Aguirre Pérez and Aracely Guillén, were former Contras who presented themselves as connected to the *Partido Resistencia Nicaragüense* (PRN). The camp was initially presented to me by them as consisting of a group of former Contras who had been in need of land. The action of grabbing the land was explained to me as having been taken in connection with the promise to Contras to be given land after the peace in 1990. This promise was hitherto not fulfilled (see also — Transition from power, p. 86). Over the months, I saw them frequently.

Raymundo Flores Genet (FSLN), outgoing mayor of Ciudad Sandino in 2008, says that the land the former Contras have taken was bought only in part by the state from the former owners after it had been nationalized during the 1980s. He, therefore, thinks it is still unclear whether the area currently occupied is state property. The land occupation organizers themselves believe Flores Genet has struck a personal deal to build expensive housing on the same land. Flores Genet is furious that the police do not follow his orders of removing the occupiers. He is also one of the first to point out to me that not all those taking part in the occupation are former Contras.

During the fall of 2008, they were largely concerned about attacks from a neighbor who claimed to own the land, as well as the bureaucratic process to receive official titles in Managua.

The FSLN mayor of Ciudad Sandino in 2008 was Raymundo Flores Genet. His term ended with the elections of that same year. He had lost the position of political secretary of the FSLN in Ciudad Sandino a year earlier (Rodríguez 2007a). He expressed opposition to the land occupation when I asked him about it. He was also angry that the police defied orders to remove them. The incoming FSLN mayor, Roberto Somoza, was said by the land occupiers not to mind them. I was never able to schedule a meeting with him, and the police of Ciudad Sandino decided not to comment on why they were not acting.

For a while, it seemed to be an extraordinary favorable treatment of Contras by the higher strata of the FSLN, even though the story told to me changed after a while when Aguirre Pérez claimed that it was not only former Contras, but also former members of the military and the police who made up the camp. "We don't go around with an ideology; we are the same," he explained. I still wanted to know why he thought that three Liberal governments did not help them as Contras and that they now expected the Sandinistas, whom they fought against for 10 years, to give them lands:

Although the police do not remove the land occupiers in Ciudad Sandino, they do not defend them either. The occupiers form their own guards to fend of the frequent attacks against them. They believe that these are ordered by former owners of the land.

> To be honest... One has to speak of reality. The Liberals were not concerned about us. They are of money, and the poor people they don't see. To be frank and say it legitimately: I am not a Sandinista. I am [part of the] Nicaraguan Resistance, but I speak about reality: They are helping us more than our people. Our people left us behind. They forgot about us. They continue with their millions and we with poverty. And these [Sandinistas] don't remove us and so here we are. [...] It's not because I have the same ideology. I am [part of the Nicaraguan] Resistance. But one has to look for who gives you their hand.

One day, I showed up earlier than what had been agreed upon, and none of the organizers were present. I waited in the line outside the main organizing tent and started to converse with some of those living on the land. This was the first time I spoke to them without any of the organizers around. Those standing there explained they were simply people with a need for land and that the organizers had offered pieces of land for a nominal fee. When I asked them about their connection with the Contras or any of the other groups mentioned, they looked at me astonished and explained that this camp had nothing to do with the Contras. Suddenly it dawned on me, that the only ones who had said they were connected to the Contras were the two main organizers. I had previously wondered why two of the land occupiers had put out red-and-black FSLN flags and no flags representing other groups were to be found anywhere, but the organizers had just brushed it off as meaning nothing. The Contra-connection of the organizers was only used to legitimize a hand out of land to poor people in general. Some studying of past news paper articles shows that the national PRN leadership had claimed in June 2008 that the two organizers were not members of their party (E. García 2008). When I showed up at the headquarters of the PRN in Managua once and asked about the land occupation, the officials I met at first tried to tell me these would be part of the 'resistance movement' but not of the PRN. When I insisted those I looked for were members of the party, they finally gave me the phone numbers of Aguirre Pérez. Only now did I understand this was an effort to hide the connection. In October 2008, a few weeks after he stated the positive words on the FSLN government, Aguirre Pérez figured as the president of the PRN in the municipio of Ciudad Sandino in the same newspaper which previously had described him as not belonging to the party, when he announced his support for the PLC candidate in the local elections (Álvarez 2008).

I encountered many similar situations of hidden party connections behind organizing efforts – with the 8th of March women's march in León, controlled by the MRS, protesting sugar and banana workers in Managua organized by people with background from the FSLN, various NGOs in connection with the anti-government protests controlled by the MRS, and student groups in León coming from the FSLN. Also all the organized indigenous people in León I met, turned out to be party members of either the PLC or the FSLN. Had I not had many years of experience in operating in a political conspiratorial environment among the far left of Norway, I would likely never have thought of investigating whether a group that claims it is independent and not connected to any political party is correct in its claim.

Power through infiltration

Some of the Sandinista political involvement may have been a lot more hidden than what anthropologists in Nicaragua have found between 1990

The *Vacas Culonas* is an event in which bulls are let loose in some streets of Managua. It is part of the annual Santa Domingo celebrations and was 'invented' by Sandinistas after they lost the 1990 elections.

and 2007. In July 2009, I witnessed a bull race in Managua as part of the catholic Santa Domingo celebrations. Erick Saul Rios Juarez, a 20 year old FSLN Sandinista and radio host had asked me to cooperate on filming the event. Different from similar activities in Spain, a whole series of bulls were involved, and (drunk) people tried to mount them rather than kill them. Also, the 'bull always wins' as Carlos Alberto Rocha Castro once put it, because only humans were seriously hurt and the bulls all went back to live in the countryside after the day was over. From the outside, this looked like many traditional celebrations in the third world. Initially, I assumed it was something the Catholic Church took from preexisting religions which it then adopted and modernized.

I was surprised, when Rios Juarez revealed to me, that all those working in the preparation of this part of the Santa Domingo celebrations were Sandinistas. I was even more surprised when I interviewed the principal person responsible for the arrangement. He revealed the Sandinista planning behind the event even more openly:

> When we lost the elections in 1990, we decided as a party we needed to infiltrate all public spaces available to us. That also included the church and the Santa Domingo celebrations. So in anticipation of the cultural import of celebrations such as Halloween from the United States, we wanted to create something altogether Nicaraguan. Cows are a traditional Nicaraguan animal, and we adopted that to the city and created the bull races.

It is appropriate in connection with my discovery of the true organization of this bull race to reconsider the findings of Babb (2004) as it seems to have been how many foreign observers saw Nicaragua during the post-Sandinista years. According to her, the political life of the previously party controlled society had in the 1990s/early 2000s turned into a large amount of independent groups and organizations, each with their own narrowly defined agenda of identity politics coming into being (see also — Post-Sandinista studies, p. xxix). Her vision was of a Nicaragua in neoliberal ruins in which the Sandinistas had disappeared from power forever. Her projection of the future of Nicaragua was one in which there was ever more hunger and postmodern lifestyle and identity politics. This did not come true. As my former student and activist Douglas Augusto Varela Vilchez mentioned, at a time while he was working unofficially for the MRS but officially for another NGO: "Nicaraguans who claim they are not into [party] politics – they are lying!" Certainly the Nicaragua Babb describes just a few years earlier was a decidedly different Nicaragua than the one I saw in terms of political power and majorities. Of course, I can not know whether Babb (2004) correctly described what Nicaraguans thought at the time, or whether she just did not manage to penetrate the social structure of the activist groups enough to realize what structures actually mattered at the time. Who knows – maybe the idea of infiltration was something the Sandinistas got after the fact, when the FSLN was in government again.

Use of paid protesters?

While all the other examples point to activism based on wanting to try to change society on the part of the participants, examples exist of paid or forced protests. Most Nicaraguans I spoke to about the issue assumed government workers were forced to participate in pro-government protests. While this may be the case, it is my experience when talking to such workers, that the pressure to participate is not articulated directly, so it is hard to verify whether they were actually being pressured to participate or whether they imagine they were. There is a much more clear-cut example of paid protesters being used by the government. In this case, I also wonder if the protesters could not be said to have some influence through this mean and get closer to achieve their own goals.

Between August and the municipal elections of November of 2008, in

Managua the rotondas were physically occupied by former banana workers. Simultaneously, the banana workers protested outside parliament for more than half a year for compensation due to work related injuries and damages. At first their protest was mounted under the MRS banner. But after what they explained to me as being extensive corruption of their initial leader, a member of the MRS or at least closely connected to them, was revealed, the FSLN took over the protest and the government provided them with food.

I interviewed some of the leaders of the banana workers a little before the elections and they said they were under MRS leadership earlier, but now they were independent. I asked them what the vast number of red-and-black Sandinista flags were doing in the camp if they were independent, and they replied that "anyone is free to put up whatever party banner they want." I then asked why there were large government posters behind the food tent. They told me: "Well, it protects us from the rain, we found it down at the John Paul the Second plaza after [government] festivities."

In order to prevent the MRS and PLC from marching, these banana workers stood in all the rotondas of Managua starting in the summer of 2008. For this, they allegedly received C$100 per day per worker (around $5 USD) to swing flags in favor of the CPCs and playing loud music. The banner they stood under, read 'love is greater than hate' – a quote of Rosario Murillo made in connection with the MRS protest in late spring 2008 (see also — *The MRS protests (May - November 2008)*, p. 117). The occupation of the rotondas lasted more than half a year, with some interruptions. At times, when the opposition was sufficiently violent, especially in the days after the elections, they were able to take control of the rotondas, at least one at a time. Arguably, those organized were used to achieve a goal rather than achieving a goal of their own. Their protest in front of the Liberally dominated parliament was in this way prolonged, as they had both a constant source of income and supply of food while camping out. In February 2011 Sandinista news media reported Ortega Saavedra had started handing out houses to these protesters (La Voz del Sandinismo 2011).

Power without organizing?

Organizing in itself seems to be a fundamental principle of Nicaraguan society and few Sandinistas are not organized in some group or another. The few examples of not being organized I find are those working as street vendors in León, such as María Elena Bustillo. Not much direct organizing takes place among them in León other than directing who is to stand where. Their ability to affect society, therefore, seems to be the most limited. The disorganization also means they are left out of channels of receiving help from the state. At one point of time, I explained to Bustillo what kinds of micro-credits are available from the government. They generally involve several people getting together to apply for a loan in a group. "So if one of them just disappears, the rest have to carry that!" was her disappointed reaction. Bustillo expected the FSLN to give more power to the poor in general. As it turns out, power is only accessible to the organized citizen.

Bustillo made me take a photo of a rotten beam in her house and write a postcard to hand to Ortega Saavedra in her name the first time I came to Nicaragua. Another time, when changing municipal governments from one FSLN mayor to the next FSLN mayor, I witnessed how Bustillo and those she hangs around talked about the personal tragedy of losing a contact in the government who "always was good to [them]." For her and others in that situation, who feel an allegiance to Sandinismo and the Ortega Saavedra government, the relationship to the government seemed to be more connected to the caudillo principle, in which a relationship to a government person with access to money and power would give them certain privileges.

Political activist education

The understanding of the collective nature of political pressure and the idea that one needs to make use of all the opportunities available at any given time, is quite ingrained in Sandinista philosophy. It was well exemplified in the reaction to the municipal elections of 2008, when not only party leaders, but grassroot Sandinista followers became involved in disclaiming charges of voter fraud.

A large part of the different understandings of whether they have been cheated or not is likely due to the difference in political education and culture of Liberals and Sandinistas. The whole setup was explained to me by Díaz: In Nicaragua at each election center, there are at least three

Liberals participate in street fights after their leaders declared they believed that fraud had taken place at the 2008 municipal elections. The young man looking towards the camera with stones in his hand wears a t-shirt that reads "I am a *fiscal*." The fiscales are the election observers that represent each party in election centers. In the background, several other stone-carrying demonstrators are identified as fiscales by their t-shirts. Those representing the Liberals at elections centers have an image of being young and without political experience. *Photo: Jorge Mejia Peralta*

people sitting at the table: a president, a vice-president and a secretary. These are supposed to be from different parties, and the local chapter of the *Consejo Supremo Electoral* (CSE), which also is made up of people from different parties and whose national leadership is appointed by parliament. In addition, each party is allowed to send one observer to witness what takes place at each electoral center. Each of those officially appointed to sit at the electoral center decide upon a number on the morning of the election. They do not announce the number to others until the electoral proceedings of the day begin. Before any ballot is given out, each of these persons needs to write their number on the ballot. The president and vice-president have to sign it. "There are six ways to make a ballot not count," Díaz explained to me. A circumstance under which one might decide to cheat could be if a personal neighbor would enter the election center, and one knew the neighbor always voted for another party than one's own, so before handing the ballot to the neighbor, one would make sure to invalidate it, so that the vote would not count. The six ways include signing with a false name, not signing at all, putting down the wrong number, etc. What all these have in common is they cannot be done unless none of the others present take notice. There seems to be quite a difference in understanding as what constitutes cheating. One young

Sandinista girl from Estelí explained it to me this way:

> See, you will typically have like a 57-year-old man representing the FSLN. He has participated in this many times before. The Liberals will be represented by a 17 year old who joined the day before.

Gómez Morales later on explained that same process to me:

> See, I went there, but I had my son around, so that he could learn how all the procedures worked.

At the same time, I was told of several Sandinista voters who had shown friends of mine that they had indeed proof that they had voted twice. This did not seem to constitute a problem to them, as long as all the procedures had been followed. When I sat outside municipal headquarters of the FSLN León during one of the days just after the elections, one of the older activists told me:

> I just don't understand how they can talk about cheating. When I see that something isn't right with a ballot, I know to put down my ID card on the table and the table is automatically closed until those from the CSE arrive and resolve the conflict.

The CSE did not receive many complaints about cheating that day, as Liberal observers had likely not known the proper procedures and had even signed off the result before naming their concerns to campaign headquarters. As this example shows, the moral behind these actions seems to be that, within the Sandinista logic, it is the responsibility of the group/party, not the individual, to ensure the individual voice gets heard by educating the individual member.

Concluding remarks

In this chapter, we saw how different Sandinista groups of different kinds work mostly autonomously with only vague ideological points connecting all the party's members. We also saw how political alliances on single issues are part of the Sandinista repertoire of politics and how this gives some limited possibilities for non-Sandinistas to take part in Sandinista processes of decision making. This does not always mean an even power sharing with the cooperating group. Thereafter we saw how wide the repertoire of politics for Sandinistas is today, but that all of those who successfully exert power follow group-based approaches.

It is not difficult to understand, then, that such a wide range of political activity leads to a wide-ranging inclusion of individuals who all entertain a feeling of ownership, a generally high level of participation, and that it permits trying out different approaches by different groups. The socioeconomic characteristics of individuals and groups may offer some explanation for the specific way in which they engage politically. These characteristics are seldom questioned and generally taken as a given. The explanations only go as far as explaining why the individual Sandinistas do what they do, given their position within Nicaraguan society in combination with their adherence to Sandinista ideology. In this sense, the Sandinismo of the 21st century seems to be much in line with the project of a Socialism for the 21st Century.

Simultaneously this chapter cannot explain all that is happening during the government of Ortega Saavedra in terms of the transformation of power structures. The neoliberal trade policies through the *Dominican Republic-Central America Free Trade Agreement* (DR-CAFTA) and the conditions the *International Monetary Fund* (IMF) debt levies upon the country have not changed much since 2007, in spite of all the Sandinistas who exert power in some way. These and similar conditions are oftentimes taken for granted and not considered much further, by either Nicaraguans or foreigners. Additionally, there may be an appropriation of large amounts of oil revenues by individual FSLN leaders—a claim which the right-wing press makes repetitively but so far has not been able to substantiate. This would hinder the free and independent development of Nicaragua the way it seems Sandinista ideology envisions it. Such differences between Sandinistas can also be seen at a lower level where they do not necessarily mean difference in access to funds, but still are quite apparent.

Sixth Chapter

Historic relations with Eastern Europe

The preceding chapters showed how Nicaraguans, and especially Sandinistas, see almost exclusively other Nicaraguans as central in political events that either happened in the past or present. This seems to be quite systematic. We have seen how this understanding of history, which puts Nicaraguan actors at the center stage of history, is effectively used to mobilize a diverse net of groups who all see themselves as acting in the name of Sandinismo. This net reaches far beyond President José Daniel Ortega Saavedra and a few people around him. Although a great percentage of the population may mobilize to participate in a general struggle for social change, their effect is somewhat limited. The wealth of the two oligarch families seems impossible to touch under all types of governments. So instead of judging the Sandinista government by how well it manages to redistribute wealth, Sandinistas judge their own policies by where they could lead, or could have led, if they were allowed to continue forever.

This chapter shows, how there is a unique historical relationship with Eastern Europe, and that it influences the current understanding of history. It gives yet another cause for the Sandinista movement to mobilize around. The uniqueness of the Nicaraguan case means, that the current tactics and strategies of the Sandinistas cannot easily be applied anywhere else, even though many other countries find themselves in a similar situation economically. This relationship is explained by presenting some of the personal stories those Sandinistas who went to a school of political leadership in the *Deutsche Demokratische Republik* (DDR, German Democratic Republic). The majority of these students presented their time in East Germany to me as having had a lasting effect on their view of politics. This chapter shows how some of them are in positions of political power whereby they are likely to shape the policies of the current government.

Nicaraguan particularities in the current global system

Besides economic issues, Nicaraguan dependency on other powers is complex terrain. Some of the cultural aspects survived from the previous phase of economic cooperation with the Soviet Union, and Sandinistas now seek to convert that into renewed economic links. Economic links to the United States were already in place by 2006. When these led the country into a global crisis, Nicaraguan actors could only influence how the crisis was managed in Nicaragua. No-one in Nicaragua could decide upon its existence nor strength. The global capitalist interdependence has a direct effect on Nicaraguan daily life which hardly can be influenced by any Nicaraguan government policies. The current financial crisis (2008–), which has clearly affected Nicaragua, made the Nicaraguan lack of influence clear once more. The Nicaraguan government can only decide where it will cut spending, not whether it will do so. On 22 January 2009, the presidential decree to confront the financial crisis was revealed (La Voz del Sandinismo 2009). According to it, government workers who made under C$20,000 a year (roughly $1000 USD) would continue to enjoy wage increases while those earning more would not, no vacant positions would be filled during the first nine months of the year, and the working day for public employees would end at 1pm, among other things. All this was part of a reaction to a lower influx of money.

Most Sandinistas believe the United States is directly responsible for the current crisis. According to some voices in the media, the crisis is stronger in Nicaragua than anywhere else in the world (AFP 2009) yet according to many of the agriculture experts at the NGO *Servicio de Información Mesoamericano sobre Agricultura Sostenible* (SIMAS), in 2009 the crisis did not show in many parts of the country. Denis Cáceres explained this:

> Well see, there are many areas where there is no substantial flow of money, but where there is a considerable amount of food security, simply because the people grow themselves.

Subsistence farming has been the target for many of the government programs, such as 'Hambre Cero.' According to Cáceres and his colleagues, it may not make the country rich, but to a certain extent, it makes farmers more independent.

It is not just Nicaragua which is unable to do much about the current increase in global dependency and the trend towards privatization going with it (Amin 2004). The socialist governments of Latin America are not all the same – the somewhat limited changes to the economy under Brazil's Lula is not as radical a change from politics as usual as Venezuela's Hugo Chavez's *Project for a Socialism of the 21st Century*. The socialism of Cuba is represented by an administration that is the same as during Soviet days, and the Cuban political and economic system has only changed to a limited extend since the 1980s (Wilm 2010). Nicaragua is different from other countries, in that it is the only one which experienced 10 years as a Soviet-allied country with a mixed economy during the 1980s and afterward much of the same neoliberal reforms as most other Latin American countries. It now tries to reestablish the revolution temporarily ended in 1990.

In Nicaragua people who are not Sandinistas and have more right-wing views on internal Nicaraguan issues, oftentimes see the state of world capitalism surprisingly critically. At the same time, the aid which comes from other countries to the Ortega Saavedra government, does not only originate in countries with Leftist governments. Today Nicaragua receives help from and cooperates with Iran (Morrissey 2007), Libya (Castro 2007)[1] and Russia (see also — *The Georgia conflict*, p. 127). One main reason for the support they receive from these countries seems to be the country's strong position against the influence of the United States in Latin America. The military protection and political links offered by these countries are combined with economic aid and development projects. Even some more right-wing groups within the third world are working with the Ortega Saavedra government.

The extent to which classic or western concepts are questioned is different in Nicaragua than many other places. In some parts of the periphery, the 'colonization of the mind,' understood as the import of concepts, ideas and moral standards from the center, is questioned. This includes the idea of western rationality – also world views such as historical materialism are questioned as being too Euro centered (Quijano 2000). This is true in several Middle Eastern countries, where religious groups, rather

---

1. In the 2011 NATO attack against Libya, Nicaragua was one of the most openly pronounced supporters of Libya and even offered to represent the country within the United Nations. Yet it is probable that due to the war the delivery of aid by Libya was ended.

than socialist ones, now make up the main part of resistance against western influence. This is not the case in Nicaragua. Here, the rhetoric and concepts of socialism most closely resemble those of Eastern European socialism/communism. These concepts were largely learned during Soviet times by Nicaraguan students studying there. Nicaragua does not seem to have followed global trends in this sense. Many international radical analysts, such as Immanuel Maurice Wallerstein, thought in the 1990s that this 'old Left' was gone forever. Wallerstein stated the following in 1997:

> Let us ponder the political consequences of the world economic difficulties of the period 1970–[95]. First and foremost, it has meant the serious discrediting of the Old Left, the erstwhile anti-systemic movements – the national liberation movements in the ex-colonial world, the populist movements in Latin America, but also the Communist parties in Europe (east and west) and the social-democratic/labor movements in western Europe and North America. Most of them have felt that, in order to survive electorally, they needed to become even more centrist than before. Their mass appeal has, as a result, seriously diminished, and their self-confidence has declined to the same degree. In any case, they can scarcely any longer serve as guarantors of Liberal reformism for impatient and impoverished populations. They are, therefore, unable to serve as a mechanism of control (previously the principal mechanism of control) of the political reactions of such populations, many of whom have turned elsewhere – to political apathy (which, however, is always a temporary way-station), to fundamentalist movements of all kinds, and in some cases to neo-fascist movements. The point is that these populations have become volatile once again, and therefore, dangerous once again from the point of view of the privileged strata in the world-system. (Wallerstein 1997)

The level of apathy seems to be somewhat different in Nicaragua than many other places, and contrary to Wallerstein's predictions, the calls for (state based) socialism are back. Among those stating some form of state socialism as their goal, globally there are differences as how one relates to previous experiments with socialism and specifically the Soviet Union. In the West and much of Latin America, there has always been a certain portion of Trotskyism among the radical Left which viewed the Soviet Union as having lost its progressive mission in the 1920s (Chilcote 2009). In the case of Nicaragua, with the FSLN's regimes comparatively not all that totalitarian character during the 1980s, most radical Soviet critics traditionally supported the Sandinista regime as well. Nowadays in turn, remarkably little criticism of anything related to the Soviet Union can be found among Sandinistas.

Connections to a former center

Trade-wise, Nicaragua can be said to be more independent from the United States through the growth of new trading partners in Latin America and Asia than it was in the years of Somoza or the first few years following electoral defeat in 1990. Given a classic Dependency Theory interpretation, in which economic links are decisive, this could explain the relative independence the country has maintained from the United States and to a lesser extent from Western Europe.

What it does not explain is, why the Sandinista ideology as worded by government officials, and a substantial part of the population, is so hostile toward the United States, and at the same time so friendly to Russia. Russia has military potency, but in terms of trade, it has relatively little impact on Nicaragua. The main event that involved Russia during my stay in Nicaragua was the war in Georgia where Nicaragua supported Russia (see also — *The Georgia conflict*, p. 127). Although the Nicaraguan involvement in that was only an action by Ortega Saavedra, it was clear among the Sandinistas the actions taken by Ortega Saavedra were something they strongly favored. The handing of the medal to the former East German minister (see also — *Award given to last Minister of Education of East Germany and alliance with Honduras (19 July 2008)*, p. 125), who at the time held no state power, seemed not to be done in connection with any now-existing power relation. The following shows how among many former Soviet Union and the Eastern bloc trained Sandinistas at various levels, continue to have a particularly powerful influence originating in their personal experiences in the 1980s when they went to Eastern Europe to study. It is this which mainly contributes to the special understanding of Russia in Nicaragua today.

It has been argued, that the Soviet Union and the Eastern bloc never represented any kind of center of accumulation in Dependency Theory sense. In the Nicaraguan perspective of things, the fact that it had the importance it did trade-wise and its position as a center for study, could make it look like a center. That is especially evident in the influence Eastern Europe has had through education. The use of western-style education by elites of peripheral countries is by many adherents of Dependency Theory seen as an integral part in the upkeep of the relationship between core and non-core (Quist 2001). Similarly in this sense, the relationship between Eastern Europe and the current Nicaragua has a lot to do with the education programs many Sandinista cadres received there in the 1980s.

Shortly after the visit of the former minister of education of the DDR to Nicaragua, a former East German student of an international school of political cadres in East Germany in the 1980s contacted me through a friend of mine in Berlin. The Nicaraguans were young Nicaraguan Sandinistas in line for taking over higher offices in the government and the party at the time of their travel. The East German student only had some false names of some of his co-students, but asked my help in finding his Nicaraguan classmates. Through the use of TV and radio, I eventually found a number of students who attended a year of study at the school.

The students

When meeting the Nicaraguans who had studied at this school in the DDR, I tried to figure out if and how their view on Eastern Europe and the country where they studied, the DDR, is still influenced by that time. In most cases, it does not seem to be a decisive factor whether they have a job or the type of job they have within the current government, when determining how they see the current government and the various political events that happen in Nicaragua. The formal interviews I made of these students were hugely different in terms of length and somewhat different in terms of contents. The amount of information they provided, and the type of information they were willing to volunteer, differed considerably. I adjusted my interview questions as I went along during each interview, to accommodate for these differences. Some of these informants gave no more information than what I heard before in the streets of León. I choose here to mention a some of the students I found, as their interviews gave me the most insight.

Ossiel Mendieta was among the first students to go to East Germany in the early 1980s. At that time, the revolution in Nicaragua was not

Ossiel Mendieta creates bracelets out of colored threads in his restaurant in Chinandega. He considers whether it makes sense to sell such bracelets to students of socialism in Germany. Here, he makes a bracelet in red-and-black, the Sandinista colors.

seen as particularly developed, so all participants received code names to use while in Germany, in case of a takeover by Contra forces.

Mendieta contacted me after reading about my project of finding students from his school in the newspaper El Nuevo Diario. I met him within 15 minutes after he called me, as he happened to be in León at the time. Mendieta now has a restaurant in front of city parliament in Chinandega. He also makes money creating bracelets out of colored threads.

Mercedes Campos Montenegro I met in the village of Malpaisillo, just a few kilometers outside of León. A former teacher in Germany wrote down her name and city even though they were encouraged not to interchange addresses. To update the addresses, I had gone to the voters' registration office in León. After explaining my plans, they found the address of Campos Montenegro and that of several of her co-students. This service on their part was likely downright illegal, but there seemed to be an understanding among the Sandinista workers at the office that it was a service they provided to a comrade representing the DDR. Like most, Campos Montenegro still lived in the same village she lived in during the 1980s.

Mercedes Campos Montenegro (center) stands in the doorway of her house in Malpaisillo together with her daughters. They urge me to take the photo quickly, as neighbors start gathering around.

> When I arrived in Malpaisillo on the bus, instead of trying to find the address, I asked the first policeman I spotted, to see if he could tell me where Mercedes Campos lived and he pointed me one block down a road. I knocked on the door, where Campos Montenegro sat with two young girls. I asked her, if she were the Mercedes Campos who went to study in East Germany. She did not seem to wonder how I would know that. She spoke to me as if she found it to be the most natural thing in the world that a foreigner would come by asking her about that. Within minutes, she was ready to give me an account of how things were back then and what had changed since.

María Antonieta Blandón Montenegro is different from many of the other students in that she no longer lives in the same village as in the 1980s. I found her house in Matagalpa, in northern Nicaragua. With the new Ortega Saavedra government, she became "something like a minister," as her sister explained to me casually. The official title is 'Directora Ejecutiva de la *Oficina de Ética Pública* (OEP)' where she is to monitor and audit the other ministries to prevent corruption. I talked to her several times later in Managua and followed her in some of her work talking to students at the *Universidad Nacional Autónoma de Nicaragua* (UNAN) in Managua on codes of ethics.

Guimar Aminta Arias also was successful. When I first met her, she worked at customs in the city of Estelí. I ran around town after her, and finally encountered her at a Sandinista meeting at departamento level. She did not have time right then, and when I met her again a few weeks later, she had just taken over as president of the *Instituto Nicaragüense de Fomento Municipal* (INIFOM) at national level in Managua. During the 16 years out of power she survived among other things through working for the Sandinista mayor of Estelí.

She went to Germany with a group of ten students and was only 18 years old. She had been a member of the *Juventud Sandinista* (JS) since she was 12 years old and was one of the group's founders. She joined because she wanted to teach as part of the literacy program. When she came back she started working with children, and anything to do with recreation. She volunteered to join the army to fight the Contras. After the lost elections of 1990, she worked in the ministry of education and secured a master degree which was crucial in obtaining her current position. During the years of opposition, she did not stop working with the Sandinista movement, and focused her work on an independent youth radio station in Estelí. She returned to work in city government in 2000, after serving as campaign leader for the FSLN. During this time, she continued with her radio job in 'civil society.'

Rogelio Antonio Selva Gonzales gave me a markedly different report of the time at the school than all the others. Selva Gonzales was still a close friend of Aminta Arias, and he also lived in Estelí, but he now identified with the MRS. He worked in the ministry of interior in the 1980s and in the early 1990s in the military, when it was still controlled by the Sandinistas. Being a Sandinista made it hard for him to get a job during the 1990s. He felt the only way to get around this was to renounce his FSLN affiliation.

Francisco Blandón Robleto was a student in the last year the school was held, 1989–90. He was also in Germany when the Berlin Wall came down. Until just before I met him, he was a lawyer in Matagalpa but had been named judge of the small village of Waslala, RAAN under the new Ortega Saavedra government. He saw no reason to hide his experiences in East Germany. Different from the others, he already

Francisco Blandón Robleto (center) is proud to have known East Germany's leader at the time of the fall of the Berlin Wall, Egon Krenz. When I ask for a picture of him, he gathers his family around.

then worked at a higher level in the party apparatus. As a leading figure inside the JS in the early 1980s, he had direct contact to Egon Krenz, the leader of the *Freie Deutsche Jugend* (Free German Youth, FDJ, the East German partner organization of the JS) up until 1983. On 18 October 1989, Egon Krenz was elected as head of state of East Germany, and Blandón Robleto claimed to have met him while he was in that position.

Amada Alvarado Soza had more of a personal tragedy related to her visit to East Germany. I met Alvarado Soza's family in Matagalpa, living further outside the center than Blandón Robleto. Alvarado Soza and her husband had bought the rights for a bus line which they operate, and they previously worked as taxi drivers. In the early 1980s, Alvarado Soza was employed in a police capacity in Managua. A car accident during that time led to her being temporarily infertile. Treatment was available, but only in East Germany. So, in addition to the political training, Alvarado Soza was sent to East Germany to receive medical treatment. Tests were made, everything was

Amada Alvarado Soza had been invited to come to East Germany to be to be treated against infertility in 1989. She claims, that upon the fall of the Berlin Wall and the taking of power of the political right, her operation was canceled and instead she was sent to pick fruit. Now Alvarado Soza and her husband operate a bus line in Matagalpa.

>prepared, and then the Berlin Wall came down. The school stopped in the middle of the year. It was offered that if anyone had the money they could continue study, but no one had the funds, and some groups like the Cubans had to leave immediately. Others, like Alvarado Soza, stayed and were sent out to harvest fruit in the country side until their scheduled trip home. Not hard to imagine, also Alvarado Soza sees East Germany very positively and West Germany as well as western-style capitalism decidedly negatively.

Víctor Ruiz is another person I found in Estelí. He studied a lot, including History, Economy and law. When I met him, he worked in the *Instituto Nicaragüense de Seguridad Social* (INSS) and taught at a university. I found him during his lunch break at his house. Ruiz is still a Sandinista, and he sees enormous advances with the current government. After he had seen my for some seconds, he immediately started lecturing me on some of the new government programs in his sector.

Víctor Ruiz (2nd from left), here with family, does not think twice about presenting his life and family during his lunch break, only minutes after meeting me.

The importance of Eastern Europe for the Sandinista Revolution in the 1980s

Most Sandinistas I spoke to in the streets on random occasions talked about the Soviet Union and its allies as allies of the Sandinista Revolution. The relationship between the two is mostly portrayed as being between even partners. In their view, the cooperation between Nicaraguan Sandinistas and other revolutionary groups around the world, was and is one of reciprocity without any one group having the upper hand. Among those who went and studied in East Germany, the relationship is at least partially seen as different because of a recognition that the Eastern European states were stronger than the Nicaraguan state.

Instead of seeing the school as a place of interchange in which even partners would come together and share revolutionary ideas, the way one could imagine for it to happen if the relationship had been totally horizontal, the students recognize the fact that the school with its study programs was created to spread a certain ideology. The most elaborate explanation of someone's view on this, I received from Mendieta. When I first met him, I explained the current status of the school they all attended. He made it clear, that he thought it was supremely valuable for ideological education to continue in East Germany. The school buildings had been sold, altogether the party only kept a few buildings scattered around East Germany, one of which was party headquarters in Berlin. "You are, however, still educating the recruits, right?" he wanted to know. I told him that, yes, there was a party youth organization with a study program connected to it, but that it did not use the same program as back then. He commented:

> Oh, I still have the books. I'll donate them for you to make copies if that means you can use them to start the program back up.

The idea of East Germany and the East German system as a place to copy and ally oneself with, seemed to be genuine as he continued along the same line after I turned off the camera at the end of one of our meetings:

> It filled me with such joy when I saw that they gave the medal to Mrs Honecker there on July 19th, for all the help they gave us back then. That was well deserved.

The statements of Mendieta are quite typical for the ex-students. In part, their comments were likely shaped by their knowledge that I was affiliated with the successor of the party that formerly ruled East Germany. Given that, in most cases, it was they who chose to contact me, and that they did present numerous points of criticism of aspects both of the Nicaraguan government and the East German system, I conclude, that most of their statements genuinely represented their views.

"See, these are things we learned over there at the school in East Germany," Blandón Montenegro explained, before she listed some points of the revolutionary tactics and theory, that the Nicaraguan group she had been with brought from Germany. Again, the picture of East Germany was a positive one, in a way which would likely surprise most Germans. She turned out to have been a friend of the first East German who started me on the search, and, in connection with that, she pointed out how grateful she is that "even though [our socialist East German class mates] have lost power, they are still trying to help us here."

Aminta Arias said that the experience in East Germany was understood differently by different people participating without specifying further. She also said: "Altogether it was the cooperation from the Eastern bloc and East Germany that made the first phase of the revolution possible," and the current 'phase of the revolution' would be very much formed by the education given back then to many of the leading cadres of the Sandinista movement. With that explanation, she is the one who seems to sum up the underlying idea of the statements of all of the former students.

The degree of positive views of the Soviet Union and socialist Eastern Europe seems not that different between the former students and the general Sandinista part of the population. A noticeable difference lies in the recognition by the former students, that the socialist ideology of the time, which the Sandinistas shared with Eastern Europe, did not flow as egalitarian or originate only in Nicaragua, the way it seems to many Sandinistas.

Comparison between Nicaragua and DDR

One of the obvious advantages in determining the relation between Nicaragua and the rest of the world, for those who have been abroad, is the ability to compare the state they went to with Nicaragua. The comparison most students made combined ideological leadership with material wealth. At one of the meetings, Mendieta realized that I and a Norwegian friend, who visited me, had never experienced East Germany. Then he explained what it had been like:

> In East Germany, everybody had read that book [Das Kapital]. When you boarded a bus, the bus driver would have read it. And the guy checking the tickets. And the person sitting next to you.

A little later, he continued describing East Germany, but this time his description had turned more to the material rather than ideological sides of the country:

> The Democratic Germany was a country where the people had just about everything. There was not one wish the people had that the government did not fulfill. ...East Germans had almost more than the West Germans.

Ruiz recognized that the standard of living in East Germany after 1990 was higher than that of Nicaragua. In common with most Sandinistas, both of the MRS and the FSLN, these former students such as Mendieta expressed an overall positive view of Eastern European socialism. However, different from others who have not seen any of these countries, there seems to be more of an admiration of these countries, and a recognition, that they had reached another level of development than Nicaragua, both ideologically and materially.

The difference between Nicaragua and the DDR was also explained by some of the former students in concrete material terms related to themselves. Campos Montenegro spent considerable time explaining that after several years of unemployment during the years of neoliberalism, she obtained employment as a teacher at a Christian school for which she had to become a Christian, with a salary of $40 USD per month. She pointed out how hard it was to obtain this employment. Then she compared her wage to the $400 USD per month stipend she was given by the DDR government while studying there.

While most Nicaraguans seemed quite aware of the differences in wages between Western Europe/the United States and Nicaragua, I cannot recall the theme of wages coming up in connection with discussing Eastern Europe in the 1980s in the same war as with Campos Montenegro. There seems to be some recognition, that Eastern Europe had the ability to send material products and economic help to Nicaragua in a way Nicaragua was not able to do. From this, it can be derived, that a certain realization of the differences between the economics is present also among those Sandinistas who did not leave Nicaragua. The difference seems to be mostly in the views of the relationship between the two in ideological terms.

Experiences with the fall of the wall and views on changes of Eastern Europe

The fall of the Berlin wall and the change away from socialism in Eastern Europe, are today seen as positive events in the history of that region of the world by most westerners, no matter what ideology they may follow. Given the positive view Sandinistas seem to have of Eastern European socialism, I thought it intriguing to ask those of the former students who had some experiences with either the fall of the Berlin wall or who had experiences with East Germany afterward, about their view of the disappearance of East Germany. The Sandinistas generally see the destruction of East Germany as a loss for the German people. From those who had experienced the time of the system change in the DDR, I had expected to hear a somewhat different view, but this was not the case. For example, Campos Montenegro was still employed by the city under the first mayor after 1990. As part of that job she was able to go to Spain and from there on to Germany once more in 1992. She summed up her experiences at that time in just one sentence: "It was a very sad sight – all that poverty and trash that was flying around."

While I have heard many people in East Germany—and some in West Germany—speak negatively about the changeover to capitalism in East Germany, I cannot recall having heard any assessment of the situation in the early 1990s quite as negative by any German as how Campos Montenegro sees it. The view Campos Montenegro's expressed of East Germany in 1992, paints a picture of post-unification Germany similar to how other Nicaraguans who visited Germany during the same period presented it to me. It seems for them, progress in Europe is directly connected to the DDR, and western-style capitalism is equal with a breakdown of society.

Two of the former students, Alvarado Soza and Blandón Robleto, experienced the fall of the Berlin Wall directly during their time as students. The events surrounding that period, are generally described as a period of partying and happiness over the changeover among Germans. The Sandinista view of that period seems to be in line with their overall view of East Germany. This may partially be explained by the somewhat limited understanding the students had of the German language and situation, and that they received a lot of information through the educators at the school. Alvarado Soza recalled the initial reaction by the school staff to the opening of the German-German border this way:

> [T]he first thing the teachers told us, was, that we should stay in the school, to prevent being attacked from neo-nazis. It was horrible. First we lost here [at national elections on 16 February 1990] and then they also lost in East Germany [at national elections 18 March 1990].

I am not in the position to say whether the possibility of attacks from neo-nazis was real or was an excuse by school staff to keep the students indoors. Had Alvarado Soza had the same access to the news and information the general German population had, her view of the situation might have been somewhat different.

A few months after the fall of the Berlin wall, and before the school year was over, the educational program at the school was suspended. The socialist East German authorities had scheduled for Alvarado Soza to be operated on using the superior East German medical equipment. Under the new, non-socialist leadership, her operation was canceled. Instead, she and some of the other students were sent to pick fruit during the first half of 1990 until their flight back to Nicaragua in the summer of that year. Alvarado Soza referred to the period as "when we had lost" in a way that sounded as if it was a personal loss. Many other Nicaraguans who themselves lost much less materially than Alvarado Soza, also refer to the period in the same manner. It seems to be an identification not only with the FSLN, but also with the socialist government of East Germany and the entire Soviet bloc.

Blandón Robleto seems not to have been quite as restricted in his movements during those days. According to him, after the wall came down, there was nothing physically stopping the students from going to West Germany and even to neighboring countries as some of the students did. Blandón Robleto told me how he only went to West Berlin and how he did so only for a short trip. When the Nicaraguan students were scheduled to go back to Nicaragua, Robleto Blandón left, even though he believed he could have stayed due to the general level of chaos. "Did you not even consider staying?" I asked him. "Well no, I had things and family here in Nicaragua" he answered me as if it would have been the strangest thing in the world to suggest. The emphasis in his explanation of his activities in 1989–90, lies in the opportunity to be able to meet people with high ranks within the East German ruling party, rather than in the possibilities connected with experiencing West-German capitalism.

Another Sandinista who also studied in Eastern Europe, but at a different school, decided to take up the question of the Berlin Wall after I ask what his experience in East Germany was like:

> See, we as the Frente Sandinista are extremely glad that the Berlin wall has come down, because that means that all the educated Marxists from the East can stream over into the rest of Germany and educate the working class there. So we truly hope, that we will win again in Germany as well, and that the entire Germany then will join the socialist camp.

Whenever I heard a Sandinista talk about the events surrounding the fall of the Berlin wall, it was always fundamentally different from how I have known it in the German discourse. Instead of being a positive event in which a more democratic and liberating system wins over a more dictatorial regime, in the Nicaraguan Sandinista perspective it is the DDR that always was the better system. Much like Alvarado Soza, many Sandinistas who have never been in the DDR are readily willing to identify with its government of the 1980s, even though they may not show the same level of interest in a country they have never seen.

Experiences after returning and the 16 years of neoliberalism

The former students told me of various parts of their life story after their return. Similar to many other Sandinistas and Nicaraguans in general, they did not stick to explaining their personal history, but gave a general overview of the history of the country (see also — *Problems understanding the discussion of Nicaraguan history*, p. 54). One particular period most Sandinistas seem to leave out of their personal life story, is the period surrounding the 1990 elections, which are often described as "then we lost the elections" or something to a similar effect. The periods left out differ from person to person. In the few cases I heard about what happened during that period, it was mostly a period of unemployment and personal depression.

Several of the students who studied in the DDR in the early 1980s spent the later 1980s in either JS or in another part of the state. Most of them seem to have been through the physically hardest time before they went to East Germany. One exception is a student who joined the military service upon return and was still too shell-shocked to be interviewed in 2009, and Blandón Montenegro who went and led the JS in the village of Rio Blanco and lost her right index finger in the confrontations with the Contras there.

The stay in the DDR was, according to how the former students described it, influential for their careers, specifically during the 16 years of neoliberalism. According to Blandón Montenegro, it was the study program in East Germany which inspired her to study law in Nicaragua during some of the earlier years of neoliberalism. She then used her education during the last years in opposition defending landless farmers in cases concerning land occupations. Many of the others had similar career paths, but admittedly this was also common for Sandinistas who did not go to East Germany.

Among these former students, the years of neoliberalism were when most left the FSLN. The one student I interviewed about this was Selva Gonzales. He explained that for the first few years after 1990, Selva Gonzales was known not for his criticism, but for his staunch support of the FSLN. It was first when he could not find work for being known as an FSLN

Rogelio Antonio Selva Gonzales believes that his Sandinista political conviction forces him to stand in opposition to President José Daniel Ortega Saavedra.

Sandinista, that he decided to change sides. Of all the students I spoke with, Selva Gonzales is the only one with direct criticism of the processes of the 1980s. He is today not part of any political, power exerting processes. I heard of at least one other case of a former student who switched sides during this period, as she was the co-student of one of the interview partners. Although I knew both her name and her whereabouts, I was never able to schedule an interview. There may be several other cases of former students who heard about my interview project who for similar reasons chose not to answer. The stay in East Germany seems not to have prevented anyone from switching political sides after their return.

Among those former students still with the FSLN when I saw them in 2008/09 and who explained how the stay in the DDR significantly improved their career or ability to help, the stories as told may have been told differently had I come in 2004/05. I first understood this when interviewing Ruiz. When Selva Gonzalez walked me to the house of Ruiz, I came unannounced and Ruiz started his self-presentation by listing an impressive number of things he had achieved, both within the state apparatus and academia. After a while, he finished the interview and left for work. Then his Nicaraguan wife explained to me, that her husband fathered a child with a German co-student while in East Germany. A few years ago, before the Sandinista takeover, he was asked to travel to Germany and get to know her, by a German TV show. "Because he had no job, he felt ashamed of not being able to give her anything," his wife said to me. In the end, he did not go. Had the same happened at the time I came by, his wife was sure that he would have made the trip.

The extensive filtering of personal life stories by those telling them, and the fact that I hardly managed to find any former students who changed party-allegiance, means, that I do not feel I can summarize much of how the experience shaped the average former DDR student and what they did in the following years. Those who stayed being Sandinistas did and do have a noticeable impact. As mentioned, among the total of under 100 students who went to this school in the DDR, several of them obtained high positions within the new Sandinista state and for a relatively high percentage of them as Blandón Montenegro pointed out, the study in Germany inspired them to continue with further studies and get more involved in Sandinista politics upon their return.

Views on the current government

Aminta Arias focused a lot on the importance the connection to the DDR and the rest of Eastern Europe had in defining development goals for the Sandinistas that the current government still sees as valid. Her personal experience in the DDR seems to be conflated with that of the general influence the Eastern bloc had on the FSLN. In connection with that Aminta Arias mentions that she thinks, it is vital to "recover our own identity, as part of a historic struggle." Some of the most crucial development factors for her are high literacy rates and access to credit for people to produce. She thinks that the literacy rate is an indicator of the level of development and that the level can be used to measure how valuable certain development strategies are:

> When we left office, we had around 12% of illiteracy. When we returned it was at 37% – almost 40%![2] For us, that in itself is an indicator of development – at least people are able to read and write.

Different from the first Sandinista government, Aminta Arias believes certain hindrances during the first Sandinista government made it impossible to achieve these goals:

---

2. While I cannot confirm the figures she cites, the direction seems to be similar to what international organizations indicate (Nicaragua Network 2009a).

> The first part of the revolution happened during a war. In times of war, no government can work; it's impossible to work on planning development.

That is different now, and she sees possibilities. One of the main misconceptions she listed about development during the '16 years of neoliberalism' and the times "which we are still living" was that development means reaching western society:

> We are a poor country... We need a much simpler model [...] It has to be local and with a lot of emphasis on the productive sector.

For Aminta Arias, relevant indicators for development are education and access to health care, rather than what type of cars or mobile phones people carry. Eastern Europe during the 1980s seems to be closer to where Nicaragua ultimately is to develop rather than current western society, according to what Aminta Arias told me.

The positive view on the current government also extended to some of those who have not found a job with the new Sandinista government, such as Campos Montenegro. The first thing she focused on, when I interviewed her, was that she still is a Sandinista. She felt a bit sad for not being employed in the public sector, but she said she believes in the current Ortega Saavedra government and that there now would be massive changes and employment opportunities even if these may not be available to her. She mentioned various examples of people from either party background who had found employment since Ortega Saavedra came to power again. "It's simply a lot more open now." According to her, in the previous years, it was hard to impossible to find employment for people known to have Sandinista tendencies. Now she explained, that she believed it would be a lot easier for her daughters to gain entrance to university than it had been in the past. Campos Montenegro seems to be one of those worst off of the ex-students in economic terms. Yet up until 2008, she continued to be active in the election campaign of the FSLN in Malpaisillo.

Blandón Montenegro's career path was decidedly different from that of Campos Montenegro. Blandón Montenegro's work for the government in Managua, with responsibilities equal to a minister, must have taken up most of her time. Additionally, there was her spare time activity during weekends, when she worked giving legal advice to landless farmers in Matagalpa. This seemed to be more relevant to her, and in line with her explanation that her work in Managua is not terribly attractive for someone who is used to be a political activist. It is essential to note, that she did not criticize the work of the Ortega Saavedra government; it was only herself, who she seemed to say was wrongly placed in that kind of job. Blandón Montenegro claimed that her goals as an activist were strongly formed by her stay in the DDR, and that they continued to be the reason why she chose to work as an activist.

Not all the former students have a positive view of the current government. As mentioned, the selection of interview partners is likely skewed by those who no longer wish to identify with the FSLN are also less likely to engage in talking about the period in which they were politically active with that party. The one person who does not mind expressing his views although he has switched away from the FSLN, Selva Gonzales, was not shy in describing what was wrong with the Nicaraguan government. Similarly to most Liberals and MRS Sandinistas, he thought Nicaragua was moving in the direction of a dictatorship. He told me, that he handed out fliers against Ortega Saavedra recently, and that he believed that it was the reason he was charged on an otherwise unrelated issue. Also Selva Gonzales claimed to have acquired political ideals in East Germany and that these continued to be valuable for him. Different from the other students, these ideals led him now to oppose the Ortega Saavedra government.

Most of the former students agreed that the time in East Germany was influential in forming their ideals as political beings. Some seemed to see this personal relation mirrored the relationship between the DDR and Nicaragua as countries. Aminta Arias stated this directly.

Predictions for Germany

Together with the view of the DDR in the past, most Sandinistas have a rather unusual view of what is likely to happen in Germany's future. That is also true for the former DDR students. Mendieta told me and my friend from Norway the following prediction about Germany's future:

> I think it is simply not likely that the Germans will allow going back to capitalism again, at least for a long time after having read that book [Das Kapital].

Blandón Montenegro rounded up my first meeting with her with this:

Nicaraguans came to East Germany to study many different things during the 1980s. This is one year of students from all over the world who received a course in political leadership at a school in the *Deutsche Demokratische Republik* (DDR, German Democratic Republic). *Photo: Undisclosed*

> I am sure that you guys will also win again in Germany soon, because the German people are a fighting people.

The view of the former students does not seem to be noticeably different from that of many other Sandinistas on this issue. It is one of the most significant conclusions I arrived at. Who influenced who in this case in their views is hard to discover, given that it seems to be such a prevalent view in Nicaragua, much more so than anywhere in the former DDR.

The experience in East Germany in perspective

The students I interviewed formed part of a small group of less than 100 students who went to that school. Their perspective is only saying something about a generalized Nicaraguan view to a limited extend. The number of Nicaraguans who went to Eastern Europe or Cuba for study purposes is somewhat larger. While I looked for students in León, I stopped at the FSLN departamento office, to ask whether they know anyone who went and received the following answer by the person responsible for propaganda: "Oh, about half of León has gone to Germany at some point of time." That figure is exaggerated, but among those involved in Sandinista politics actively, it was never difficult to find someone who studied in one of the allied countries during the 1980s. On the day when I confronted the FSLN members in León in connection with the medal to the former East German minister of education Margot Honecker, they quickly found someone sitting around who had been in East Germany, to present to me as an expert on the matter. He was just a person waiting in the front room, but he was readily available to defend the former ally. He started out telling me how they went to East Germany and how they saw snow for the first time and how welcome they were, and then made the statement about the Berlin wall having been a hinder for the spread of ideology from East Germany that I mentioned above.

Blandón Montenegro and Mendieta's idea of a possible revival of Eastern European socialism can be found among many other Sandinistas. They believe the development Nicaragua has gone through, with a loss of power of the socialist forces in 1990s and then a reversal almost two decades later can be redone many places, including Germany. They also believe it would be desirable for this to take place. In this sense, many Sandinistas seem to have a world view in which the movements in and history of Nicaragua is connected with and an essential part of the general history of the world, including that of Eastern Europe. Speaking to other Nicaraguans, also those who never left the country, the Soviet Union is seen as beneficial to the world by those positive to the Sandinistas, and negative by those opposed to the Sandinistas. Even though Sandinismo is seen as a decidedly independent and national project, a clear connection between the ex-Soviet Union and Sandinismo seems to exist.

Where this idea about Eastern Europe and the Soviet Union originated for the general Sandinista population is hard to define. Students who went abroad and talked about their experiences likely formed one of several parts. Somehow the difference in which part in the Nicaraguan-Eastern European connection was on the receiving end of ideological education and who was spreading an ideology, seems to be less clear for many Sandinistas who received information about their allies abroad as second hand information.

Dependence on Russia?

From the above interviews and the economic analysis, it is quite clear the political and cultural/social closeness to Russia is not a direct reflection of current trade links, but rather of past economic realities and personal learning experiences. The current understanding of the world, with such a central focus on the Soviet Union/Russia, is most of all the result of power constellations as they existed 20–30 years ago. That was the time when most adults made their political affiliations. It is also a period that stood out from the periods before and after it for all political groups in Nicaragua. The Sandinistas seem to have spread among themselves an idea that there was a more or less nonhierarchical relationship between themselves and their allies abroad. The popular discontent internally within Eastern European with their regimes during the 1980s, is almost never communicated.

Although many Sandinistas see things this way, it does not automatically follow that the trials of Ortega Saavedra to ally Nicaragua with Russia again are an expression of this. We cannot know whether Ortega Saavedra and his advisers have the same idea about the world as most Sandinistas and whether the government's politics are substantially influenced by this. Another reason could be that the current expansion in relations towards Russia is a conscious Nicaraguan trial of diversifying its relations to other countries. Ortega could just make use of pre-existing sentiments. It is impossible to determine this as an anthropologist, if one does not have direct access to all of Ortega Saavedra's meeting. I did not have access to any of his meetings nor did I ever speak to Ortega Saavedra in person. In any case, the freedom to build relations with Russia is likely originating in the fact that the United States does not have the dominance it previously had over the region.

Concluding remarks

We have seen that there is a particular Nicaraguan interpretation of world events, also those taking place in Europe which is mirrored by those students who went to study there during the 1980s. The Soviet Union and its Eastern European allies did represent for several of the students who went there, a center of ideological diffusion they still believe has influenced much of their current doings. Several of them have gained valuable posts within the current Sandinista run government. While the Soviet Union may not have been a center in the Dependency Theory sense, as a center for the accumulation of material wealth, the Soviet Union and the Warsaw Pact countries had a similar effect in terms of the production of ideology and allegiance through its relations with Nicaragua during the 1980s.

This does not explain why Nicaragua objectively has different options than other peripheral countries in a similar situation, but it may give some indications as why the options available to Nicaragua are perceived as being different by Nicaraguans. It is the past relation to an ideological center that, although the center may be nonexistent today, has had a lasting effect on Nicaraguan ideas about the world and the repertoire of possible actions Sandinistas believe are available to themselves.

Seventh Chapter

Factors that differentiate Sandinistas

As to be expected in any modern-day society, several factors distinguish Nicaraguans. This also applies to the part of the population identified as Sandinistas. Geography is one key factor in determining differences. Sandinistas in the countryside tend to be less academically minded, and their understanding of Sandinismo differs somewhat from that of Nicaraguans who live in cities. The latter sometimes describe rural conceptualizations of Sandinismo as resembling a religion, complete with shrines built to commemorate José Daniel Ortega Saavedra and Carlos Fonseca Amador. Between different cities, an immense variety exists in the strengths of belief in Sandinismo, and the meaning of being a Sandinista.

León is seen as the capital of Sandinismo. That is because León was liberated by Sandinistas from the Somoza regime before Managua. Additionally, the city has only had Sandinista city governments since the insurrection of 1979. Very few Liberals reside in León, and it seems the León Sandinistas manifest more self-confidence than those in Managua. When I showed a video of Sandinista protests in León to Sandinista informants in Managua, they were surprised by how articulate the protesters in León were and how devoted they seem to the cause of Sandinismo. In Managua, with Sandinista mayors only since 2000, Sandinistas tend to be more critical of the various things that have been done in the name of Sandinismo.

The differences in other cities and places are numerous: In Granada, Sandinismo is a minority position. On the Atlantic coast in the 1980s, Contras outnumbered Sandinistas. The *Frente Sandinista de Liberación Nacional* (FSLN) has only recently been able to make a pact with influential groups

One group of Sandinista veterans who fought in the revolutionary insurrection, took control of a building in downtown León after their victory. Previously, the building had been the local command center of the *Guardia Nacional* (GN). It now serves as their meeting space—mostly used to watch TV together—and it contains a photo exhibit which they use to teach foreigners about their struggle in exchange for a small fee.

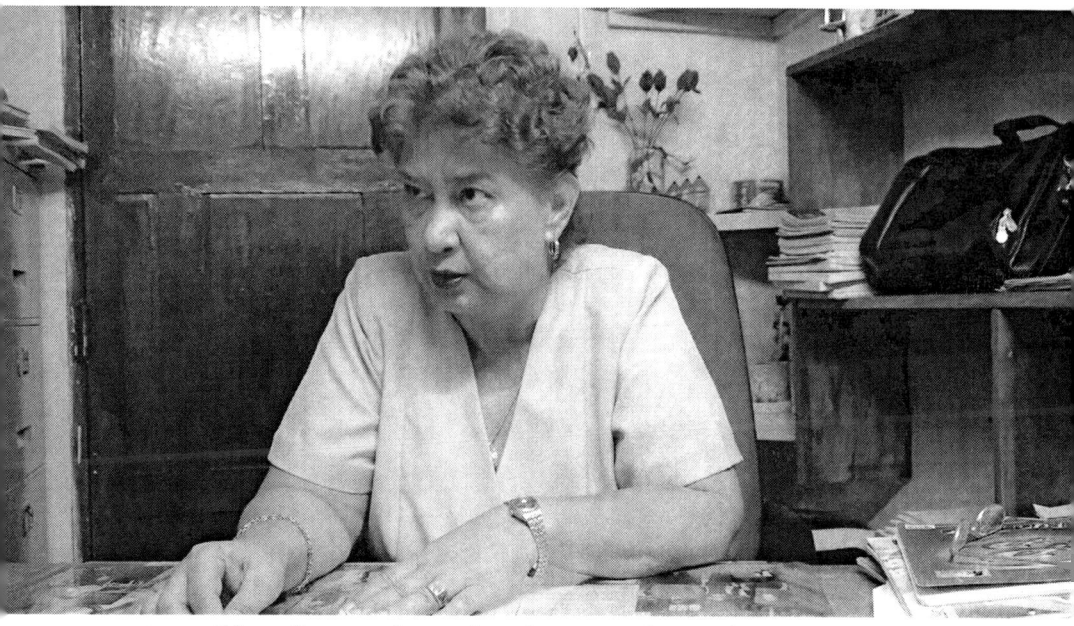

Petronilá Davila, a teacher and Sandinista in El Rama (eastern Nicaragua), explains that when she and her coworkers heard shots three days before the triumph of the revolution 19 July 1979, they could not imagine what it could be. Some thought it could be related to the celebrations of the annual day of the teacher. She herself thought it may be part of the religious festivities that start in late summer. The revolutionary movement had not arrived in El Rama before it triumphed. Later Davila participated in the organization of Sandinista education programs for some of the most remote villages.

there. The island Ometepe and much of eastern Nicaragua did not experience the revolutionary insurrection and does not have the same relation to this event as most other places. The northernmost cities like Estelí and Matagalpa were close to areas with physical battles in the 1980s, and did not experience a Sandinista government in a relatively peaceful environment as was the case for Managua and León. It is not hard to imagine how geographical factors make a difference in what it means to be a Sandinista.

Another important distinction between Sandinistas is socioeconomic class. Although Sandinismo entails an ideal of equality, not all Sandinistas come from the same socioeconomic background and differences between different social classes have not been eliminated since 1979.

My first landlord in León, Rigo Sampson Davila, is the son of a former Sandinista mayor and a member of the FSLN. He owns a relatively large downtown house with several employees. He works for a Norwegian student exchange organization, and he travels both in Latin America and Europe. On the side, he also works as a tourist guide for both European and US American tourists. His explanation for why things have not worked out as well for Nicaragua as for Costa Rica historically is, that the

José Roberto Cutbert Ramírez, *Frente Sandinista de Liberación Nacional* (FSLN) mayor of Laguna Perla in the *Región Autónoma del Atlántico Sur* (RAAS), explains to my coworker Carlos Alberto Rocha Castro and me, that while the FSLN has managed to obtain support amongst indigenous and blacks on the east coast in recent years where the party traditionally was weak, the party now lacks support amongst migrants from the Pacific coast, because the party is seen as representing a program of regional autonomy and indigenous people's rights. Other regional differences in the role of the FSLN exist in other parts of Nicaragua. Photo: Carlos Alberto Rocha Castro

ethnic makeup of Nicaragua with its many indigenous influences has been a hindrance to progress and that Costa Rica with its significantly higher percentage of European immigrants has enjoyed much better conditions. One of Sampson Davila's greatest concerns is that the José Daniel Ortega Saavedra government puts up gigantic billboards advertising itself to the Nicaraguan population, instead of using the money to advertise Nicaragua as a tourist destination in some leading US American magazine. Sampson Davila emphasizes that he does not want this just to help his own business. He makes it clear, that he sees the historic role of Sandinismo as one of improving all Nicaraguans' lives. He sees this as achievable, not by abolishing capitalism, but by making Nicaragua a place that attracts investment by promoting Nicaraguan products worldwide. At first, I saw Sampson Davila's ideas as lying far away from socialist ideology and what I have come to understand as making up Sandinismo. With time, I understood that he is not the only Sandinista with such beliefs. For many wealthy Sandinistas in Managua and León, Sandinismo seems to be most of all a nationalist Nicaraguan ideology. Some of them told me Sandinismo is an ideology that only Nicaraguans can believe in and does not extend beyond the borders of Nicaragua. They also explained, that they believed the socialist or communist elements found in the politics of the FSLN historically, were something that the Soviet Union imposed on Carlos Fonseca Amador.

According to this logic, socialist elements do not actually constitute a part of the 'real' Sandinismo.[1] Sandinismo for them seems to be not much more than the nationalist belief in the possibility of developing Nicaragua and giving Nicaraguans a nationalist perspective.

Some Sandinistas own extremely little in material terms, such as the veterans who fought in the revolution and now keep up a museum in the town center of León. Every time I saw them, they expressed an interest in explaining the different aspects of their struggle during the 1970s and 1980s to me. They blast out the same recordings of a few FSLN revolutionary songs across the town square using an unusually loud sound system. Economically, they have likely not won anything through the revolution. Their ideology emphasizes the insurrection of the 1970s and the plan for social change that the FSLN stood for in the 1980s. I heard other Sandinistas say they were drugged most of the time. Most likely, this is said in a bid to discount their ideology.

Such urban/rural differences and socioeconomic class are tremendously powerful factors in determining how a member of a political movement thinks and acts in most places in the world. It is also true in the case of Nicaragua. I here present three other factors I found to be surprisingly influential in determining how an individual Sandinista informant showed his political identity and what the political identity of Sandinismo meant to him. These differences it seems are the ones most talked about among Nicaraguans today.

I feel it is safe to say that there is a concept a prototype Sandinista that is shared within Nicaraguan society. This prototype has to do with the rhetoric used in mainstream society. The prototype is what every individual Sandinista relates and is compared to. This is true even for those who acknowledge that they differ a lot from this prototype. Asking the 25 year old daughter of Sandinistas Helen Maydelin Salmerón Vásquez if she thought a prototype Sandinista existed, she agreed and defined this prototype:

> It is someone who attended military service [in the 1980s],

---

1. Similar to Sandinista explanations of the influence of the United States on Nicaragua, explanations of Soviet Union influence are also described as mechanical in the sense that they are not the result of the decisions of individuals that divert history from its natural path—which would constitute historical agency (Graeber 1996)—but rather that it is part of the natural flow of history, as an empire that is spreading an ideology that is subservient to its own national interests.

Francisco Isidoro Sobalvarro Baldelomar from La Esperanza, El Rama fought during the insurrection of the late 1970s. After the triumph of the revolution, he retired to civilian life. In 1983, the party asked him to return to the military, as responsible of organizing the military service of which he believes to have had a deciding importance in its implementation. He continued to stay with the party after the electoral loss. This makes him fulfill several of the criteria of being a prototype Sandinista the way younger Sandinistas have defined it for me. Sobalvarro Baldelomar has, however, not been compensated for his help during the years of opposition with a 'good job' but instead runs a grocery store in Managua. He also forms part of the 'Amigos' network of Bayardo José Fonseca Galo, who sends Sobalvarro Baldelomar to accompany me to El Rama at one time.

> who worked for the revolution, who then cried and got drunk with the loss of 1990, who continued to work with the party during the 16 years the Frente wasn't in power, and who now has been compensated with a good position.

The way those who resemble this prototype Sandinista speak, resembles how those close to Ortega Saavedra express themselves in public events. The senior citizens in León I mentioned above fall within this category, although what unites them is their engagement in the guerrilla fighting of the 1970s, not the military service of the 1980s. The life-stories of these currently dominate among Sandinistas. The other types of Sandinistas I will present here are always defined through how they differ from this group. As said, all of them are aware of this concept of a Sandinista prototype and oftentimes describe themselves in terms of how they differ from it. All four types of investigative projects helped in gaining knowl-

Agapito Laguna describes to me how his father, although identifying with the Conservatives, came into trouble with the military and ended up fighting together with Augusto Nicolás Calderón Sandino. When his father was about to die, he asked Laguna to continue the struggle. Also Bayardo José Fonseca Galo tells me that his grandfather revealed to him that he had fought together with Calderón Sandino. They are the exception. Fonseca Galo says about Laguna that he 'forms the link' from their to the older generation. Most Sandinistas who were active starting in the 1970s or earlier, claim to have initiated their struggle themselves, independently of the family.

edge about these differences. I encounter the generational gap through conversing with several main informants in depth, and the journalistic project put me in touch with several of the younger currently politically active Sandinistas.

Age as a defining factor

The Nicaraguan revolution is the youngest revolution in Latin America. The relatively short time that has passed since the beginning of the Sandinista movement (1961 or 1979, depending on how one sees it) is not further in the past than that it would allow for many Nicaraguans to have participated in it from its inception to the present. The reality is, that the period in which a Sandinista is or was politically active or someone close to him was or is active, is not the same for all Sandinistas. Many

Sandinistas have not participated in political life for one or several longer periods of time. Some informants have been active in all recent political phases as Sandinista from the 1970s until now, and others have only been active recently. Others were active during parts of the 1980s, then drifted into other projects, and only recently became involved again. Not all phases are equally relevant in determining where a Nicaraguan stands politically at present. For most informants, where they stand politically is determined by what side that person's family stood on in the 1980s. In this sense, participation in politics, which is presented by the informants as in the 1960s and 1970s having been a largely individualistic choice, is now for many a matter of family membership and alliances. Carolina Fonseca Icabalzeta and Salmerón Vásquez both are second generation Sandinistas and agree on this view.[2]

Fonseca Icabalzeta explained the transition from voluntary to biological definition of becoming a Sandinista this way:

> Many of those who had become Sandinista through an individual choice of their own looked for another Sandinista to marry. Their kids often became Sandinista by birth.

Tatar (2005, 192) in his brief anthropological overview of the first phase of the Sandinista revolution portrayed family ties as one of the most significant factors in determining whether someone would participate in insurrectionist action in 1979. His field-study of Nicaragua took place in 1999, 20 years after the insurrection in the village of Monimbó outside Masaya, and he relied on some oral accounts collected and written down in the early 1980s by the Nicaraguan research institute *Instituto de Estudio del Sandinismo* (IES). A high number of personal accounts among my informants of the 1970s go contrary to the description of Tatar, especially among Sandinistas with an urban background. These Sandinistas emphasize personal choice rather than family ties to have been important in making them Sandinistas. It seems that Tatar's description does likely not cover the kinds of Sandinistas I have most contact with. I cannot out-rule

---

2. What makes out a family for my urban Nicaraguan informants does not seem to differ that much from many parts of Europe. When I asked them to define the term for me, Fonseca Icabelzeta and Salmerón Vásquez defined the meaning of 'a family' slightly differently – Fonseca Icabelzeta believes most Nicaraguans define it as "all the people who live in one house together" whereas Salmerón Vásquez defines it as the "those [biological family members] who are geographically closest". According to either way of measuring, they arrive at family sizes of two to 15 people.

that it may have been different for other Sandinistas. The distinction may be part of the difference between urban and rural Sandinistas mentioned initially.

The literacy campaign celebration

The first time I became aware of the discrepancy between older and younger Sandinistas was, when the Nicaraguan Literacy Campaign celebrated its 30th birthday with a mobile edutainment museum that moved around the country and placed in different cities for several weeks to months. I caught it in León and was present at the day of its inauguration. The center consisted of a few containers which had various computers and a TV with multimedia contents describing the experience of those who went out in the countryside as part of the literacy campaign in the early 1980s. The idea behind this museum, I was told by the Sandinistas running it, was to encourage young Nicaraguans today to sign up and volunteer for the current literacy campaign 'Yo sí, puedo.'

At the inauguration ceremony in León, almost all the attendants were adults. The speaker asked all the audience to stand up and sing the hymn of the literacy campaign originally used in the 1980s. Everybody present knew it by heart. When we were to inaugurate the museum, I was put together with the first ones to enter – a small group of high-ranking León Sandinistas, who all seem to have backgrounds from higher education. As we entered, I realized that what we were seeing was a campaign that formed an extraordinarily prominent part of the life of most of those I was with. The stories presented in the museum were about individual experiences of youngsters acting as teachers, and how they individually decided to participate in the campaign in 1980. In some cases, the youngsters participated in the program against their parents' will, in other cases they seem to have had their parents' approval; nevertheless, it was the participant's own decision to enter the program. Most stories talk about things that were unrelated to their teaching obligations, that the youngsters learned on their trip. It was quite clear, this was a generational movement of Nicaraguans who acted rather independently of their parents and grandparents.

The situation for today's youths is quite different. Parents now seem much more preoccupied with the safety of their children compared to the stories from the 1970s/80s. It is now the parent generation that encourages the youths to do as they did and go out into the countryside, to teach for a while. This is decidedly different from how it was back then, when the youths did something new which their parents had not done.

The museum stayed at that same place for quite a while, and I did not see many Nicaraguan youths enter it who had not been sent there by the school. Although the idea behind its creation likely was to encourage today's youths to participate in the current literacy campaign, it seemed to function mostly as a place of self-celebration for the older generation of Sandinistas that now ran the country. Given the focus on the campaign of the 1980s in everyday discourse, I initially did not think to question whether the current campaign is the same as the one in the 1980s.

Finally one day, Gerardo Antonio Santamaria Rosales, a 24 year old radio worker involved with the FSLN for 12 years, explained to me for the first time how the 'voluntary' participation in this program is organized under the current government:

> Before [during the time of neoliberal governments], in the 5th grade of the secondary [school], students would write a long monograph that no-one cared about and that ended up being thrown on the floor. Now they are sent into the countryside, to the least developed zones of the country, to teach other how to read and write.

It is with this experience in mind, I started to investigate the generational gap as one of the factors differentiating Sandinistas. My conclusion is that families now seem to have become more of a unit, rather than acting individually in matters of politics as appears to have been the case in the 1970s and 1980s.

The lack of ideological models among younger Sandinistas

The family of Fonseca Icabalzeta, one of my main informants in Managua, presented to me one of the clearest examples of inner-family differences in what it means to be a Sandinista. Fonseca Icabalzeta was in her late 20s and a student of philology and communication at the *Universidad Nacional Autónoma de Nicaragua* (UNAN), and she lived in a poor and rather dangerous area of Managua with her parents and a sick grandmother in a wooden house with the roof falling off. Next door lived her father's brother, Bayardo José Fonseca Galo, and his wife, in a house in equally serious condition. All four of the parents generation were active in the student

Ana Milagro Matargo Diez (age 16) from Somoto declares she is "Sandinista by blood." Her entire family has been Sandinista and so that made also her Sandinista. This seems to be the most common form to become Sandinista for younger Nicaraguans. Half a year before I talk to her, she started being involved in the *Juventud Sandinista* (JS). She believes one of the main objectives with her involvement is to help young people leave drug addictions. She hopes this will lead to a 'better' Nicaragua. She sees the contribution of the JS as indispensable in developing the course of the revolution: "Young people are the ones who have to do revolutions, because they do not fear change."

movement of the 1970s. In the 1980s Fonseca Icabalzeta and her parents moved to a small and even poorer village in southern Nicaragua for some years, as part of political work for the party. At the time her mother, Carolina Icabalceta Garay, worked as an English and history teacher and her father in an NGO. During my time there, Fonseca Icabalzeta worked now and then at a kindergarten or school, but was just as often unemployed.

Her parents have read a lot of theoretical literature, but none of that trickled down to Fonseca Icabalzeta. She is well aware of Nicaraguan history and some recent European history. She associates Eastern Europe with values of solidarity and Western Europe with values of competition. Even without having studied any of the theoretical models the older generation sees as fundamental to Sandinismo, she readily identifies as a Sandinista. The combination of much knowledge of Nicaraguan historical events but little knowledge of theoretical debates on ideology is something found in many younger Sandinistas. The explanation given by many Sandinistas is due to a period during the years of neoliberalism in which the older generation kept the ideology secret, or did at least not talk about it openly. This, in part, seems to be a valid reason.

When I finally managed to convince Fonseca Icabalzeta after several months that her mother was interesting enough to interview, the mother started out by explaining the part about her seeing herself most of all as an anarchist or anarcho-syndicalist. "A what?" Fonseca Icabalzeta asked afterward, when I summed up what her mother had said. I had not thought this could be something she possibly could not have known of beforehand. From the interview, it seemed to be a vital part of her mother's identity. Fonseca Icabelzeta asked me several times afterward what exactly makes an anarcho-syndicalist, until I explained it in detail.

Icabalceta Garay notices the lack of knowledge in the younger generation in other areas than where her daughter lacks knowledge. She mentioned during the interview that, as a history teacher, she noticed how many of the youths of today "confuse Carlos Fonseca [Amador] with [Calderón] Sandino" due to insufficient knowledge. She also said she was delighted some new programs had recently been put on TV about the time before the revolution, how life was under Somoza and the Sandinista insurrection of 1979. She continued to be concerned there was not enough of that. She explained it would be essential to put emphasis on teaching history: "If they don't know about their past, how can they have a perspective for the future?"

Icabalceta Garay believes her own daughter has listened so much to the discourse on Sandinismo in her parents' house, that she has started questioning it. "Well great, [through that she creates] another alternative," Icabalceta Garay tried to sound accepting of her daughters conduct.

Little focus on theoretical knowledge among organized Sandinista youngsters

Although Fonseca Icabelzeta is a Sandinista, she attends no meetings of any structure of the FSLN. I wondered whether I should speak to some young Sandinistas who do attend FSLN meetings.

One of the few members of the *Juventud Sandinista* (JS) I met more often is Ninfa Patricia Ramos. Ramos is the friend of Fonseca Icabalzeta and they studied together at the UNAN in Managua. While Fonseca Icabalzeta was still a student during my entire stay, Ramos already graduated and taught Spanish at the UNAN. Different from Fonseca Icabalzeta, she engaged in

Ninfa Patricia Ramos is said to have inside knowledge of the *Juventud Sandinista* which she does not always share with her friends, in order to protect the party.

student politics and the JS during her time at university. The rest of her family supported her and is also Sandinista, but she seemed to be more of a driving force in that respect than Fonseca Icabalzeta in her family.

Ramos clearly belongs to those on the inside of the Sandinista student movement. That does not mean that she is theoretically more versed than Fonseca Icabalzeta. Both seem to agree on this. The difference between her and Fonseca Icabalzeta in their relationship to the FSLN can be noted in the amount of access they have to up to date information on strategic/tactical moves of the Sandinista controlled *Unión Nacional de Estudiantes de Nicaragua* (UNEN) in which Ramos was active for several years prior to my arrival to Nicaragua. At one time, I asked Fonseca Icabalzeta about certain student-politics related disagreements within Sandinismo. We quickly realized, that these things had occurred without her hearing about them. Instead of being able to answer me, she commented in a frustrated voice: "Sometimes, Ninfa just won't tell me about things that happen." Ramos is selective in her forwarding of internal political details.

Around the municipal elections of November 2008 (see also — *FSLN won local elections (November 2008)*, p. 130), I saw Ramos more in connection with party political events, such as on election night at youth election head quarters. When I came to met up with her, the first youngster who saw me directed me immediately to mount on the back of a pickup truck to act as part of a victory parade around Managua. My connection to Ramos was likely what placed me there. The other youngsters in those days all seem remarkably similar to Ramos: extremely active and practically minded, but not particularly schooled theoretically with the books older Sandinistas studied (Karl Heinrich Marx, Lenin, Ernesto 'Che' Guevara, Carlos Fonseca Amador, etc.).

Term redefinitions

One of the main differences I noticed between old and young Sandinistas, was the way they use certain terminology. The older Sandinistas use the definitions of the international radical movement, something which hints of their being aware of the same theories as radicals globally. The younger generation seems to use mostly self-created definitions. In any society, the young learn from the elder, but it seems that the Nicaraguan case is particular in that the absence of ideological schooling after the 1980s meant that concepts related to revolutionary activity are used differently or at times not used at all among younger Sandinistas. The overall value seen in studying ideology and using an ideological analysis openly seems to have changed for the younger generation. The level of schooling of classic Marxist theory is not as high among younger Sandinistas as among older Sandinistas, some radical-theoretical terminology that the older generation uses, is still used by the younger people, although in a slightly different way. The fact that the terms are used at all by younger Sandinistas at first makes it appear as if no substantial difference between younger and older Sandinistas exists. The difference in usage points to how the theoretical underpinnings of socialist ideology used by the older generation have not been transferred to the younger generation. Of all the radical-revolutionary terms I encountered, 'vanguard' and 'tendency' seem to be the ones taken most out of their original context and as having acquired a new meaning. Terms such as 'anti-imperialism,' 'socialismo,' and 'cadres' are used without much of any definition in common for them, or one that is somewhat distant from the international and historical usage.

These terms were likely introduced into widespread usage during the 1970s and 1980s, at a time when the Sandinistas and their struggle formed part of an international and theoretical radical discourse. Subsequently the terms continued to be part of the Sandinista internal discourse, though much more disconnected from the international one. Thus, these terms developed their own meaning.

Vanguard

One of the most central terms in this connection is 'vanguard.' The young Sandinistas use it just as much as the older ones, but they tend to use it in other settings. With time, it became clearer to me, that for younger Sandinistas, it can be used quite independently from the context in which it was originally employed.

The term originally is known for its usage by Lenin and designated a section of the population that would lead intellectually and had a certain insight into the working of society which the majority of the population lacked (Lenin 1902, chapter 4) (see also — *The FSLN structure*, p. 14). In the 1980s membership in the FSLN was strictly controlled and only available to a small elite. Under these circumstances, the term 'vanguard' was used by Sandinista leaders to refer to themselves. Borge Martínez used it during a speech addressing the second anniversary celebration of the revolution like this:

> ...For this reason, all the efforts of those born in Nicaragua but now want to go back to the past ...will fail. They will never be able to separate the people from their vanguard. (Borge Martínez 1981, 129)

The vanguard as used by Tomás Borge Martínez and the Sandinistas of his generation is clearly a separate entity than 'the people.' Borge believes it is close, but it is clearly not the same thing. The way many young Sandinistas use it today, gives it a meaning of all those organized with the FSLN, independently of whether they act strictly in political works, not considering membership in the JS and the FSLN are no longer restricted to a handful of selected people. Erick Saul Rios Juarez and his friends from the JS who run a radio show (see also — *Power through infiltration*, p. 176) use the term 'vanguard' to describe themselves and the entire JS on air and when discussing with me. It is not always in the political sense. When I asked why the JS had to participate in the celebrations of the catholic holiday Santa Domingo, it was explained, "Because we are the vanguard."

When I asked him to define the term, Rios Juarez explained it this way:

> The vanguard, it's to be in the first line at the hour of combat, to be awake at any moment, it is to be prepared for the new responsibilities. The combatant can be in any of the fronts: in the cultural, in the communicative, in sports, etc.

Erick Saul Rios Juarez has been involved in Sandinista politics since the age of eight by bringing food to Sandinistas working during elections. At age 12 he "started working 100%, on a daily basis within the *Juventud Sandinista.*" He and his fellow activists describe themselves as the 'vanguard.'

When I instead asked a female friend of Rios Juarez who is about 10 years older than him, she explained it to me as:

> It can mean two things: In the revolutionary struggle, it is essential always to be ahead what the enemy does. The enemy can be the United States or the political right... It is also a literary movement. I think around the end of the 1920s, beginning of the 1930s – here in Nicaragua it was done by some oligarchs in the city of Granada... For the Sandinistas it also means: to be alert, to be in front, to be the best student, etc.

Although both of them use the term, they seem to have developed their own definitions for it that do not always match up. Rios Juarez's friend experienced the 1980s as a child and claimed her usage originates from that period. About the definition Rios Juarez gave me, she said:

> Oh yes, it's because the Chayo [Rosario] Murillo[, the wife of Ortega Saavedra,] is using the term again. So that's why Erick repeats it.

I tried to find where either Rosario Murillo or Ortega Saavedra used this term in another sense than the original one, but was not able to find it. Rios Juarez's older friend is at times a bit annoyed by him for various personal

Two groups of Sandinista students fight over the administration building of the *Universidad Nacional Autónoma de Nicaragua–León*. A student who fights with the group from León, who are attacking in this photo, tells me that the Managua students who are in the building are "terrorist students." Various Sandinista groups blame one-another for the event. The Somocistas of León are mostly concerned about the door that is being attacked here, because the building was built during the government of Anastasio Somoza Debayle.

reasons, so some of her comment regarding Rios Juarez's usage of the term may have been biased. It is fascinating to note, that she believes that the term was used mainly in the 1980s and then again currently. This seems like a probable development of the amount the usage of the term.

Tendency

At another point, there was disagreement on strategy between one of the longtime national leaders of the biggest student unions, César Pérez of the UNEN, and some of the leading figures of the *Centro Universitario de la Universidad Nacional-León* (CUUN–León). Also the CUUN–León is informally Sandinista controlled. It started during the election campaign of November 2008 (see also — FSLN won local elections (November 2008), p. 130). I was not present when it happened, but was told it started out with some UNEN students throwing fliers into lecture rooms at the *Universidad Centroamericana* (UCA) in Managua, when they decided not to allow the UNEN students to distribute their material on campus. Pérez announced he wanted to 'take' the university, which is the most prominent privately owned university that receives public funding of the same 6% of the Nicaraguan budget that is designated for students and which is the source

For some of the younger Sandinistas, the shooting of firecracker with mortars seems to be an integral part of any Sandinista event.

of income of all public universities, and turn it into a public institution. He and his group showed up with mortars once, and promised to be back physically to take control over the university campus at a later date. With that announcement, all evening classes were canceled for a few months and stricter entrance control were employed to ensure only UCA students were permitted access. Many of my Managua based Sandinista informants were strongly against the actions of Pérez, because they felt he had treated the UCA unfairly. Additionally, they felt he was not serving the Sandinista cause. Simultaneously, he was criticized by leading figures of the CUUN-León for the same reasons. The conflict culminated about a half year later in a physical confrontation between CUUN-León and UNEN at the *Universidad Nacional Autónoma de Nicaragua-León* (UNAN–León). The UCA was officially not part of the conflict. It was the national leadership of the UNEN which decided to occupy the central building of the UNAN–León as a protest against the budget of that university presented that day. Formally, all those who are members of the CUUN-León are also members of the UNEN at a national level, but the individual students I interviewed defined themselves as being part of one of the two. I was at the university and watched as CUUN-León affiliated students tried to enter the already occupied building and chase out the UNEN students who traveled to León from Managua.

At this point no-one seemed to try to define the difference as being based on different ideological lines. The UNEN affiliated students from Managua claimed they were taking control of the building as a protest against the annual university budget. The CUUN-León students complained that they had not informed and that their authority was being undermined. They attacked Pérez for having stayed in office for too long time. It was quite clear at this stage that this was nothing more than retaliation against the CUUN-León statements as concerned the UCA.

When students explained the conflict to me, they used the language of the internal ideological struggles of the FSLN in the 1970s and most specifically the word 'tendency' (see also — *The FSLN divided into three tendencies*, p. 7). Ramos told me quite plainly: "They are different tendencies" when I asked about the conflict. The students around Rios Juarez and the JS who a few months later came into conflict with Pérez explained it the same way. This does not seem to stand in contrast for them with personal career based conflicts. Fonseca Icabalzeta told me while Ramos listened and nodded approvingly:

> He [César] just wants to show that he can move the people, so that Ortega [Saavedra] makes him a member of the national assembly.

When I asked Ramos what she meant by the term 'tendency,' she explained her usage in detail:

> They are different subgroups. There is one group that [Reinaldo Gregorio] Lenín Cerna [Juárez][3] manages. Bayardo Arce[4] manages another one. A third one is run by the Chayo [Rosario Murillo]. All believe in Daniel. Nevertheless, each have their own economical and political interests. For example, Lenin Cerna wants to run the UNEN and the Juventud Sandinista. Later on they will serve them as their shock troops.[5] The more people you manage, and the more people that notice you, the more power and support you will have. At the same

---

3. Reinaldo Gregorio Lenín Cerna Juárez is known for his role within the secret police in the 1980s and is by many right-wing critics today seen as someone who secretly controls Ortega Saavedra and turns Nicaragua into a communist state.

4. Bayardo Arce is a longtime Sandinista and economic adviser of the Ortega Saavedra government.

5. Wondering whether I misunderstood, and whether the FSLN works somewhat more hierarchical than what I had thought, I asked whether all these groups of young Sandinistas then only act when they receive orders by people like Bayardo Arce. Ramos denied this in the case of the conflicts I saw: "No, At times they just act on their own."

Carolina Fonseca Icabalzeta, one of my main younger Sandinista informants, mostly met me at the shopping center Metrocentro in Managua. In the 1990s, several larger shopping centers were opened in Managua. They have since served as some of the main meeting points for Managuans. Most visitors just stand around, as prices are high.

> time, they all have something in common: Daniel unites them.

I then asked Ramos how these new tendencies were different from those before 1979. She replied:

> Well, for now I sense that all Sandinistas see ourselves like one gigantic family. The distinctions are not as large as they once were. Within the FSLN one already knows who is in charge, because Daniel unites the Sandinista family. Ideologically there is no difference; the ideology is now the same.

'Seriousness' and acceptance of younger Sandinistas

One difference between younger and older Sandinistas relates to the level of theoretical schooling and the way they express themselves. The younger generation of Sandinistas rarely speak positively about the Ortega Saavedra government. Many times during first encounters with younger Nicaraguans, I mistook their constant criticism or ridicule of current government policies as opposition to Sandinismo. When I asked them whether they see themselves as Liberals, I was often surprised to find they would never con-

Age as a defining factor

sider voting anything other than FSLN. Fonseca Icabalzeta once explained the conflict with her parents' generation on this matter:

> They just don't understand, that when one makes a joke about Daniel [Ortega Saavedra] or his wife, it doesn't mean that one is against the revolution. They are just so much more serious about everything.

One of the most serious Sandinistas I met is Fonseca Galo. Icabalceta Garay decided to introduce me to him after I finished interviewing her. Fonseca Galo was unemployed at times, but spent most of his time at an institute for social research of the UNAN with which he was loosely affiliated. His wife worked for the FSLN mayor of Managua's office. He saw his own actions as relating to Marxist theory more than any of the family members. He described himself as a Leninist. This was another fact Fonseca Icabalzeta was unaware of until I told her about it. Fonseca Galo is one of the first Sandinistas I met who made an explicit distinction between himself and other people who fought in the insurrection 1979, and those who just called themselves Sandinista without ever having any position of importance within the Sandinista movement. He said the following, after I told him, that I wanted to study 'the Sandinistas' today:

> Well yeah, but there are people who are just Sandinistas, because that's how they feel. And there are those of us, who have fought for this.

Although he was one of extremely few people who made the distinction explicitly, I noticed that two distinct ways exist of understanding the term 'Sandinista':

- Those who have not fought in the revolution and are younger, define being a Sandinista as something one can choose to be if one generally agrees with some principles. Even though this definition clearly is based around individual choice, the vast majority choose the same as their parents.

- Many of those who fought in the revolution or held noteworthy posts in the 1980s or have them currently, see only themselves as the Sandinistas and the general Sandinista-positive population as their support base.

From the many different situations I have heard the term 'Sandinista' used, the common denominator seems to be that a Sandinista is a socially conscious actor who leads and affects society. Fonseca Galo then invited me to interview his comrades from 1979 and presented me with his list of 300 combatants who lived spread out through the country. Fonseca Icabalzeta was quite embarrassed by her uncle and this project of documenting his fellow combatants afterward. "I am so sorry my uncle is using you like this," she told to me after I had spent time talking to Fonseca Galo's comrades in the city of Managua. I had to explain many times, that part of what I wanted to do in Nicaragua was to talk to these kinds of people. For many from Fonseca Icabalzeta's generation who define themselves as Sandinistas, it seems embarrassing to talk too much and too seriously about the revolution or Sandinista politics.

The relationship between Fonseca Icabalzeta, her parents and her uncles and aunts seems to be rather typical of many Sandinistas I met. All members of a family call themselves Sandinistas, but there is a marked difference between the generation that participated in the insurrection and the one that did not. Not all Sandinistas have a background in higher education, and that may have made the difference in knowledge about theory obvious. It is notable, that oftentimes the older generation seems interested in teaching the younger generation about theory and considers that important. For some reason, however, they have not engaged in doing just that. It may be speculated that this is related to the 16 years of neoliberalism during which older Sandinistas did not see the same value in teaching about those things. Fonseca Icabalzeta and her peers proposed similar theories, when I asked them about the gap.

Current studies of political theory

It took me a long time to find organized youngsters who also have some interest in political theories. That has to do with the training and organizing of Sandinista youngsters, which for the most part did not start before 2008. When I asked about what schooling existed at the local headquarters in León in the summer 2008, I was sent to the small lecture series arranged in cooperation with the UNAN-León. I attended some of these lectures, but found them exceedingly broad and aimed at students in general rather than specifically at educating young Sandinistas. For most of my first year in Nicaragua, I met members of the JS when going from León to Managua on a bus headed to some demonstration. None of them seemed to be of the type who is interested in political theory. It was not before the last two months of my stay, that I came into contact with members of the JS, who had received some fundamental training in political theories. This was 2.5 years into the presidency of Ortega Saavedra, and a limited amount of schooling in political theories on a national level had been organized.

The teaching included both theoretical and practical elements. Those teaching the practical aspects were paid through different institutions not necessarily have anything to do with the Sandinista struggle, but who got utilized to teach theory. I met a team of Mexican and Spanish media educators who taught people from the national leadership of the JS who specialize din journalism, how to perform media coverage. The educators were paid through a fund associated with the United Nations and told me the point of their program was to teach youngster who may get involved in street violence how to express their rage through the media. They understood that the group they worked with was political, but it did not seem they saw that their training was meant to further the revolutionary cause. "I will teach them how to do objective journalism," a Mexican told me, "these youngsters here all seem extremely political and that is not the best way of doing good journalism."

In the 1980s, theoretical schooling existed all over the country. It was much smaller at the time when I left in 2009; the only teaching facilities were in Managua. Additionally, only those at the upper leadership at a national level participated.

Professionals and Sandinismo

Besides generational age grouping, another decisive factor that seems to change how a Sandinista expresses himself that was noticeable to me among my informants is whether the person works as a professional, i.e. a person with a university degree who works within his field of study or one closely related. Most professionals at high levels seem to work in Managua and oftentimes they have to work quite closely with government entities.

When dealing with both young professionals in the Nicaraguan free software movement, the NGO *Servicio de Información Mesoamericano sobre Agricultura Sostenible* (SIMAS), or similar groups that made up social spaces, the cooperation with the Sandinistas is communicated in a much more subtle way than average. In my experience, in Managua Sandinistas of all kinds are much more openly critical towards the Ortega Saavedra government than in León. Among professionals, their allegiance with the Sandinistas is communicated in an even less direct form. Not speaking about political affiliation or saying "I am not very political," in Nicaraguan society means, that one associates with the Liberals. I assumed the same when I first entered into contact with professionals working in the Nicaraguan capital, as they did not spend as much time talking about their political affiliation as most Nicaraguans do. After a while, I learned how Sandinista affiliations within these circles are communicated differently. The average Sandinista will usually say something like this when asked about what political party is most likely to develop the country:

> Only we, the Sandinistas, are building this country! In the 1980s, we sent students to study to the Soviet Union, to the DDR [*Deutsche Demokratische Republic*, German Democratic Republic] and to Cuba. Now we build roads, have ended the power outages and teach the poor how to read and write. [Heard at a Sandinista celebration after electoral victory in León, Fall 2008]

I heard similar statements many times by Sandinistas. The person uttering them does not need to have been involved in any of the actions mentioned or in any further way be associated with the FSLN. Many times the statement is augmented by a long list of current programs the Ortega Saavedra government is implementing or has announced as starting in the near future.

As a contrast, when I asked one of Fonseca Galo's work colleagues, Freddy Enrique Quezada Picado, who Fonseca Galo had presented to me as a Sandinista compañero and insurrectionist fighter and who also agreed to be interviewed as such, whether all parties were equally interested in the social development projects his organization developed, I received the following answer:

> The parties of the right, their doings are partidarian.
> ...There is no... I do not anywhere see that there are propositions of development, propositions of production in the communities. All they are looking for, is votes. The activity of development I see as only coming from the government, from the party of the government.

Freddy Enrique Quezada Picado works as a professional and is presented to me as a Sandinista. Like many professional Sandinistas, Quezada Picado is not as direct as other Sandinistas when expressing his support for the policies of the current government.

> I don't see any initiative of those political parties [on the political right] towards social or economic development. There are members of the national assembly... All the members of the national assembly have a part [of their budget] assigned to advertise their image. They distribute that to social activities, right? As a part... as a political party, I do, however, not see it.

Quezada Picado showed just as much as any other FSLN Sandinista that he favored the FSLN and he had nothing pleasant to say about any of the other parties. He just uttered his views in a more hidden or subtle fashion. He even avoided calling any of the political parties by their name or to mention any concrete action or program of any present or former government, the way it is usually done in Nicaragua. This way Quezada Picado spoke I found to be more common within professional circles.

Through the Linux group of Managua to which I maintained contact through most of my time in Nicaragua, I learned that Quezada Picado is not just a particularly strange case. On the evening of the first Linux conference I attended between the different Linux groups in Managua, I was invited to go drink with some of the core organizers of the Linux events in Managua. During the entire day, no mention of party politics was made, even though several strategies related to how one could influence government politics to use more free software were presented and discussed. I was transported to the home, where we were to drink, in the car of the only Costa Rican participant of the group. At one point, we were alone in the car, and we discussed how it was strange, that no-one had mentioned party politics all day long. We both guessed where the Nicaraguans are situated politically – he guessed *Movimiento Renovador Sandinista* (MRS) and *Alianza Liberal Nicaragüense* (ALN), and I guessed MRS. Later that night, when everybody was more or less drunk, someone finally brought the question of political affiliation up. The question, as it was originally phrased, was: "Who here does not belong to the Sandinista movement?" The Costa Rican reformulated it quickly: "Why not make it easier: 'What party did you vote for?' ?" The result was, that, among the 10–15 programmers present, there was no-one who claimed not to have voted either for the FSLN or the MRS. This happened in late spring 2008, when the national news were mostly about MRS leaders and activists claiming the FSLN was trying to establish a dictatorship. The programmers instead tried to emphasize the common Sandinista tradition that lies in both parties. The initial phrasing of the question may well have been an expression of that.

For over a year, the image I developed of these young professionals did not change fundamentally in character. Some of the programmers started a group blog called Barricada.com.ni, named after the former FSLN party newspaper *La Barricada* (see also — *The FSLN as an opposition force*, p. 21). It used the red-and-black logo of the paper. Almost all of them said they had nothing to do with the original paper. The exception was one contributor, who was also heavily contributing comments on both Nicaraguan newspaper sites and the foreign language sites related to Nicaragua. He was singularly anti-FSLN and much in favor of anything other than the FSLN. All contributors seemed to be critical of the governments doings, but also in support of most of its chief ideological lines. To this day, it is to my knowledge the only independent Spanish-language site for discussion of politics in Nicaragua. The hiding of ideological affiliation with the Sandinista cause may have to do with the position of professionals during the 16 years of neoliberalism. The anthropologist Lundgren (2000) studied this and described how many of those educated during the Sandinista years tried to hide their Sandinista past in the 1990s. The state needed the service of these professionals, and as long as one did not openly show

Sandinista sympathies during those years many could continue to work within their field. Quezada Picado confirmed that the stigma of being a Sandinista was not exactly helpful during those years. It does, however, not fully explain why there is a resistance to the usage of direct Sandinista rhetoric even today, with all state institutions allegedly taken over by the FSLN.

In the following example, we see how at times the typical Sandinista rhetorics are seen as misplaced, when they are uttered in a professional setting even though those are dominated by Sandinistas. Shortly after I was hired to help create a new information system for the ministry of agriculture through SIMAS, Denis Cárceres and I went to the ministry of agriculture to hear about their wishes and present our plan for the system. I thought of how to present our plans and to make it understood to the ministry that we wanted to create a system to their advantage. I considered what spin I should give to my presentation and took the following two main factors into account: Cárceres, who originally initiated contact with me, is one of the administrators of `http://barricada.com.ni`, a Facebook-group member of the various Sandinista groups and in every other sense a supporter of the Sandinista ideology. Second, the criticism of Nicaraguan public institutions by Liberals is mostly that the Sandinistas insert their people to control them and make those who already work there participate in various Sandinista arrangements. Considering all these factors, I decided to argue for the programming of a new information system altogether controlled by Nicaragua. I used all the Sandinista ways of saying things with which I had grown familiar on the streets of León. I argued that in order to build a self-sustaining country, without any interference from the dominant imperialist powers, it was necessary to create a system which could be programmed on and extended by Nicaraguans. After the meeting, Cáceres pulled me aside and told me:

> You know, you cannot use that language everywhere around here. This time it was okay, because we know where they stand [politically], but some Liberals also work here and they are not supposed to hear that.

I was surprised, and asked Cáceres in the future to warn me when Liberals were present in the room to avoid any such problems. At the various meetings over the next eight months with different parts of the ministry, I learned the word 'Sandinista' was almost never said directly in this group

Members of the *Movimiento Renovador Sandinista* (MRS) frequently compare President José Daniel Ortega Saavedra with the Somoza dictators as part of their protests against the government.

of professionals. At best, the chief of SIMAS, Falguni Guharay, a biologist from India who came to Nicaragua in the 1980s as part of the solidarity movement and truly pro-FSLN, invoked references to the current FSLN jokingly. That happened when he did things such as telling a lady at the counter at the entrance of a government build: "I like the color of your shirt," when she wore a shirt in the pink-color which the current government uses and which is hated by a large part of Sandinistas who prefer the classic red-and-black of the 1980s. And he started meetings by saying things such as: "This system we program is situated in the Soviet Union" because the domain name we use for it is http://marx.su. These types of comically meant comments I only heard from Guharay. And they were laughed at. Adult Nicaraguans do not usually employ such humor, and younger Nicaraguans, such as students, keep it to themselves.

MRS Sandinismo

A third critical distinction between Sandinista informants seems to be whether they are FSLN or MRS affiliated. The MRS is a party started in 1994 by FSLN dissidents. This party is much better at communicating their views to western media, although they are much smaller than the FSLN (7% versus 38% in the elections of 2006), and their outreach is mainly limited to professionals and university students. Given that this target

The *Movimiento Renovador Sandinista* (MRS) protest in front of their own city headquarters at a time when they claim to lead in opinion polls in León during summer 2008.

group is rather limited in size it limits the amount the MRS could grow. The members of the MRS also claim to be Sandinistas, and often speak about their party representing the 'real' Sandinismo. At other times, they talk about those connected to the FSLN as the Sandinistas and themselves as something else. Among its members are some former *comandantes* of the FSLN, and when they started the party they were able to recruit the majority of Sandinista members of parliament, so for a short while they had more seats in parliament than the FSLN.

For the most part, I tried to seek out FSLN Sandinistas and during most of my time in Nicaragua, most of my informants belonged to that tendency. When I arrived, the political party MRS was in the process of losing their right to participate in the 2008 municipal elections, and arranged various marches in Managua, a hunger strike, and once openly confronted students at the UNAN–León. The events dominated the coverage of Nicaragua in the international news media. During that period, I maintained closer contact to the MRS office in León (see also — *The MRS protests (May - November 2008)*, p. 117) than to the FSLN.

Although I knew the percentages in the elections in 2006, I did not initially understand quite where in the socioeconomic spectrum their members were located and what potential for growth they had. They gave a clearly false impression of poll numbers ("Latest poll shows that our candidate has over 48% support here in León"), and they exaggerated the "oppression" by the FSLN. At one time, I was told the beans given out cheap through the government controlled *Empresa Nicaragüense de Alimentos Básicos* (ENABAS) would only be available to FSLN sympathizers. I was even told that I would be able to verify this easily by going to the village of Telica just outside of León. Upon closer inspection of the site in Telica, I realized this was not true. When meeting with the local MRS leader in Telica I was told: "Oh no, everybody can get it, but the beans are just very hard."

I had taken it as a given that each political party fought for a majority of votes in the popular elections. Not before I interviewed Icabalceta Garay some months into my stay, did I realize, that it may not be that simple. During the interview, Icabalceta Garay was quite critical of the FSLN and seemed to agree much with the official party line of the MRS. When I finally asked her why she did not switch to the MRS, she explained her view that there are different concepts of parties in Nicaragua:

> The MRS is a party that has drifted to the right. They don't defend the popular masses. They are convinced they are the intelligentsia and that the intelligentsia should be in charge. Very Plato-like, but for me, Plato never was the best philosopher.

I initially misunderstood the nature of the disagreement with the FSLN. By the MRS, it was always presented as an ideological struggle in which the FSLN had left behind its old roots and now only the MRS represented the 'true' cause. The ever recurring proof was the issue of 'therapeutic abortion' (abortion in case the mother's life is in danger) which was removed shortly before the 2006 elections. The MRS had been the only party in parliament who had been in favor of keeping the right in place. Upon closer inspection, the picture turned out to be quite different (see also — *Therapeutic abortion*, p. 148).

The marches organized by the MRS in 2008, which they marketed to foreigners as being about the only party in favor of a right to abortion being forbidden, in reality gathered not only MRS sympathizers, but everyone who held any grudge against the FSLN. I understood after a while, that although political demonstrations in Nicaragua are always held under the pretense of being about some concrete political issue, in the end they are in reality about FSLN Sandinistas vs. the Liberals. This was also the case this time. In this case, the Liberals thought it made sense for them to support the MRS, even though the Liberal parties voted against the therapeutic abortion right themselves. The MRS activists at all levels knew this, and the therapeutic abortion issue was only focused upon when communicating with foreigners and international media as the most crucial issue. It was not a theme of the marches in Nicaragua. I notice over the summer of 2008, that most of the militants of the MRS in León had some personal grudge against the FSLN, rather than an ideological argument against its policies. I had assumed the two were separate issues and that it would be frowned upon to combine the two. This belief was also due to the heavy influx of radical, academic terminology in the explanatory models of some MRS activists.

One prominent character of the MRS during that period was Ronald Vargon, universally known as 'the Horseman' for one of his costumes in which he rides a toy horse, while being in his late 30s or early 40s. For a while in 2008, he appeared in many newspaper articles and TV interviews in relation with the MRS protests, because he was the only adult doing street theater. The MRS paid him a modest amount during this period, and he walked around town with his toy horse, which was to symbolize something or another which neither I nor most other people I asked ever quite understood. He also played guitar on buses that were set up for protests in Managua, and he spray painted the letters 'MRS' on many downtown businesses many times in July 2008. For all his engagement against Ortega Saavedra, its source was personal hate more than a political motivation: He traveled through much of Europe and spoke French with his dog in the absence of any other French speaking person. He explained to me, that once during one of his travels he went to Cuba studying together with one of Ortega Saavedra's sons. Ortega Saavedra's son apparently always had $300 USD a month available and had lots of girls, while Vargon did not. This was his sole source of hatred of Ortega Saavedra he readily explained to me one day after I had hung around him for an extended period.

The group of MRS militants in León was rather small. Only 5–7 people would loiter around the MRS head quarters, and even these few could not agree on actual politics other than that they all hated Ortega Saavedra. I initially tried to find out what the MRS was about in terms of political demands, thinking it should be seen as just another stream of Sandinismo. By September 2008, however, when the MRS officially called for voting for the main Liberal party, the PLC, whom they hitherto had been accusing in the world press of having a pact with the FSLN to rule the country dictatorially in-between them (see also — *El pacto*, p. 149), it became clear

Ronald Vargon is present during most protests against President José Daniel Ortega Saavedra. Here, he protests the agreement Ortega Saavedra has allegedly made with former President José Arnoldo Alemán Lacayo of the *Partido Liberal Constitucionalista* (PLC) to split all power between them in the 1990s. Fall 2008 Vargon campaigns for the PLC when Alemán Lacayo and the PLC have come to an agreement with Vargon's party, the *Movimiento Renovador Sandinista* MRS, to work together in the municipal elections of 2008.

that most statements made by them were of a strategic nature. In León, Vargon explained to me, the MRS would have received five jobs in the city council, had the PLC won the local elections of that year.

Another under-communicated fact internationally is that it was the MRS who started out by officially leaving the principles of class war (Fonseca Terán 2008b) and anti-imperialism (Fonseca Terán 2008e), while the FSLN continued with the original party line. Today, the MRS accuses the FSLN simultaneously of being ultra leftist and not conducting a true revolution. They also hold that a revolution is not possible at the current stage, yet they believe they and not the FSLN carry on the legacy of the 1980s (Fonseca Terán 2010b, 2010d). The rhetoric of the MRS may seem contradictory to the outside observer, and are portrayed as such by FSLN spokesperson Fonseca Terán, yet almost never is it explained this way outside of Nicaragua.

Because the MRS-members are known for being intellectuals, I initially expected them to have more discussions about politics than what most FSLN connected youths engage in, but I found remarkably little of that. The first time I sat with a small group of them, I engaged them all in discussion, asking what they thought went wrong in the 1980s. One of them, an older and quite central gentleman, claimed the problem was that Ortega Saavedra had done all he could to upset the United States by allying with the Soviet Union and helping the *Frente Farabundo Martí para la Liberación Nacional* (FMLN) in El Salvador. At this point, I was accustomed to that Nicaraguans were used to and expected political disagreement and showing that one knew internals about Nicaraguan politics worked to my advantage when I tried to have people open up, even when they disagreed with me. So I said, that the way I had heard the story was, Ortega Saavedra first tried to go to the United States to find help before turning to the Soviet Union.

Different from what I had experienced in similar political discussions with people in the streets, this was not the start but the end of the discussion. He simply said: "Well, that's what I think." No-one else commented on it any further. I was quite astonished these political activists seemed to be much less interested in discussing politics than the general populace. After interviewing several of the older activists individually about their personal, political outlook, I understood why they could not talk about concrete politics: They simply did not agree on anything among themselves. All they had in common is that they did not like Ortega Saavedra.

Their candidate for mayor never spoke of anything concrete about what he wanted to realize when together with those working on his campaign. When I asked him about what he wanted to do in the context of an official interview, he explained that he studied marketing in the United States, and his plan was to squeeze more money out of the students who come to León from the surrounding countryside. Other MRS activists explained they were 'theoretical Marxists,' angry with the reformism that forms an inherent part of the Sandinismo of the second Ortega Saavedra government. Other MRS activists said the 'class war' against the rich, which they claimed Ortega Saavedra stood for, should be ended.

The MRS youths seem to have no idea of their own what they wanted to happen, according to some of the older MRS-people who raised points of criticism about them, when I spoke to them individually. The only two MRS activists in León who were in their 30s and 40s seemed most cynical: One of them told me a lot of the internal secrets of the group and that "of the youngsters here, there is not one who has even touched a book" and that "all [they] have in their head is just sex, sex, sex." He explained how the one girl who showed up at all their demonstrations was involved "in some sex game with her boyfriend" that involved her showing up at party headquarters all the time.

The second MRS activist in the same age range was responsible for the economics of the MRS León and before one demonstration he called me and said I should come to their headquarters immediately. I ran downtown. He explained they needed C$500 from me, because they would otherwise not be able to pay for the sound equipment for an upcoming demonstration, and that if they did not have that, their fate would likely be sealed. I later found out he told the others I donated $C30–40 for a can of spray paint and pocketed the rest. "You know he is a cocaine addict," was the explanation given to me. The internal corruption did not seem to worry anyone. The MRS activists in León may not be representative of anything beyond themselves. During those months, however, the MRS at a national level claimed León was where they had the most support. Together with their loss of license to run in national elections it meant that there was a lot of focus on the party in León by national and international media. It was even more surprising that things were so badly organized and shows how little emphasis was placed on ideological studies by the MRS, especially given that they could not even muster a single youth in the country's second biggest city interested in theoretical studies.

Concluding remarks

As shown in this chapter, the types of Sandinistas that exist are many. While the general Nicaraguan population seems terribly interested in political discussions, there are certain limits as to how political concepts are communicated. Among those with a background of higher education, this seems related to a generational disconnect between FSLN Sandinistas who have experienced the insurrection and/or the Sandinista rule of the 1980s, and those who have not experienced that time. This may be due to a period in which Sandinista politics were not discussed during the years of neoliberalism. Among professionals who work within high ranks of the state apparatus, a less direct way of communicating some political concepts is used. Third, the MRS Sandinista party, which consists mainly of people with a university background, does not talk about politics, probably due to a large number of internal differences.

A heavy contrast between the level of organization among the youths in the 1980s and now exists, but not necessarily in the initial level of political education of the majority of Sandinistas. I spoke to one of the East Germans highly active at the Wilhelm Pick school and who studied together with Nicaraguans there in the mid-1980s. He described the Nicaraguan JS of the time this way:

> It was the grand maneuver of the DDR – Nicaraguans and West Saharans were put in the same group of students who were studying at a very basic level [because they did not have that schooling from home] and in that way influenced what direction the movement went.

In the 1980s, a remarkable effort was made in spreading theoretical knowledge by the Eastern European powers. In the current period, only a limited amount of knowledge emanates from Venezuela. During my time in Nicaragua, I did not see a single instance of a student going to Venezuela. Some went to Cuba, but that was also the case in the years with neoliberal governments. The agreements with Russia include some scholarships to study in Russia, which I only hear referred to as "scholarships for the Soviet Union" with the most enthusiasm shown for them by older Sandinistas who went to study in the Soviet Union in the 1980s. If more education is employed with the JS, this may change. It seemed that in the last months of my stay, there was a stronger emphasis on ideological schooling within the

JS. This description of a generation of politically uneducated Sandinistas may, therefore, possibly only fit the first few years of the current phase of the Sandinista revolution.

Conclusion

Nicaraguans and specifically Sandinistas see Nicaragua as very central to world-history. For them, politics is a very important part of their life, and that includes more than just showing up to vote every few years – it means going on marches, working in different types of organizations and at times participating in physical confrontations. I hope this book can contribute some to the understanding of foreigners who get to know Nicaragua the first time, and who all-to-often seem to believe in a simplistic version according to which the 1980s were about honesty and communism and the current period is only about corruption and a president turned caudillo.

In short we could summarize the findings of this books this way: In Nicaragua, historical agency tends to be interpreted as residing in Nicaraguan hands both in the past and currently. In many occasions, views from outside of Nicaragua would instead likely identify some historical agency which is foreign and which has influenced Nicaraguan reality. Additionally there is a marked difference between the interpretation by different Nicaraguan groups of symbolic-political acts. The economical plans and realities that existed during the time of past regimes which different groups of Nicaraguans still identify with, are each judged according to their own criteria. The criteria that are used to judge the success any particular regime oftentimes cross these different groups. Similarly, support for a particular types of economic policy goes across political groups. Whereas Sandinismo internationally may be seen as synonymous with a certain type of socialist planning and the opposition with free-market capitalism, the differences in economic preferences among those identifying with opposing political groups is not as sharp. What economic policies one proposes or economic class one belongs to does not seem to be directly linked with political affiliation, although the *Frente Sandinista de Liberación Nacional* (FSLN) is the party that most directly addresses the poorer layers of society. The difference in how regimes in the past are judged is related to whether one looks at the actual existing economic reality during its time, or whether one focuses on what plans for economic development a given government had. The second view provides for the history of a certain government to be seen as positive, even though their proposed goal never materializes. This is specifically true for the FSLN government of the 1980s.

The development of Sandinista political activities takes place constantly, and to a high degree are either the response to, or of the origin of international involvement. The repertoire of Sandinista activities is wide-ranging and mostly a collective process is involved, not exclusively controlled by one entity such as the President. Society may be more fragmented than in the 1980s because more smaller independent groups exist, each of which have a unique view of things. At the same time, family relations have in recent years often been stronger than the will to take individual choices, if we are to believe the older Sandinistas.

The Sandinista perspective of world politics is unique. This is at least in part due to the unique historical past of Nicaragua and the Sandinista movement. It is this particular Nicaraguan history, connected with Nicaraguan understandings of global geo-politics, and the dynamics of leftist groups in power, which mean that Nicaragua seems to have other options available than other countries that in economic terms seem rather similar. It seems Nicaraguans have developed a particular type of understanding of freedom of historical agency, which is compatible with most basic points of Dependency Theory, even if such theoretical points are made much less now than in the 1980s.

One possible interpretation of Dependency Theory leads to a world view which effectively makes any historical agency for individuals impossible. Actors within countries such as Nicaragua, which is peripheral and does not produce anything of considerable importance, cannot possibly influence their own situation. This is not the view that most Sandinistas seem to have, at least not about many issues. The understanding that exists within Sandinismo in relation to Dependency, although not formulated explicitly, seems for a long time to have followed the line of the Egyptian Dependency Theorist Samir Amin. In most of his writings, he expresses a believe in the possibility of changing the current worldwide setup fundamentally, and his analysis generally end with a call for action, directed towards third world countries. His view of the trajectory of third world socialists changed in recent decades. In *Class and nation* Amin declared autonomous capitalism in the countries of the periphery is impossible. Therefore, the national liberation movements should be seen as part of the development of socialism on a world scale rather than part of regional development of capitalism (Amin 1980, 131). Ten years later, in The social movements in the periphery, he declared the national liberation fronts' dead with their promise of nothing beyond national independence not being enough for the masses of the south, who feel everyday exploitation by capitalism (Amin 1990, 97–98). Another 14 years later, in *The liberal virus*, he called for renewed politicization in the global South and the building of new Internationals and creating links with Europe to organize against the 'neo-nazis' in the United States government Amin (2004).

Similarly in 1980, the Sandinistas had great hopes of achieving socialism with the help of the FSLN. By 1990, they had lost the hope they would achieve much of anything at the government level, and instead involved themselves in various social struggles. After the turn of the millennium, once again the belief in leftist internationalism grew. The view expressed by Amin in 2004 did not spell out what possibilities for historical agency existed in the current historical phase, in which the national liberation front FSLN did not disappear as predicted and instead is back in power with the backing of other third world countries rather than the Soviet Union and without having turned entirely into a system-abiding party. What limits for political changes and maneuvers exist today, seems to be something that is being discovered in everyday practice, not only be the government, but by many smaller groups of Sandinistas. There does not seem to exist the same type of theoretical framework such as that upon which Carlos Fonseca Amador and the Sandinistas before 1979 used to legitimize their revolutionary project and argue for its viability. Even though material development indicators largely have improved since the 1980s, the United States seems less likely to intervene militarily due to its other obligations, and the material foundation in terms of computational power and the skills to development advanced web applications that could accommodate a planned economy at least of some aspects in some sectors is present in Nicaragua as the project of creating a national information system for the *Ministerio Agropecuario y Forestal* (MAGFOR) showed, there seems to be a general consensus among most Sandinistas—possibly with the exception of some of their intellectual leaders—that they no longer see it as viable to create an economic system markedly different from capitalism as it exists everywhere else in the immediate future. This can likely at least in part be attributed to the disappearance of the Soviet bloc and possibly also as a long-term reaction to the war of the 1980s.

It cannot be said for certain where the Sandinista movement will go, although I try to make some guesses below. The movement is not a democratic-centralist political party as what is common many places in Europe, in which an internal democratic process regulates the forming of most party-endorsed policies, nor is it a small cheerleader-group around President José Daniel Ortega Saavedra. Instead, it is a network of semi-independent groups of various sizes, with some overlap of personnel. The determination of Sandinista policy happens in an ad-hoc fashion. When conflicts exist, these are played out in the open in Nicaraguan daily life, and at times reach the point of physical fights. This structure seems to allow for extreme broad participation in political processes for people from very different backgrounds, including economical class and age.

Possibly due to this difference in structure that I had not anticipated, the question of whether there is pressure for radical change from below on Ortega Saavedra or whether the Sandinistas are a radicalized elite that try to impose radical policy on the population against the population did not seem as relevant. The pressure on Ortega Saavedra that exists does not originate from only one direction. While it is true that many of the policies of the current government were drafted by urban professionals, such as those relating to poverty reduction, other policies, such as those maneuvering around the question of therapeutic abortion, seem to be unpopular first and foremost among these same urban professionals. The totality of all government policies seems to be a compromise of the different groups that together make up the Sandinista movement.

Developments since...

Since I left Nicaragua in September 2009, some important things have occurred. The two most important issues are:

In October 2009, the *Corte Suprema de Justicia* (CSJ) decided the constitutional restrictions against reelections were in conflict with the right of equality before the law to stand as a candidate and be elected to public office. The restrictions against reelections had not been part of the original constitution of 1987 and were added through constitutional reform in 1995 (Púlsar 2009; ANN 1987, 2005). This was the period when the *Frente Sandinista de Liberación Nacional* (FSLN) temporarily had lost most of its members of the *Asamblea Nacional* to the newly established *Movimiento Renovador Sandinista* (MRS). The court also considered similar decisions that permitted reelections in Colombia and Costa Rica in recent years (EP 2009). The opposition, and specifically the MRS, has since claimed this is simply a first move to establish a lifetime dictatorship by President José Daniel Ortega Saavedra (Potosme 2011) and have openly asked for the military to intervene in a way that can be interpreted as a call for a military overthrow (Silva 2010). Opinion polls half a year before the presidential elections to be held on 6 November 2011 started showing that Ortega Saavedra would win a landslide victory (Radio La Primerísima 2011) and that picture has not changed since.

In Honduras an agreement was reached in May 2011 between President Porfirio 'Pepe' Lobo Sosa, elected in November 2009 in elections arranged by the coup d'etat regime, on one side and former President José Manuel Zelaya Rosales and the *Frente Nacional de Resistencia Popular* (FNRP) on the other side. The agreement allowed for Zelaya Rosales and his supporters to return to Honduras from exile, the formal recognition of the FNRP as an organization by state institutions to be permitted to participate in elections and the formal recognition of the principles of human rights. After Zelaya Rosales returned to Honduras on 28 May 2011, Honduras was readmitted to the *Organization of American States* (OAS) with the vote of Nicaragua, and against the no-vote of Ecuador with Venezuela abstaining. The representatives of Ecuador claimed a state of democracy had not been reestablished in Honduras yet and readmitting the country would represent a 'dangerous precedent' (Canales 2011). Some Honduran activists who campaigned against the coup d'etat, with whom I continued to be in contact over the Internet, also claimed the state of human rights in Honduras was not likely to change with this agreement signed. Nicaraguan FSLN activist were angry that during the same week Rosales Zelaya was readmitted into Honduras, the Nicaraguan opposition, mainly through the organization *Unión Nicaragüense Americana* (UNA) with a seat in Miami and supported by various inner-Nicaraguan opposition groups such as the *Movimiento por Nicaragua* (MpN), organized a 'forum' in the Managua Holiday Inn hotel with the title 'Antidote to the Socialism of the 21st Century' on 26 May 2011, which had as one of its speakers via Internet, Roberto Micheletti Baín, the Honduran politician who took charge as 'de-facto president' when Rosales Zelaya was removed (Flores 2011).

...and into the future

If there are no major changes in the next few years ahead, Nicaragua seems to be slowly bur surely improving according to most development indicators. This development has sped up during the current government, but even before that, during the times of Liberal governments, a marked improvement in several indicators could be measured. This realization goes somewhat counter to both sides in Nicaraguan, who generally like to claim that the country went to hell during the time the other governments of other parties were in charge.

I think from this one can conclude various things, although it is impossible to predict precisely where Nicaragua will be in just a few years. Currently four different scenarios seem most probable to me:

- The Sandinistas may stay in power for a long time with an administration of some social justice policies and otherwise build upon models of capitalist expansion. This may actually work in bettering living standards for most Nicaraguans for a while. If the necessary stability and guaranteed infrastructure is provided, a positive investment climate at a local level may arise even though capitalism at a world scale is in a slump. Tourism may shift from more expensive locations such as Costa Rica to Nicaragua. Many Nicaraguans seem to have an extreme faith in being able to advance by selling something or other at a world-scale. This would obviously not be a model adaptable by other countries, as it would rely on business shifting from other places to Nicaragua. Also, some of the faith in world-capitalism that some Sandinistas and other Nicaraguans have, seems somewhat misplaced, and the debt to the *International Monetary Fund* (IMF) and others Nicaragua is building up again seems frightening. In the worst case scenario, the FSLN could indeed turn into another *Partido Revolucionario Institucional* (PRI). Let's not forget that some of the greatest revolutionary advances celebrated in Mexico today came not at the beginning, but rather some decades into the revolution, with Lázaro Cárdenas (1934–40).

- The Sandinistas could also stay in power and turn to a more radical course after taking over the majority of parliament or after they feel they have built up sufficient independent energy production, infrastructure, etc. Also President Hugo Chavez of Venezuela did not nationalize big industry before several years into his government period. Given the size of the Nicaraguan economy and the continued dependence on foreign aid to pay for part of the national budget, this would be a difficult situation. If, in addition, the United States continues to have military personnel stationed both north and south of Nicaragua, in Costa Rica and Honduras who both could cut off all trade routes, then not even Russia or Venezuela may be able to help Nicaragua. If it is done as part of a larger plan in which more South American countries participate, then it may have better chances for success. If the Sandinistas want to nationalize, why have they not said that until now? One of the lessons they may have learned from the 1980s is that nationalizations have to happen immediately and swift and not be pre-announced. If nationalizations are announced on beforehand, the owners will only try to find out how to move money out of the company and neglect reinvestments, as what the case with the *Ingenio San Antonio* (ISA) in the 1980s. Although much of Sandinista politics is done with different levels of secrecy and trickery, due to the character of Sandinismo and the fact that it entails mass participation, any such secrets are always likely to leak out to a certain degree. Planning something like nationalizing major businesses would likely have to happen without any chance of the plans leaking, and would, therefore, have to be a decision of only Ortega Saavedra and a few personal advisers. Such a move may anger many Sandinistas, because they would feel they were not involved.

- Another possibility may be the Liberal opposition and the secret services of the United States stage some kind of coup or civil war. The actions around the municipal elections of 2008 looked frighteningly similar to what happened in Chile 1970–73. Yet somehow this did not transform into a coup. The question is – why not? The intent of the Nicaraguan opposition seemed pretty clear that they wanted to provoke something like this. Maybe the US administration was just hesitant to get involved too deeply in Nicaragua. Maybe their analysis was that opposition leaders did not have the popular support necessary to stage a coup. What we know is that 1.5 years later the US administration staged/permitted a coup in Honduras. Should the United States ever decide to stage something similar in

Nicaragua, it would surely be disastrous and would be a setback. At times, it seems that some opposition groups do not quite realize what they would be inviting. If the Liberals indeed would be put back into power with extensive military deployment in Nicaragua or with the cooperation of some local military force, then it will not be the same as Nicaragua before 2007. The amount of Sandinistas is large, and similar to Chile, the only way to prevent them from taking the country back physically would be harsh repression. Different from Chile, the Nicaraguan military is known to be very loyal to the Sandinistas. But whether that will always remain that way is questionable. If enough of them determine that President Ortega Saavedra's reelection in 2011 is unconstitutional, then this may look quite different.

- A last likely possibility would be the growth of a democratic opposition. The current opposition is not democratic because it seeks to gain power through all types of means other than winning in open elections – intervention by the United States, military coup, etc. In fact, the main problem as far as lack of democracy goes in current Nicaragua, seems not to be that opposition parties are not allowed to spread their propaganda, but that just about everything said by the opposition is part of some grand trickery scheme. There seems to be a complete lack of ideology and the opposition parties do not present a coherent alternative to the government policies of the Sandinistas.

If the FSLN stays in power, the inner-party democracy of the FSLN will obviously be an issue for all Nicaraguans. If Ortega Saavedra ends up as president for 40 years, the way some older informants of mine have said they hoped, it will be justified to talk of caudillismo. The criticism that comes concerning this now from the west is rather silly, given that very few of them limited their leaders to only sit for 5 years, and that in practice major players such as United Kingdom and Germany have seen heads of governments sit for over a decade even in recent years. Ortega Saavedra never was allowed to single-handedly pick all members of CSJ and *Consejo Supremo Electoral* (CSE). The FSLN never since 1990 had such a majority that it could have done that by itself. When the members of these two institutions who were sent there by the Liberals chose to vote in favor of accepting a reelection, I can only see three possible reasons: Possibly they are corrupt and sold themselves to the FSLN. Another possibility is that the FSLN managed to trick the Liberals into thinking some candidate was a Liberal when really he was a Sandinista. Alternatively the FSLN Sandinistas were correct in their assessment of the legal situation, the prohibition of running twice was indeed unconstitutional, and the protests by the opposition are just made to instigate problems for the government. None of these cases look very good for the opposition.

The most important conclusion I have reached is at least for now Nicaragua is a country with an extremely high amount of freedom of speech – not matched by any other country known to me. The great number of people willing to volunteer information for this book—many times without knowing me or anything about me, immediately ready to say exactly what they thought of their government—was quite impressive. Sure, many of them were somewhat concerned with how they themselves would look. But whether the government liked what they said almost never seemed to be an issue. That is something I have not experienced in any First World country of the world.

What is to be done?

It is seldom clear how an anthropological study can be useful for those involved in a certain social constellation more than giving the informants who read a study access to information about how their views and the perspectives of those they live and work with which they otherwise would not have had access to.

Another aspect studies of revolutionary movements in Third World countries may be useful for is the secret services and general intelligence communities of First World countries who seek to quell these movements. While I believe I have found quite a lot of information which may be interesting to these, I have tried to write around this material and not include anything of value harmful to the Sandinista movement.

Over the almost 4 years I worked on this project (2007–11), I had ample opportunity to speak with Sandinistas at different levels and of different types (FSLN and MRS) and have continuously tried to contribute with my analysis and criticism based upon the great amount of interviews and informal conversations I had with Nicaraguans. The value of this study writing process for the Sandinista movement I believe lies mainly in these comments which various decision makers can react to if they so desire.

Glossary

AC - The *Alternativa por el Cambio* (Alternative for Change) is a small Nicaraguan party which in the 2011 elections was one of several small parties that formed part of an alliance led by the *Frente Sandinista de Liberación Nacional* (FSLN).

ALBA - The *Alternativa Bolivariana para los pueblos de nuestra América* (Bolivarian Alternative for the people of our America) is an alternative trade- and cultural network between Nicaragua, Cuba, Venezuela, Ecuador, Bolivia, Antigua and Barbuda, the Commonwealth of Dominica and Saint Vincent and the Grenadines.

Albanisa - *ALBA de Nicaragua, S.A.* (ALBA of Nicaragua) is a Nicaraguan privately held company that handles the Nicaraguan side of the economic parts of the *Alternativa Bolivariana para los pueblos de nuestra América* (ALBA) agreement. Government-critics claim that this is a major source of enrichment of the leadership of the *Frente Sandinista de Liberación Nacional* (FSLN). Pro-government commentators often claim that *Albanisa* has been set up to circumvent the Liberal majority in parliament and restrictions set by the *International Monetary Fund* (IMF) on the use of public funds.

ALN - The *Alianza Liberal Nicaragüense* (Liberal Nicaraguan Alliance) is a Liberal party formed in 2005 by Eduardo Montealegre Rivas and other members of the *Partido Liberal Constitucionalista* (PLC) who were in disagreement with the leadership of the PLC.

AMNLAE - The *Asociación de Mujeres Nicaragüenes Luisa Amanda Espinoza* (Association of Nicaraguan Women Luisa Amanda Espinoza) is a famous Sandinista women organization.

ATC *Asociación de Trabajadores del Campo* (Association of Rural Workers)

BANIC *Banco Nicaragüense de Industria y Comercio* (Nicaraguan Bank of Industry and Commerce)

BD - The *Banca Democratica* (Democratic Bench) was formed by Eduardo Montealegre Rivas after the 2008 municipal elections. Montealegre had run as a candidate for the *Partido Liberal Constitucionalista* (PLC) but decided to form his own fraction in the national parliament and city council of Managua after the elections.

BIS - The *Bank for International Settlements* is an international bank that controls loans to central banks.

BRD - The *Bundesrepublik Deutschland* (Federal Republic of Germany) was the official name of West Germany until 1990, since then the official name of the entire current German state.

C$ - See *Cordoba*.

caudillo - A *caudillo* (strong-man) is a term used to describe a type of political-military leader in Latin America. Caudillos are authoritarian and they are often seen as a father-figure by the public.

CDSs - The *Comités de Defensa Sandinista* (Committee for Defense of Sandinismo) were an organization in the 1980s which formed local committees in neighborhoods of all of Nicaragua during the 1980s which aimed to hinder Contras from sabotage. Critics claim that it at times acted like the East German *Staatssicherheit* (StaSi).

CEPAL - The *Comisión Económica para América Latina y el Caribe* (Economic Commission for Latin America and the Caribbean) is a United Nations Institution that is known for its adoption of *Dependency Theory* in the years after the *Second World War* (WWII).

CIA - The *Central Intelligence Agency* is an agency of the US government which aims to collect foreign intelligence.

CIPRES - The *Centro para la Promoción, la Investigación y el Desarollo Rural y Social* (Center for Promotion, Investigation and Rural and Social Development) is an NGO which has worked close with the current *Frente Sandinista de Liberación Nacional* government in designing several of its agriculture-related policies. CIPRES is allegedly mainly comprised of Sandinistas who stopped working in the state after the 1990-elections.

CLSs - The *Consejos de Liderazgo Sandinista* (Sandinista Leadership Councils) make out the lowest level of leadership within the *Frente Sandinista de Liberación Nacional*. CLSs can be found in neighborhoods all throughout the country.

CMEA - The *Council of Mutual Economic Assistance* was the economic network of the Soviet Union and its allies.

CONPES - The *Consejo Nacional de Planificación Económica y Social* (National Council for Economic and Social Planning) is a Nicaraguan government institution.

Contras - The *Contras* (Counter-revolutionary) is a term that designates all the groups who took up arms against the Sandinista-dominated government in the 1980s. Nowadays former *Contras* more often use the term *Resistencia* about themselves.

Cordoba is the official currency of Nicaragua. The exchange rate to the *US Dollar* has been around 20:1 in the period 2007–11.

CPCs - The *Consejos de Poder Ciudadano* (Councils for Citizen Power) make out an organization which aims to organize direct democracy in Nicaragua. It was started by President José Daniel Ortega Saavedra of the *Frente Sandinista de Liberación Nacional* (FSLN) in 2007.

CPoC - The *Communist Party of China* has been the ruling party of the *People's Republic of China*, the larger of the two Chinas, since 1949. It bears the name 'communist' for historic reasons. Very few radicals outside of China see it as representing a program that would lead toward communism.

CSE - The *Consejo Supremo Electoral* (Highest Election Council) is a Nicaraguan government institution which organizes elections.

CSJ *Corte Suprema de Justicia* (Highest Court of Justice)

CUUN–León *Centro Universitario de la Universidad Nacional–León* (University Center of the National University, León)

CW - The *Cold War* was the military stalemate between the Soviet Union and its allies with the United States in its allies in the period between the end of the *Second World War* (WWII) in 1945, and the *Fall of the Berlin Wall* in 1989.

DDR - The *Deutsche Demokratische Republik* (German Democratic Republic) was East Germany, the Soviet-allied part of Germany during the time of the *Cold War* (CW) up until 1990.

DN - *Disnorte* is one of two companies that *Unión Fenosa, S.A.* created in order to bid for the administration of the Nicaraguan electricity net.

DR-CAFTA - The *Dominican Republic-Central American Free Trade Agreement* is a free trade agreement between the United States and Guatemala, El Salvador, Nicaragua, Honduras Costa Rica and the Dominican Republic. Nicaragua joined the DR-CAFTA in 2006.

DS - *Dissur* is one of two companies that *Union Fenosa, S.A.* created in order to bid for the administration of the Nicaraguan electricity net.

ENABAS - The *Empresa Nicaragüense de Alimentos Básicos* (Nicaraguan Company for Basic Food Items) is a state-owned company used in the 1980s to organize cheap food for poor Nicaraguans in times of crisis. It is again used by the current government.

EPZ - An *Export Production Zone* is an area which is regulated by special laws (unfavorable to labor unions) and with specially low tax codes. EPZs have in recent years been established in many third world countries with the aim to bring cash to the country.

FADCANIC - The *Fundación para la Autonomía y el Desarollo de la Costa Atlántica de Nicaragua* (Foundation for the Autonomy and Development of the Atlantic coast of Nicaragua) is an NGO that works with development projects on the Nicaraguan Atlantic coast.

FDJ - The *Freie Deutsche Jugend* (Free German Youth) was the socialist youth organization of the *Deutsche Demokratische Republik* (DDR)

FIDEG - The *Fundación Internacional para el Desafío Económico Global* (International Foundation for the Global Economic Challenges) is a Nicaraguan NGO formed in 1990. It has a self-declared goal of creating alternative economic development plans for Nicaragua that focus upon combining economic growth with diminishing economic differences and keeping in mind questions of democracy, gender and the environment. The annual study on economic development and poverty FIDEG has published in 2010 and 2011 were financed through Dutch and Swiss aid.

first world - See *third world*.

FLN - The *Frente de Liberación Nacional* (National Liberation Front) was the name of the of *Frente Sandinista de Liberación Nacional* (FSLN) 1961-63.

FMLN - The *Frente Farabundo Martí para la Liberación Nacional* (Farabundo Martí National Liberation Front) is a sister-party of the *Frente Sandinista de Liberación Nacional* (FSLN) in El Salvador.

foco strategy - The *foco strategy* (focus strategy) is a strategy that originated with Ernesto Guevara and the Cuban revolution. Its concern was how to organize for a revolution. Instead of waiting to start an insurrection until one had organized a large amount of factory workers in the cities to be able to confront the military and political leadership of the country through the mass of people involved, instead the strategy stated that one should initially attack in certain strategic points with small and mobile paramilitary guerrilla units. These attacks should then develop into the 'focus' of the movement of discontent with the regime among the general population. The way the strategy seems to have been understood a lot of places, including Nicaragua at least initially, was that attacks needed to be organized and launched from the countryside.

FSLN - The *Frente Sandinista de Liberación Nacional* (Sandinista National Liberation Front) has been the main Sandinista party since 1963.

GDP - The *Gross Domestic Product* is the market value of all final goods and services produced within a country in a given period.

GN - The *Guardia Nacional* (National Guard) was the Nicaraguan military that was trained by the United States in the late 1920s and upon which the Somoza dictatorship built it strength until 1979.

GNI - The *Gross National Income* is the *Gross Domestic Product* (GDP), plus income received from abroad, minus payments made to receivers abroad within a certain period.

GP - The *Grupo Pellas* (Pellas Group) is the collection of businesses belonging to one of the richest Nicaraguan families.

GPP - The *Guerra Popular Prolongada* (Prolonged Popular War) was one of three ideological tendencies within the Sandinista movement of the later 1970s which emphasized the need to organize peasant farmers.

ICJ - The *International Court of Justice* in Den Haag, Netherlands is the main judicial part of the United Nations and its decisions are in theory binding.

IDB - The *Inter-American Development Bank* is a bank that has given multilateral loans to countries in the Caribbean and Latin America since 1959.

IEEPA The *International Emergency Economic Powers Act* is a 1977 US law which gives the US President the right to regulate commerce in the case of an emergency.

IES - The *Instituto de Estudio del Sandinismo* (Institute for the Study of Sandinismo) was an institute that existed in the 1980s and which had an aim of investigating and documenting everything available related to Augusto Nicolás Calderón Sandino.

IMF - The *International Monetary Fund* is a bank that gives multilateral loans which is known for its harsh conditions of privatization towards indebted countries.

INIFOM - The *Instituto Nicaragüense de Fomento Municipal* (Nicaraguan Institute for Municipal Development) is an institute whose mission it is to aid local governments in achieving development and independence.

INSS *Instituto Nicaragüense de Seguridad Social* (Nicaraguan Institute for Social Security)

ISA - The *Ingenio San Antonio* (San Antonio Plant) is Nicaragua's largest sugar plantation, which belongs to *Nicaragua Sugar Estates Limited* which in turn is part of the *Grupo Pellas* (GP).

JS - The *Juventud Sandinista* (Sandinista Youth) is the youth organization of the FSLN.

latifundio - A *latifundio* is a large farm of over 500 hectares. It is part of a very common structure of agriculture in Latin America.

MAGFOR - The *Ministerio Agropecuario y Forestal* (Ministry of Agriculture and Forestry) has been the name of the ministry dealing with agriculture since 1998. It underwent many administrative changes for the past 4 decades.

MCCA - The *Mercado Común Centroamericano* (Common Central American Market) is a 1960 trade agreement between Guatemala, Honduras, El Salvador, Nicaragua and Costa Rica. The market was in part non-operational during the 1980s.

MICE - The *Ministerio de Comercio Exterior* (Ministry of Foreign Trade) was given responsibilities to control foreign trade during the 1980s.

MINED *Ministerio de Educación* (Ministry of Education)

minifundio - A *minifundio* is a small farm of under 5 hectares. It is part of a very common structure of agriculture in Latin America.

MINSA *Ministerio de Salud* (Ministry of Health)

MpN - The *Movimiento por Nicaragua* (Movement for Nicaragua) is a right-wing NGO that organizes protest marches under the banner 'pro-democracy' as they claim that the current government is anti-democratic.

MpRS - The *Movimiento por el Rescate del Sandinismo* (Movement for Rescue of Sandinismo) is a group of Sandinistas who are not happy with the control of President José Daniel Ortega Saavedra of the *Frente Sandinista de Liberación Nacional* (FSLN). During the years 2006–09, they formed an alliance with or were part of the *Movimiento Renovador Sandinista* (MRS). Different from the MRS, the members of the MpRS have a goal of taking power in the FSLN. They are seen as standing to the left of the MRS in economic questions.

MRS - The *Movimiento Renovador Sandinista* (Movement for Sandinista Renovation) is a political party formed in 1994 which has given up on class-war as part of its program and sees itself in a tradition with European social democratic parties. It claims to be more democratic than the *Frente Sandinista de Liberación Nacional* (FSLN) and to be in favor of the establishment of a right of *therapeutic abortion*.

NGO - *Non-governmental organization* is a term usually used for organizations if they work on a nonprofit basis and do some work that under other circumstances could have been done by a government entity.

OEP - The *Oficina de Ética Pública* (Office of Public Ethics) is a government institution which aims to monitor corruption within the public sector.

PDVSA - *Petróleos de Venezuela, S. A.* (Petroleum of Venezuela) is the state-owned oil company of Venezuela.

Petrocaribe is a treaty between countries of the Caribbean, South America and Central America, all of which are accessible by water, with Venezuela to collaborate on energy issues and obtain oil at discounted prices. *Petrocaribe* has some different members than the *Alternativa Bolivariana para los pueblos de nuestra América* (ALBA) and membership seems to have less ideological implications than what membership of the ALBA means. At times, there seems to be some confusion as to which treaty is being used between countries with dual membership in ALBA and *Petrocaribe*. Current members of *Petrocaribe* are Antigua and Barbuda, Honduras, Bahamas, Jamaica, Belice, Nicaragua, Cuba, Dominican Republic, The Commonwealth of Dominica, San Cristobal and Nieves, Granada, San Vicente and the Granadinas, Guatemala, Santa Lucía, Guyana, Suriname, Haiti and Venezuela.

PLC - The *Partido Liberal Constitucionalista* (Liberal Constitutionalist Party) has been the main Liberal parties since the late 1990s.

PLI - The *Partido Liberal Independiente* (Independent Liberal Party) is a Liberal party which is mostly known for having been formed in opposition to the Somoza-regime in 1944. Eduardo Montealegre Rivas called for his supporters to join this party after the 2008 municipal elections.

PPP Int. $ - *International Dollars* are not a real currency. It is a measurement used by international organizations. The value of 1 PPP Int. $

in any country is defined as the amount of local currencies that has the same purchasing power as USD1$ in the United States(WHO 2005).

PRI - The *Partido Revolucionario Institucional* (Institutional Revolutionary Party) is a party in Mexico which held the presidency between the 1930s and the year 2000. It is known amongst leftists as a political party which started as idealistic and radical and ended as corrupt and conservative.

PRN - The *Partido Resistencia Nicaragüense* (Party of the Nicaraguan Resistance) is a party which represents those who were *Contras* in the 1980s.

PSN - The *Partido Socialista Nicaragüense* (Nicaraguan Socialist Party) was up to the founding of the *Frente Sandinista de Liberación Nacional* (FSLN) the party of most Nicaraguan radicals. During this period, it held contact with the Soviet Union and several of the later members of the FSLN started their political career in the PSN. During the 1979 insurrection, parts of the FSLN cooperated with PSN. In 1990, the PSN formed part of the anti-Sandinista opposition group *Unidad Nicaragüense Opositora* (UNO).

RAAN - The *Región Autónoma del Atlántico Norte* (Autonomous Region of the Atlantic, North) is a region bordering the northern part of the Atlantic coast which enjoys certain rights of political autonomy from the administration in Managua. It was established in 1986, but the autonomy has not been respected at all times since.

RAAS - The *Región Autónoma del Atlántico Sur* (Autonomous Region of the Atlantic, South) is a region bordering the mid-southern Atlantic coast which enjoys certain rights of political autonomy from the administration in Managua. It was established in 1986, but the autonomy has not been respected at all times since.

Resistencia (Resistance) is another term for *Contras*, preferred by many former Contra fighters.

revolution - See *Sandinista revolution*.

revolutionary insurrection - The *revolutionary insurrection* is Sandinista terminology the war between Sandinistas and Somoza's forces up to the point of the *triumph of the revolution*. See also *Sandinista revolution*.

rotonda (roundabout) - The roundabouts of Managua were constructed in the 1990s and have obtained strategic importance for political groups who try to control the capital physically.

Sandinista revolution - The *Sandinista revolution* has in the Sandinista view gone on since the start of the Sandinista movement. The start is put somewhere after 1961 and before 1979 and a lot, but not all, Sandinistas see the revolution as still continuing. Those who do not see it as still going on, mostly believe that the revolution ended in the later 1980s or with the electoral defeat in 1990. The Sandinista understanding of this term is at times contrary to the terminology used by many foreigners, who use it only to define the actions in the year 1979 that led to the overthrow of the Somoza dictatorship and up to the point of Sandinista take-over. The point of take-over of power is in the Sandinista terminology called the *triumph of the revolution*. The war between Sandinistas and Somoza regime are called the *revolutionary insurrection*. I have chosen to stick to the terms as they are used by those Sandinistas who see the revolution as still in process.

SAP - *Structural Adjustment Programs* are programs by the *International Monetary Fund* (IMF) that are to govern the politics of indebted countries. SAPs are notorious for ordering privatizations of publicly owned goods.

SED - The *Sozialistische Einheitspartei Deutschlands* (Socialist Unity Party of Germany) was a party governing the *Deutsche Demokratische Republik* (DDR) until 1990. The SED was started by Communists and Social-democrats after the *Second World War* (WWII).

SIMAS - *Servicio de Información Mesoamericano sobre Agricultura Sostenible* (Mesoamerican Information Service about Sustainable Agriculture) is a Managua-based NGO advising about sustainable agriculture and the use of open source software to aid the agriculture sector.

StaSi - The *Staatssicherheit* (State Security) was the secret police of the *Deutsche Demokratische Republik* (DDR). The StaSi is mainly known for its policies of excessive spying on the population of the DDR, which created an overall climate of distrust.

therapeutic abortion is abortion in case only either the life of the mother or the fetus can be saved. A right for abortion under these circumstances existed for 100 years in the Nicaraguan constitution until it was removed in 2006.

third world - The *third world* was originally part of much-used model that divided of the world of countries that belonged to the *first world*, which were relatively rich and allied with the United States; countries that belonged to the *second world*, which were part of or very close allies of the Soviet Union and somewhat wealthy; and third world countries, which were formally not allied with either one of the two blocks and very poor. There are, however, some parts that are unclear about this – for example Nicaragua was allied with first the United States and then the Soviet Union, yet was at all times categorized as part of the third world. Cuba on the, other hand, was seen as part of the second world. Since the end of the of the Soviet Union, the concept has been even less clear. In much of Latin America, there is an understanding that all Latin American countries are part of a less developed third world, and that western European countries and the United States make out the first world. Additionally some argue that Africa represents a fourth world of countries that are not developing. There seems to be no clear understanding as to whether a second world still exists and what countries would belong to it.

TP - The *Tendencia Proletaria* (Proletarian Tendency) was one of three ideological tendencies within the Sandinista movement of the later 1970s which emphasized the need to organize factory workers.

triumph of the revolution - The *triumph of the revolution* is in Sandinista terminology the point when the Somoza regime was defeated by Sandinistas in summer 1979. See also *Sandinista revolution*.

TT - The *Tendencia Tercerista* (Third [Way] Tendency) was one of three ideological tendencies within the Sandinista movement of the later 1970s which emphasized the need to organize across class divides and for acting rather than studying theories.

UABJO *Universidad Autónoma "Benito Juárez" de Oaxaca* ("Benito Juárez" Autonomous University of Oaxaca)

UCA - The *Universidad Centroamericana* (Central American University) is the most famous private university of Managua. The UCA receives public funding.

UdeM León *Universidad de Managua, León* (University of Managua, León campus)

UF - The *Unión Fenosa, S.A.* is a Spanish company which has a contract to run the Nicaraguan electricity net. The UF is universally hated by Nicaraguans who claim that the UF has been shying away from necessary investments in order to make a larger profit.

UNAG *Unión Nacional de Agricultores y Ganaderos* (National Union of Farmers and Ranchers)

UNA The *Unión Nicaragüense Americana* is a right-wing organization operating out of Miami.

UNAN - The *Universidad Nacional Autónoma de Nicaragua* (National Autonomous University of Nicaragua) is the most prestigious public university in Nicaragua.

UNAN–León - The *Universidad Nacional Autónoma de Nicaragua, León* (National Autonomous University of Nicaragua, León campus) is the unit of the Universidad Nacional Autónoma de Nicaragua in León. The UNAN–León enjoys certain institutional independence from the main university in Managua.

UNEN - The *Unión Nacional de Estudiantes de Nicaragua* (National Student Union of Nicaragua) is the central organization representing all Nicaraguan students.

UNESCO *United Nations Education, Science and Culture Organization*

United States is a short form of *United States of America*.

United States American as an adjective means something pertaining to the *United States of America*. It can also mean citizen of the *United States of America*. This is a term I have decided to use myself as the term mostly used, 'American,' is confusing in that it may also denote the inhabitants of all the Americas or things related to any part of the Americas.

UNO - The *Unidad Nicaragüense Opositora* (United Nicaraguan Opposition) was an electoral alliance of 14 parties, mostly from the political right, who won the 1990 presidential elections.

USC - The *US Congress* is the parliament of the United States, consisting of the two chambers *US House of Representatives* (USHR) and the *US Senate*.

USD - The *US Dollar* is the official currency of the *United States of America*. It is extensively used in Central America. El Salvador uses the USD as official currency. In Nicaragua, professionals, as well as others with high income, oftentimes receive their wages in USD rather than the national currency *Cordoba*.

USD05 are USD adjusted for inflation to 2005 levels, using the *US Urban Consumer Price Index* (USCPI-U).

USHR - The *US House of Representatives* is one of two chambers of the *US Congress* (USC). Elections are separate from elections for *President of the United States*, and at times some political disagreement exists between the two.

USCPI-U - The *US Urban Consumer Price Index* is a measure of inflation for all urban consumers in the US. Official statistics over the USPCI-U are released annually by the *US Department of Labor, Bureau of Labor Statistics*.

VcE - *Vamos con Eduardo* (Let's go with Eduardo) is a supporter group around Eduardo Montealegre Rivas, the 2006 presidential candidate of the *Alianza Liberal Nicaragüense* (ALN) and 2008 candidate for mayor of Managua of the *Partido Liberal Constitucionalista* (PLC) who after the 2008 formed the *Banca Democratica* (BD) amongst city council members and then asked his supporters to join the *Partido Liberal Independiente* (PLI). VcE seems to be used for organizing politically whenever Montealegre is not a member of another party.

voto duro (hard vote) - A Sandinista who votes for the *Frente Sandinista de Liberación Nacional* (FSLN) even when he disagrees with the politics of the leadership, is counted as someone giving a *voto duro*.

voto oculto (hidden vote) - A person who does not want to disclose to pollsters who he voted for at elections is seen as part of the *voto oculto* and Nicaraguan pollsters assume the person voted for a different party than the *Frente Sandinista de Liberación Nacional* (FSLN).

WB - The *World Bank* is a foundation which spreads western development policies.

WWI - The *First World War* was a war between most major world powers (1914–18).

WWII - The *Second World War* was a war between most major world powers (1939–45).

Bibliography

Abu-Lughod, Deena I. 2000. Failed buyout: Land rights for Contra veterans in postwar Nicaragua. *Latin American Perspectives* 27 (3): 32–62. ISSN: 0094582X, http://www.jstor.org/stable/2634080.

Adler Lomnitz, Larissa, and Ana Melnick. 2000. *Chile's political culture and parties: An anthropological explanation.* Trans. from the Spanish by Barbara Robledo. Notre Dame, Indiana: University of Notre Dame Press. ISBN: 026800840X.

AFP. 2009. Nicaragua sufre mayor impacto por la crisis financiera [in Spanish]. *El Nuevo Diario* (Apr. 16). http://www.elnuevodiario.com.ni/nacionales/45361 (accessed June 4, 2011).

Agence France-Presse. 2008. Russia retaliates against Georgia. *Sydney Morning Herald* (Aug. 9). http://www.smh.com.au/news/world/russia-retaliates-against-georgia/2008/08/08/1218139076806.html (accessed Apr. 9, 2011).

Aguilera, Amparo. 2009a. Minsa no hace abortos... sólo terapéuticos [in Spanish]. *El Nuevo Diario* (July 31). http://www.elnuevodiario.com.ni/nacionales/53637 (accessed July 4, 2011).

———. 2009b. Minsa practica abortos [in Spanish]. *El Nuevo Diario* (July 29). http://www.elnuevodiario.com.ni/nacionales/53469 (accessed May 29, 2011).

Alegría, Claribel, and D. J. Flakoll. 2004. *Nicaragua: la revolución sandinista: Una crónica política / 1855–1979* [in Spanish]. 1st ed. Ed. Erick Flakoll Alegría. Managua: Anamá Ediciones Centroamericanas.

AlianzaBolivariana.org, ed. 2011. Alternativa Bolivariana para los pueblos de nuestra América: Tratado de comercio de los pueblos. http://www.alianzabolivariana.org/ (accessed May 30, 2011).

Álvarez, Leonor. 2008. Desgrane no necesita trámites técnicos en CSE [in Spanish]. *El Nuevo Diario* (Oct. 23). http://www.elnuevodiario.com.ni/politica/30492 (accessed May 29, 2011).

Amin, Samir. 1980. *Class and nation: Historically and in the current crisis.* Trans. from the French by Susan Kaplow. 292. New York and London: Monthly Review Press. ISBN: 0853455228.

———. 1990. The social movements in the periphery: An end to national liberation? In *Transforming the revolution.* New York: Monthly Review Press. ISBN: 0853458073.

———. 2004. *The liberal virus.* Trans. from the French by James H. Membrez. London: Pluto Press. ISBN: 9780745323596.

Arévalo Alemán, Raúl. 2011. Lenin Cerna sustituido por Ortega en la Secretaría de Organización del FSLN [in Spanish]. *La Jornada* (May 17). http://www.lajornadanet.com/diario/archivo/2011/mayo/17/1.php (accessed Aug. 19, 2011).

Arrien, Juan B. 2006. *Literacy in Nicaragua.* Background paper. United Nations Educational, Scientific and Cultural Organization. http://unesdoc.unesco.org/images/0014/001459/145937e.pdf (accessed May 6, 2011).

Asamblea Nacional de Nicaragua. 1987. *Constitución de Nicaragua* [in Spanish]. Managua. http://www.constitution.org/cons/nicaragu.html (accessed June 2, 2011).

———. 2005. *Constitución de 1987, con las reformas de 1995, 2000 y 2005* [in Spanish]. Managua. http://pdba.georgetown.edu/Constitutions/Nica/nica05.html (accessed June 2, 2011).

Babb, Florence E. 2001. *After revolution: Mapping gender and cultural politics in neoliberal Nicaragua.* University of Texas Press. ISBN: 9780292708990.

———. 2004. Recycled Sandalistas: From revolution to resorts in the new Nicaragua. *American Anthropologist,* New Series, 106 (3): 541–555. ISSN: 00027294, http://www.jstor.org/stable/3567618.

Bahen, D., and A. Hernández. 2007. Huelga petrolera 1937 [in Spanish], ed. Frente de Trabajadores de la Energía de México. *Energía* 7 (83). http://www.fte-energia.org/pdf/e83-34-39.pdf (accessed Jan. 28, 2011).

Bambirra, Vania. 1978. *Teoría de la dependencia: Una anticrítica* [in Spanish]. México: Ediciones Era.

Banco Central de Nicaragua. 2007. *Nicaragua en cifras 2006* [in Spanish]. survey. Banco Central de Nicaragua. http://www.bcn.gob.ni/estadisticas/economicas_anuales/nicaragua_en_cifras/2006/Nicaragua_en_cifras_2006.pdf (accessed May 6, 2011).

———. 2009. *Nicaragua en cifras 2008* [in Spanish]. survey. Banco Central de Nicaragua. http://www.bcn.gob.ni/estadisticas/economicas_anuales/nicaragua_en_cifras/2006/Nicaragua_en_cifras_2006.pdf (accessed May 6, 2011).

———. 2010a. Balanza de pagos 1960–2009 [in Spanish] [in Spanish]. http://www.bcn.gob.ni/estadisticas/economicas_anuales/50_anios/BD/Capitulo_VII-Sector_externo/VII-1.pdf (accessed June 18, 2011).

———. 2010b. Estadísticas macroeconómicas 1960-2009: Vii-sector externo [in Spanish] [in Spanish]. http://bcn.gob.ni/estadisticas/economicas_anuales/50_anios/BD/Capitulo_VII-Sector_externo/sector_Externo.xls (accessed June 21, 2011).

———. 2011. *Nicaragua en cifras 2010* [in Spanish]. survey. Banco Central de Nicaragua. http://www.bcn.gob.ni/estadisticas/economicas_anuales/nicaragua_en_cifras/2006/Nicaragua_en_cifras_2006.pdf (accessed May 6, 2011).

Baran, Paul Alexander. 1957. *The political economy of growth*. First Modern Reader Paperback Edition. New York and London: Monthly Review, 1968.

Barbosa, Francisco J. 2005. July 23, 1959: student protest and state violence as myth and memory in León, Nicaragua [in English]. *The Hispanic American Historical Review* 85, no. 2 (May): pp. 187–221. ISSN: 00182168, http://www.jstor.org/stable/40268840.

Bartoszko, Aleksandra. 2009. "I'm not sick, I just have pain": Silence and (under)communication of illness in a Nicaraguan village. In *Probing boundaries: the patient*, ed. Aleksandra Bartoszko and Maria Vaccarella. Oxford: Inter-disciplinary Press.

———. 2010. Kunnskap uten verdi: Opplevelse og forståelse av formell utdanning i Nicaragua [in Norwegian] [in Norwegian]. Article pending publication.

Beachy, Ben. 2006. Swindling the sick: The IMF debt relief sham. Common Dreams.org. Jan. 27. http://www.commondreams.org/views0 6/0127-32.html (accessed May 12, 2011).

Berger, Timo. 2008. Interview: wir sind Sandinisten und wir sind autonom [in German]. *Junge Welt* (Jan. 8): 3.

Berrios, Ruben. 1985. Relations between Nicaragua and the socialist countries. *Journal of Interamerican Studies and World Affairs* 27 (3): 111–139. ISSN: 0022-1937.

Biderman, Jaime. 1983. The development of capitalism in Nicaragua: A political economic history. *Latin American Perspectives* 10 (1): 7–32. ISSN: 0094-582X, http://links.jstor.org/sici?sici=009 4-582X%28198324%2910%3A1%3C7%3ATDOCIN%3E2.0.CO%3B 2-V.

Bochove, Jeroen van. 2008. Direct democracy in León, Nicaragua: Citizen participation, empowerment, and the influence on the democratic character of local governance. Master's thesis, Utrecht University.

Borge Martínez, Tomás. 1976. *Carlos, el amanecer ya no es una tentación / Carlos, now the dawn's no fond illusion* [in spanish/english]. Trans. Dinah Livingstone. Manchester: KATABASIS, 1996. ISBN: 0904872254.

———. 1980. On human rights in Nicaragua. In *Sandinistas speak: Speeches, writings, and interviews with leaders of Nicaragua's revolution,* ed. Bruce Marcus, trans. from the Spanish by Intercontinental Press. New York: Pathfinder Press, 1982.

———. 1981. The second anniversary of the Sandinista Revolution. In *Sandinistas speak: Speeches, writings, and interviews with leaders of Nicaragua's revolution,* ed. Bruce Marcus, trans. from the Spanish by Intercontinental Press. New York: Pathfinder Press, 1982.

———. 1990. *La paciente impaciencia* [in Spanish]. Edición corregida, disminuida y aumentada. Managua, 2010. ISBN: 9789992409275.

Bossert, Thomas John. 1984. Nicaraguan health policy: The dilemma of success. *Medical Anthropology Quarterly* 15 (3): 73–74. ISSN: 07455194, http://www.jstor.org/stable/648794.

Bourgois, Philippe. 1986. The Miskitu of Nicaragua: politicized ethnicity. *Anthropology Today* 2, no. 2 (Apr.): 4–9. ISSN: 0268-540X, http://links.jstor.org/sici?sici=0268-540X%28198604%292%3A2%3C4%3ATMONPE%3E2.0.CO%3B2-M.

Brown, Timothy C. 1994. Review: the United States and Nicaragua: inside the Carter and Sandinista administrations. *Journal of Interamerican Studies and World Affairs* 36 (2): 207–219. ISSN: 00221937, http://www.jstor.org/stable/166178.

Bukharin, Nikolaĭ Ivanovich. 1920. *Economics of the transformation period.* Bergman Publishers, 1971.

Bureau of Labor Statistics, ed. 2011. Labor force statistics from the current population survey: Where can I find the unemployment rate for previous years? Feb. 11. http://www.bls.gov/cps/prev_yrs.htm (accessed May 6, 2011).

Calderón Sandino, Augusto Nicolás. 1929. El general Benjamín Zeledón [in Spanish]. *El Nuevo Diario* (Oct. 4). http://archivo.elnuevodiario.com.ni/1998/octubre/04-octubre-1998/opinion/opinion1.html (accessed May 29, 2011).

———. 1933. To abolish the Monroe Doctrine. http://historymatters.gmu.edu/d/4988/.

Canales, Diana. 2011. Honduras vuelve a OEA, con el voto en contra de Ecuador y reserva de Venezuela [in Spanish]. *América Latina en Movimiento* (June 1). http://www.alainet.org/active/47000&lang=es (accessed June 2, 2011).

Castro, Ivan. 2007. Nicaraguan president to visit Iran in Gaddafi's. *Reuters* (June 3). http://www.reuters.com/article/2007/06/04/us-nicaragua-iran-idUSN035318220070604 (accessed Feb. 6, 2011).

Castro Ruz, Fidel. 1990. Una análisis sobre la derrota [in Spanish] [in Spanish]. Chap. 6 in *Nicaragua Sandinista: ¿un conflicto de baja intensidad?* By Fabián Escalente Font, ed. Ricardo Barnet Freixas, 280–289. Fragments of a speech given at the 5th Congress of Cuban Women in the Convention Palace, Havanna. Havanna: Editorial de Ciencias Sociales, Instituto Cubano del Libro, 2009. ISBN: 9789590611582.

Central Intelligence Agency. 2011a. The World factbook: Nicaragua. https://www.cia.gov/library/publications/the-world-factbook/geos/nu.html (accessed Apr. 11, 2011).

———. 2011b. The World factbook: Distribution of family income - gini index. https://www.cia.gov/library/publications/the-world-factbook/fields/2172.html (accessed May 6, 2011).

———. 2011c. The World factbook: Inflation rate (consumer prices). https://www.cia.gov/library/publications/the-world-factbook/fields/2092.html (accessed May 10, 2011).

Centre for Research on Globalization, ed. 2008. Georgian attack against South Ossetia: 8 august 2008. http://www.globalresearch.ca/index.php?context=va&aid=20550 (accessed Apr. 9, 2011).

Chilcote, Ronald H. 2009. Trotsky and development theory in Latin America. *Critical Sociology* 35 (6): 719–741. doi:10.1177/0011392109343058, http://crs.sagepub.com/content/35/6/719.abstract.

Childs, Matt D. 1995. An historical critique of the emergence and evolution of Ernesto Che Guevara's foco theory. *Journal of Latin American Studies* 27 (3): 593–624. ISSN: 0022216X, http://www.jstor.org/stable/158485.

Clark, Paul Coe, Junior. 1992. *The United States and Somoza 1933-1956: A revisionist look.* Westport: Praeger.

Consejo Supremo Electoral, ed. 2006. Escrutinio: Elecciones nacionales 2006 [in Spanish] [in Spanish]. http://www.elecciones2006.net.ni/escrutinio/general_dn.html (accessed Jan. 13, 2008).

Cuadra Núñez, Arlen Jahoska, and Carlos Fonseca Terán. 2010a. Logros de la Revolución Sandinista en su segunda etapa. [In Spanish] [in Spanish]. In *The left in government: Latin America and Europe compared.* Vol. II. Speech sent by private email by Fonseca Terán. Bruxelles: Rosa Luxemburg Foundation, June.

———. 2010b. Logros de la Revolución Sandinista en su segunda etapa. parte excluida por falta de espacio [in Spanish] [in Spanish]. private document, Part of presentation that had to be cut out due to time constraints. Sent by private email by Fonseca Terán.

Cuenca, Alejandro Martínez. 1992. *Sandinista economics in practice.* Trans. from the Spanish by Nick Cooke and Hamlet Translations. With a forew. by Roberto Pizarro. Boston: South End Press. ISBN: 0-89608-431-0.

Cupples, Julie. 1992. Ownership and privatisation in post-revolutionary Nicaragua. *Bulletin of Latin American Research* 11, no. 3 (Sept.): 295–306. ISSN: 0261-3050, http://links.jstor.org/sici?sici=0261-3050%28199209%2911%3A3%3C295%3AOAPIPN%3E2.0.CO%3B2-M.

Diario Granma. 2007. Instalan en Nicaragua los Consejos del Poder Ciudadano [in Spanish]. *Diario Granma* (Dec. 1).

Dieterich, Heinz. 2007. *El socialismo del siglo xxi* [in Spanish]. Bogota: Fundacion Para La Investigacion Y La Cultura.

Dijkstra, A. Geske. 1999. Technocracy questioned: Assessing economic stabilisation in Nicaragua. *Bulletin of Latin American Research* 18 (3): 295–310. ISSN: 02613050, http://www.jstor.org/stable/3339167.

Donahue, John M. 1989. International organizations, health services, and nation building in Nicaragua. *Medical Anthropology Quarterly,* New Series, 3 (3): 258–269. ISSN: 07455194, http://www.jstor.org/stable/648642.

Ejército de Nicaragua. 2009. Antecedentes históricos [in Spanish] [in Spanish]. In *30 años de vida institucional 1979–2009*. Managua: Ejército de Nicaragua. ISBN: 978-99924-973-0-2, http://www.ejercito.mil.ni/contenido/relaciones-publicas/publicaciones/docs/memoria-1979-2009-026-049.pdf (accessed Jan. 27, 2011).

Enriquez, Laura J. 1997. *Agrarian reform and class consciousness in Nicaragua*. Gainesville: University Press of Florida.

Equipo Envío. 1990. ¿cómo votó Nicaragua?: Los resultados electorales [in Spanish]. *Revista Envío* (Managua), no. 102 (Apr.). http://www.envio.org.ni/articulo/621 (accessed Feb. 28, 2010).

———. 1991. La amistad de Estados Unidos con el gobierno Chamorro [in Spanish]. *Revista Envío* (Managua), no. 120 (Oct.). http://www.envio.org.ni/articulo/687 (accessed Feb. 28, 2010).

Equipo Envío Nitlápan. 2006a. Daniel Ortega presidente: Del poder 'desde abajo' al gobierno [in Spanish]. *Revista Envío* (Managua), no. 296 (Nov.). http://www.envio.org.ni/articulo/3418 (accessed Feb. 28, 2010).

———. 2006b. Herty Lewites: now a "spiritual candidate" [in Spanish]. *Revista Envío* (Managua), no. 300 (July). http://www.envio.org.ni/articulo/3324 (accessed Jan. 29, 2011).

Equipo Correo. 2010. El repligue táctico a Masaya: Una lección de audacia [in Spanish], ed. Scarlet Cuadra Waters. *Correo de Nicaragua*, no. 10 (June–July): 13–15.

Equipo Envío Nitlápan. 1996. How Nicaraguans voted. *Revista Envío* (Managua), no. 185 (Dec.). http://www.envio.org.ni/articulo/1990 (accessed Feb. 28, 2010).

Europa Press. 2009. La corte suprema de Nicaragua da vía libre a la reelección de Ortega [in Spanish]. *El Pais* (Oct. 20). http://www.elpais.com/articulo/internacional/Corte/Suprema/Nicaragua/da/via/libre/reeleccion/Ortega/elpepuint/20091020elpepuint_5/Tes (accessed June 2, 2011).

Evans, George. 2007. The deaths of Somoza [in English]. *World Literature Today* 81 (3): pp. 36–43. ISSN: 01963570, http://www.jstor.org/stable/40159408.

Everingham, Mark. 2001. Agricultural property rights and political change in Nicaragua. *Latin American Politics and Society* 43 (3): 61–93. ISSN: 1531426X, http://www.jstor.org/stable/3177144.

Federal Research Division. 1993. A country study: Nicaragua: The UNO electoral victory. The Library of Congress. Dec. http://lcweb2.loc.gov/frd/cs/nitoc.html (accessed May 30, 2011).

Field, Les. 1998. Post-Sandinista ethnic identities in western Nicaragua. *American Anthropologist,* 2nd ser., 100, no. 2 (June): 431–443. ISSN: 0002-7294, http://links.jstor.org/sici?sici=0002-7294%28199806%292%3A100%3A2%3C431%3APEIIWN%3E2.0.CO%3B2-J.

Flores, Judith. 2011. Foro: antídoto para el socialismo del siglo xxi [in Spanish]. *La Prensa* (May 12). http://www.laprensa.com.ni/2011/05/12/politica/60295 (accessed June 2, 2011).

Fonseca Amador, Carlos. 1964. *Desde la carcel yo acuso a la dictadura* [in Spanish]. León, Nicaragua. http://www.sandinovive.org/carlos/desdelacarcel.htm (accessed June 29, 2010).

———. 1969. Nicaragua: Zero hour. In *Sandinistas speak: Speeches, writings, and interviews with leaders of Nicaragua's revolution,* ed. Bruce Marcus, trans. from the Spanish by Michael Taber and Will Reisner. New York: Pathfinder Press, 1982.

Fonseca Terán, Carlos. 2007. El proyecto revolucionario en marcha [in Spanish]. *El Nuevo Diario* (Dec. 7). http://www.elnuevodiario.com.ni/variedades/3207 (accessed June 4, 2011).

———. 2008a. Balseros y mojados [in Spanish]. *El Nuevo Diario* (Dec. 29) (accessed June 4, 2011).

———. 2008b. Canciones, flores y banderas [in Spanish]. *El Nuevo Diario* (Aug. 6). http://www.elnuevodiario.com.ni/opinion/23435 (accessed June 4, 2011).

Fonseca Terán, Carlos. 2008c. La infamia paso a paso [in Spanish]. *El Nuevo Diario* (Dec. 17). http://impreso.elnuevodiario.com.ni/2008/12/17/opinion/91675 (accessed June 4, 2011).

———. 2008d. No pasarán [in Spanish]. *El Nuevo Diario* (Nov. 27). http://www.elnuevodiario.com.ni/opinion/33642 (accessed June 4, 2011).

———. 2008e. Realidades [in Spanish]. *El Nuevo Diario* (Nov. 8). http://archivo.elnuevodiario.com.ni/2008/11/08/opinion (accessed June 4, 2011).

———. 2008f. Revolución socialista o reformismo socialdemócrata [in Spanish]. *El Nuevo Diario* (Dec. 11). http://www.elnuevodiario.com.ni/opinion/34851 (accessed June 4, 2011).

———. 2008g. Zorros del mismo piñal [in Spanish]. *El Nuevo Diario* (July 16). http://www.elnuevodiario.com.ni/opinion/21537 (accessed June 4, 2011).

———. 2009a. El felicismo [in Spanish]. *El Nuevo Diario* (Jan. 11). http://www.elnuevodiario.com.ni/opinion/37259 (accessed June 4, 2011).

———. 2009b. La democracia cubana [in Spanish]. *El Nuevo Diario* (Jan. 1). http://www.elnuevodiario.com.ni/opinion/36430 (accessed June 4, 2011).

———. 2010a. A la V Internacional: Para globalizar la lucha y la esperanza [in Spanish], ed. Scarlet Cuadra Waters. *Correo de Nicaragua,* no. 7 (December 2009–January 2010): 43–56.

———. 2010b. ¿es neoliberal el gobierno del FSLN? si los perros ladran es que cabalgamos [in Spanish] [in Spanish]. May 5. http://larepublica.es/firmas/blogs/index.php/carlosfonseca/2010/05/05/ies-neoliberal-el-gobierno-del-fsln-si-l (accessed July 15, 2010).

———. 2010c. Posición del FSLN respecto al tema del aborto y otros aspectos vinculados con temas de género [in Spanish] [in Spanish]. private document, Talking points used in international conferences. Received by private email.

———. 2010d. Ser o no ser revolucionarios [in Spanish] [in Spanish]. July 11. http://larepublica.es/firmas/blogs/index.php/carl osfonseca/2010/07/11/ser-o-no-ser-revolucionarios (accessed July 15, 2010).

Font, Fabián Escalente. 2009. *Nicaragua Sandinista: ¿un conflicto de baja intensidad?* [In Spanish]. Ed. Ricardo Barnet Freixas. Havanna: Editorial de Ciencias Sociales, Instituto Cubano del Libro. ISBN: 9789590611582.

Food and Agriculture Organization of the United Nations, ed. 2010. Country profile: food security indicators: Country: Nicaragua. http://www.fao.org/fileadmin/templates/ess/documents/food_se curity_statistics/country_profiles/eng/Nicaragua_E.pdf (accessed May 5, 2011).

Fundación Internacional para el Desafío Económico Global. 2010. *Encuesta de hogares para la medición de la pobreza en Nicaragua* [in Spanish]. survey. Fundación Internacional para el Desafío Económico Global. http://fideg.org/files/doc/1283290135_Resultados%2 0FIDEG%202009web.pdf (accessed May 6, 2011).

———. 2011. *Informe de resultados de la encuesta de hogares para medir la pobreza en Nicaragua* [in Spanish]. survey. Fundación Internacional para el Desafío Económico Global, June 8. http://fideg.org/files/do c/1307568030_Resultados%20FIDEG%202010.pdf (accessed Sept. 17, 2011).

García, Ernesto. 2008. PRN desautoriza a invasores de tierras [in Spanish]. *El Nuevo Diario* (June 18). http://www.elnuevodiario.com.ni/nacionales/19078 (accessed May 29, 2011).

García, Nery. 2007. Han importado 66 millones de galones [in Spanish]. *El Nuevo Diario* (Nov. 17). http://impreso.elnuevodiario.com.ni/2007/11/17/nacionales/64075 (accessed June 4, 2011).

Garfield, Richard. 1984. Revolution and the Nicaraguan health system. *Medical Anthropology Quarterly* 15 (3): 69–70. ISSN: 07455194, http://www.jstor.org/stable/648791.

Gaynor, Tim. 1999. Daniel Ortega: Tim Gaynor in Nicaragua talks with one of the key architects of the Sandinista revolution. *New Internationalist* (July).

George Washington University, ed. 2010. Eduardo Montealegre Rivas. http://www.gwu.edu/~clai/recent_events/2006/060615%20-%20Montealegre%20bio.pdf (accessed Feb. 27, 2010).

Gilbert, Dennis. 1997. Rewriting history: Salinas, Zedillo and the 1992 textbook controversy. *Mexican Studies / Estudios Mexicanos* 13 (2): 271-297. ISSN: 07429797, http://www.jstor.org/stable/1052017.

———. 2003. Emiliano Zapata: Textbook hero. *Mexican Studies / Estudios Mexicanos* 19 (1): 127-159. ISSN: 07429797, http://www.jstor.org/stable/1052173.

Gooren, Henri. 2010. Ortega for president: The religious rebirth of Sandinismo in Nicaragua. *European Review of Latin American and Caribbean Studies*, no. 89:11-27.

Gould, Jeffrey L. 1987. 'for an organized Nicaragua': Somoza and the labour movement, 1944-1948. *Journal of Latin American Studies* 19, no. 2 (Nov.): 353-387. ISSN: 0022-216X, http://links.jstor.org/sici?sici=0022-216X%28198711%2919%3A2%3C353%3A%27AONSA%3E2.0.CO%3B2-K.

Graeber, David. 1996. Epilogue to the disastrous ordeal of 1987. http://www.hartford-hwp.com/archives/36/010.html (accessed Feb. 24, 2011).

Grigsby, William. 2005. ¿por qué hay tan poca movilización social? [In Spanish]. *Revista Envío* (Managua), no. 280 (July). http://www.envio.org.ni/articulo/2980 (accessed Feb. 28, 2010).

Gunder Frank, André. 1969. La estructura de clases en América Latina [in Spanish] [in Spanish]. In *Clases y revolución en América Latina,* ed. André Gunder Frank et al. Montevideo: Tauro.

Hanemann, Dr. Ulrike. 2005. *Nicaragua's literacy campaign.* UNESCO Report. Hamburg, Germany: UNESCO Institute for Education. http://portal.unesco.org/education/fr/files/43486/11315380511Hanemann_U.doc/Hanemann_U.doc (accessed May 9, 2011).

Harding, Luke, and Mark Tran. 2008. Georgia under all-out attack in breakaway Abkhazia. *The Guardian* (Aug. 10). http://www.guardian.co.uk/world/2008/aug/10/georgia.russia3 (accessed Apr. 9, 2011).

Harris, Richard L. 1988. Marxism and the transition to socialism in Latin America. *Latin American Perspectives* 15 (1): 7–53. ISSN: 0094-582X, http://links.jstor.org/sici?sici=0094-582X%28198824%2915%3A1%3C7%3AMATTTS%3E2.0.CO%3B2-J.

Helgheim, Rakel. 2009. El trasfondo político de la penalización del aborto terapéutico en Nicaragua en 2006, y su relación con los derechos humanos de las mujeres [in Spanish] [in Spanish]. Master's thesis, University of Bergen.

Heston, Alan, Robert Summers, and Bettina Aten. 2011. Penn World Table version 7.0. May 1. http://www.iadb.org/en/about-us/debt-relief,6898.html (accessed June 19, 2011).

Hoefer, Michael, Nancy Rytina, and Bryan C. Baker. 2009. Estimates of the unauthorized immigrant population residing in the United States: January 2009. Department of Homeland Security. http://www.dhs.gov/xlibrary/assets/statistics/publications/ois_ill_pe_2009.pdf (accessed Apr. 17, 2011).

Holbig, Heike. 2006. Ideological reform and political legitimacy in China: Challenges in the post-Jiang era. *GIGA Research Program: Legitimacy and Efficiency of Political Systems*, no. 18 (Mar.).

Hüeck, Bosco Matamoros. 2006. *La Contra: Movimiento nicaragüense* [in Spanish]. 3rd ed. Ed. Alicia Caso Guido. Managua: Editorial HISPAMER. ISBN: 9789992457818.

Hurtado, Jorge. 2008. FSLN gana las elecciones municipales [in Spanish]. *El Nuevo Diario* (Nov. 21). http://www.elnuevodiario.com.ni/nacionales/32980 (accessed Jan. 29, 2011).

Index Mundi, ed. 2010. México – tasa de desempleo – cuadros de datos históricos annuales [in Spanish] [in Spanish]. http://www.indexmundi.com/g/g.aspx?c=mx&v=74&l=es (accessed May 6, 2011).

Inter-American Development Bank. 2011. About us: Debt relief. http://www.iadb.org/en/about-us/debt-relief,6898.html (accessed May 12, 2011).

International Monetary Fund, ed. 2000. World Economic Outlook Database: Inflation (annual percent change) all countries. http://www.imf.org/external/pubs/ft/weo/2000/02/data/pcpi_a.csv (accessed May 9, 2011).

———, ed. 2010. World Economic Outlook Database: 5. report for selected countries and subjects, Nicaragua inflation. http://www.imf.org/external/pubs/ft/weo/2010/02/weodata/weorept.aspx?pr.x=64&pr.y=5&sy=1980&ey=2015&scsm=1&ssd=1&sort=country&ds=.&br=1&c=278&s=PCPI%2CPCPIPCH%2CPCPIE%2CPCPIEPCH&grp=0&a= (accessed May 9, 2011).

Irvin, George. 1982. The Nicaraguan economy: Legacy and perspectives. *Social Scientist* 10, no. 1 (Jan.): 36–43. ISSN: 0970-0293, http://links.jstor.org/sici?sici=0970-0293%28198201%2910%3A1%3C36%3ATNELAP%3E2.0.CO%3B2-P.

Jamieson, Mark. 2002. Ownership of sea-shrimp production and perceptions of economic opportunity in a Nicaraguan Miskito village. *Ethnology* 41 (3): 281–298. ISSN: 00141828, http://www.jstor.org/stable/4153029.

Jansen, Robert S. 2004. *Resurrection and reappropriation: Political uses of historical figures in comparative perspective.* paper. University of California, Aug. http://www2.asanet.org/sectioncbsm/Jansen-aug-2004.pdf (accessed Jan. 15, 2008).

Johnson, Dale L. 1981. Economism and determinism in dependency theory. *Latin American Perspectives* 8 (3/4): 108–117. ISSN: 0094582X, http://www.jstor.org/stable/2633473.

Jones, Adam. 2002. Beyond the barricades: Nicaragua and the struggle for the Sandinista press, 1979-1998. *Ohio University Research in International Studies, Latin American Series*, no. 37.

Kay, Cristóbal. 1989. *Latin American theories of development and underdevelopment.* London and New York: Routledge.

Kester, Paul. 2010. Hambre Cero: ¿desarrollo o gotas de lluvia? [In Spanish]. *Revista Envío* (Managua), no. 334 (Jan.). http://www.envio.org.ni/articulo/4121 (accessed Feb. 28, 2010).

Kodrich, Kris. 2008. The role of state advertising in Latin American newspapers: Was the demise of Nicaragua's Barricada newspaper political sabotage? *Bulletin of Latin American Research* 27 (1): 61-82. doi:10.1111/j.1470-9856.2007.00257.x, http://www.blackwell-synergy.com/doi/abs/10.1111/j.1470-9856.2007.00257.x.

Leiva, Roberto Cajina. 1982. La coyuntura de 1926 y el surgimiento y desarollo de la primera etapa del Movimiento Revolucionario Nicaragüense [in Spanish] [in Spanish]. In *Apuntes de historia de Nicaragua, tomo 1*. Managua: Universidad Nacional Autónoma de Nicaragua.

Lenin, Vladimir Ilyich. 1902. What is to be done? In *Lenin collected works*, 347-530. Vol. 5. First published as separate works. Moscow: Foreign Languages Publishing House, 1961.

———. 1914. The right of nations to self-determination. In *Lenin collected works*, 393-454. Vol. 20. First published in the journal Nos. 4, 5 and 6. Moscow: Progress Publishers,

———. 1917a. Chapter 11 "can we go forward if we fear to advance towards socialism?" in "the impending catastrophe and how to combat it". In *Lenin collected works*, 360-363. Vol. 25. First published in pamphlet form. Moscow: Progress Publishers, 1977.

———. 1917b. Chapter 22 "resolution on the current situation" in "the seventh (april) all-Russia conference of the R.S.D.L.P.(B.)" In *Lenin collected works*, 309-313. Vol. 24. First published as Supplement to Soldatskaya Pravda No. 13. Moscow: Progress Publishers, 1964.

———. 1917c. Imperialism, the highest stage of capitalism. In *Lenin collected works*, 185-304. Vol. 22. First published in pamphlet form. Moscow: Foreign Languages Publishing House, 1964.

———. 1921. The tax in kind. In *Lenin collected works*, 329-365. Vol. 32. First published in pamphlet form. Moscow: Progress Publishers, 1965.

Leogrande, William M. 1996. Making the economy scream: US economic sanctions against Sandinista Nicaragua. *Third World Quarterly* 17, no. 2 (June): 329-348. ISSN: 0143-6597.

Levy, Clifford J. 2008. Russia backs independence of Georgian enclaves. *New York Times* (Aug. 27). http://www.nytimes.com/2008/08/27/world/europe/27russia.html (accessed Apr. 9, 2011).

Liberación Sandinista, Frente Sandinista de, ed. 2002. Estatutos fsln 2002 [in Spanish] [in Spanish]. http://idbdocs.iadb.org/wsdocs/getdocument.aspx?docnum=35321509.

Lowy, Michael and Denner, Arthur. 1987. A new type of party: The Brazilian PT. *Latin American Perspectives* 14 (4): 453-464. ISSN: 0094-582X, http://links.jstor.org/sici?sici=0094-582X%28198723%2914%3A4%3C453%3AANTOPT%3E2.0.CO%3B2-Y.

Lundgren, Inger. 2000. *Lost visions and new uncertainties: Sandinista profesionals in northern Nicaragua.* Stockholm: Almquiest & Wiksell Intl.

Luxemburg, Rosa. 1908-1909. *The national question: Selected writings.* Ed. Horace B. Davis. Originally published in Przeglad Socialdemokratyczny. Progress Publishers, 1976.

———. 1913. *The accumulation of capital.* London: Routledge / Kegan Paul Ltd, 1951.

———. 1922. The problem of dictatorship. In *The Russian Revolution.* New York: Workers Age Publishers, 1940.

Madrigal, Vargas. 2006. Labor migration in Costa Rica. Department of Labor Migration. http://www.sedi.oas.org/ddse/migrantes/contenidos/Presentaciones/Dia%201%20-%20Nov.28/Costa%20Rica%20ING.ppt (accessed Apr. 17, 2011).

2009. Ma highlights Taiwan-Nicaragua ties (July 5). http://www.chinapost.com.tw/taiwan/foreign-affairs/2009/07/05/214944/Ma-highlights.htm (accessed Nov. 17, 2009).

Mahoney, James. 2001. Radical, reformist and aborted liberalism: Origins of national regimes in Central America. *Journal of Latin American Studies* 33 (2): 221-256. ISSN: 0022216X, http://www.jstor.org/stable/3653684.

Manzanares Calero, J. Salomón. 2002. 23 de Julio, historia para nunca olvidar [in Spanish]. *El Nuevo Diario* (July 23). http://archivo.elnuevodiario.com.ni/2002/julio/23-julio-2002/variedades/variedades3.html (accessed June 4, 2011).

Martínez, Moisés, and Sergio León. 2011. Ortega arrebata tres municipios a la RAAS [in Spanish]. *La Prensa* (Apr. 8). http://www.laprensa.com.ni/2011/04/08/nacionales/57301 (accessed Apr. 16, 2011).

Marx, Karl Heinrich. 1867. *Kapital.* First German Edition [in German]. Vol. I.

———. 1881. First draft of letter to Vera Zasulich. *Marx Engels Collected Works* (Moscow) 24:346.

Mayorga, Jorge Loáisiga. 2007. ¿los CPC serán los nuevos 'soplones'? [In Spanish]. *La Prensa* (July 30).

McNaughton, Heathe Luz, Marta Maria Blandon, and Ligia Altamirano. 2002. Should therapeutic abortion be legal in Nicaragua: The response of Nicaraguan obstetrician-gynaecologists. *Reproductive Health Matters* 10 (19): 111–119. ISSN: 09688080, http://www.jstor.org/stable/3775779.

McNaughton, Heathe Luz, Ellen M. H. Mitchell, and Marta Maria Blandon. 2004. Should doctors be the judges?: Ambiguous policies on legal abortion in Nicaragua. *Reproductive Health Matters* 12 (24): 18–26. ISSN: 09688080, http://www.jstor.org/stable/3776112.

Metoyer, Cynthia. 2000. *Women and the state in post-Sandinista Nicaragua.* Lynne Rienner. ISBN: 9781555877514.

Ministerio de Educación, ed. 2009. *Informe final campaña nacional de alfabetización "de Martí a Fidel": Programa estratégico del gobierno de reconciliación y unidad nacional: "un programa del pueblo".* paper. Ministerio de Educación, June 30. http://unpan1.un.org/intradoc/groups/public/documents/icap/unpan039103.pdf (accessed May 6, 2011).

———, ed. 2011. Gobernantes de Nicaragua [in Spanish] [in Spanish]. http://www.mined.gob.ni/gobernant.php (accessed Jan. 27, 2011).

Miranda, Pedro, José Daniel Ortega Saavedra, and Stephen Gorman. 1979. Interview with Daniel Ortega. *Latin American Perspectives* 6 (1): 114–118. ISSN: 0094-582X, http://links.jstor.org/sici?sici=0094-582X%28197924%296%3A1%3C114%3AIWDO%3E2.0.CO%3B2-B.

Morales A., Roberto. 2009. Buses rusos pasan los primeros exámenes [in Spanish]. *La Prensa* (Aug. 13). http://archivo.laprensa.com.ni/archivo/2009/agosto/13/noticias/nacionales/343461_print.shtml (accessed Apr. 9, 2011).

Morrissey, Siobhan. 2007. Iran's romance of Nicaragua. *Time Magazine* (Sept. 10). http://www.time.com/time/world/article/0,8599,1660500,00.html (accessed Feb. 6, 2011).

Muro Rodríguez, Mirtha, et al. 1984. *Nicaragua y la Revolución Sandinista* [in Spanish]. Ed. Alfonso Iglesias García. Havana: Editorial de Ciencias Sociales.

Navas, Lucía. 2010. Taiwán dona US$400 mil a Usura Cero [in Spanish]. *La Prensa* (Feb. 13). http://www.laprensa.com.ni/2010/02/13/economia/16060 (accessed Feb. 28, 2010).

Nicaragua Network, ed. 2009a. Nicaragua network hotline: August 25, 2009. http://www.nicanet.org/?p=771 (accessed Nov. 16, 2009).

———, ed. 2009b. Nicaragua network hotline: November 3, 2009. http://www.nicanet.org/?p=857 (accessed Mar. 8, 2010).

El Nuevo Diario. 2007. Cuba, Venezuela, Bolivia y Nicaragua crearán empresa de telecomunicaciones [in Spanish]. *El Nuevo Diario* (Nov. 6). http://www.elnuevodiario.com.ni/nacionales/1754 (accessed June 4, 2011).

NYT, ed. 2008. Nicaragua recognizes independence of South Ossetia and Abkhazia. *New York Times* (Sept. 4). http://www.nytimes.com/2008/09/04/world/americas/04iht-georgia.4.15904253.html (accessed Apr. 9, 2011).

Ortega, Humberto. 1980. Nicaragua: The strategy of victory. In *Sandinistas speak: Speeches, writings, and interviews with leaders of Nicaragua's revolution*, ed. Bruce Marcus, trans. from the Spanish by Granma. New York: Pathfinder Press, 1982.

Ortega Saavedra, José Daniel. 1979. Nothing will hold back our struggle for liberation. In *Sandinistas speak: Speeches, writings, and interviews with leaders of Nicaragua's revolution*, ed. Bruce Marcus, trans. from the Spanish by Intercontinental Press. New York: Pathfinder Press, 1982.

Paguaga, Néstor Delgadillo, ed. 2006. Censo 2005: Características educativas. Instituto Nacional de información de desarollo. http://www.inide.gob.ni/censos2005/VolPoblacion/Volumen%20Poblacion%201-4/Vol.II%20Poblacion-Caracteristicas%20Educ.pdf (accessed May 6, 2011).

Pallmeyer, Hannah. 2009. *Beyond corporatism and liberalism: State and civil society in cooperation in Nicaragua.* Hispanic Studies Honors Projects, Macalester College.

Palmer, Steven. 1988. Carlos Fonseca and the construction of Sandinismo in Nicaragua. *Latin American Research Review* 23 (1): 91–109. ISSN: 0023-8791, http://links.jstor.org/sici?sici=0023-8791%281988%2923%3A1%3C91%3ACFATCO%3E2.0.CO%3B2-N.

Pantoja, Ary. 2007. CPC fuera de la ley [in Spanish]. *El Nuevo Diario* (Nov. 21). http://impreso.elnuevodiario.com.ni/2007/11/21/nacionales (accessed June 4, 2011).

Pantoja, Ary, and Eduardo Marenco. 2007. Convencionales PLC dicen no al pacto [in Spanish]. *El Nuevo Diario* (July 12). http://archivo.elnuevodiario.com.ni/2007/07/12/politica/53574 (accessed June 4, 2011).

Patten, George P. 1971. Dairying in Nicaragua. *Annals of the Association of American Geographers* 61 (2): 303–315. ISSN: 00045608, http://www.jstor.org/stable/2562447.

Perez, Andres. 1992. The FSLN after the debacle: The struggle for the definition of Sandinismo. *Journal of Interamerican Studies and World Affairs* 34 (1): 111–139. ISSN: 00221937, http://www.jstor.org/stable/166151.

Policía Nacional. 2010. *Anuario estadístico 2009: A tu servicio siempre* [in Spanish]. police report. Policía Nacional de Nicaragua. http://policia.gob.ni/cedoc/sector/estd/Anu2009%20PN.pdf (accessed July 8, 2011).

Pollin, Robert, and Alexander Cockburn. 1991. The world, the free market and the left. *Social Scientist* 19 (7): 18–38. ISSN: 09700293, http://www.jstor.org/stable/3517668.

Potosme, Ramón H. 2009. Regalados salen caros [in Spanish]. *El Nuevo Diario* (June 3). http://www.elnuevodiario.com.ni/nacionales/49231 (accessed Apr. 9, 2011).

———. 2011. Dirigentes históricos del FSLN rechazan reelección de Ortega [in Spanish]. *El Nuevo Diario* (Mar. 20). http://www.elnuevodiario.com.ni/politica/97542_dirigentes-hist%C3%B3ricos-del-fsln-rechazan-reelecci%C3%B3n-de-ortega (accessed June 2, 2011).

Powell, Anna I. 1928. Relations between the United States and Nicaragua, 1898–1916. *The Hispanic American Historical Review* 8 (1): 43–64. ISSN: 00182168, http://www.jstor.org/stable/2505819.

Pozas, Víctor S. 1988. *La Revolución Sandinista (1979-88)* [in Spanish]. Madrid: Editorial Revolución, S.A.L. ISBN: 84-85781-72-4.

Prebisch, Raúl. 1950. *The economic development of Latin America and its principal problems.* New York: United Nations.

La Prensa. 2005. El pacto sigue [in Spanish]. *La Prensa* (Mar. 10).

———. 2008. Corte avala Consejos del Poder Ciudadano [in Spanish]. *La Prensa* (Jan. 11).

President of the International Development Association. 1980. *President's report and recommendation to the executive directors on a proposed credit to the republic of Nicaragua for a preinvestment fund project.* P-2916-NI. World Bank, Dec. 1. http://www-wds.worldbank.org/external/default/WDSContentServer/WDSP/IB/1999/08/04/000178830_98101902363447/Rendered/PDF/multi_page.pdf (accessed Aug. 22, 2011).

Púlsar. 2009. Corte Suprema de Justicia habilita la reelección de Ortega en Nicaragua [in Spanish]. *Agencia Púlsar* (Oct. 21). http://www.agenciapulsar.org/nota.php?id=16045 (accessed June 2, 2011).

Pytko, Aleksandra. 2008. Vi er ikke dumme, vi er fattige!: Om vitenskap, eksperter, utdanning og barrierer for folkelig deltakelse i en nicaraguansk landsby [in Norwegian] [in Norwegian]. Master's thesis, University of Oslo.

Quesada, James. 1998. Suffering child: An embodiment of war and its aftermath in post-Sandinista Nicaragua. *Medical Anthropology Quarterly*, New Series, 12 (1): 51–73. ISSN: 07455194, http://www.jstor.org/stable/649477.

Quijano, Aníbal. 2000. Colonidad del poder y clasificacion social [in Spanish]. Festschrift for Immanuel Wallerstein Part I, *Journal of World-Systems Research* 11 (2): 342–386.

Quist, Hubert O. 2001. Cultural issues in secondary education development in West Africa: Away from colonial survivals, towards neocolonial influences? *Comparative Education* 37 (3): 297–314. ISSN: 03050068, http://www.jstor.org/stable/3099748.

Radio La Primerísima. 2011. Cid Gallup también da como ganador a Daniel y al FSLN [in Spanish]. *Radio La Primerisima* (May 26). http://www.radiolaprimerisima.com/noticias/general/99435 (accessed June 2, 2011).

Reed, Jean-Pierre. 2004. Emotions in context: Revolutionary accelerators, hope, moral outrage, and other emotions in the making of Nicaragua's revolution. *Theory and Society* 33 (6): 653–703. ISSN: 03042421, http://www.jstor.org/stable/4144905.

Reuters, ed. 2009. Nicaragua approves purchase of Union Fenosa stake. Feb. 12. http://www.reuters.com/article/2009/02/12/unionfenosa-nicaragua-idUSN1248107320090212 (accessed Apr. 27, 2011).

RIA Novisti, ed. 2010. Russia set to donate 250 buses to Nicaragua. *RIA Novisti* (Aug. 18). http://en.rian.ru/russia/20100818/160241986.html (accessed Apr. 9, 2011).

Ricardo, David. 1821. *On the principles of political economy and taxation*. 3rd ed. London: John Murray. http://www.econlib.org/library/Ricardo/ricP.html.

Ripp, Joseph L. 1984. Revolutionary Nicaragua: An arena for research in medical anthropology. *Medical Anthropology Quarterly* 15 (3): 68–69. ISSN: 07455194, http://www.jstor.org/stable/648790.

Robinson, William I. 1996. Globalization, the world system, and "democracy promotion" in US foreign policy. *Theory and Society* 25, no. 5 (Oct.): 615–665. ISSN: 0304-2421.

Rodgers, Dennis. 2008. An anthropologist in a Managua gang. In *Gangs of Nicaragua*, ed. Dennis Rodgers and José Luís Rocha. http://www.bwpi.manchester.ac.uk/aboutus/staff/rocha-rodgers_gangs_of_nicaragua.pdf (accessed May 25, 2011).

Rodríguez, Heberto. 2007a. Quitan poderes de partido a alcalde de Ciudad Sandino [in Spanish]. *El Nuevo Diario* (Aug. 27). http://impreso.elnuevodiario.com.ni/2007/08/27/nacionales/57356 (accessed May 29, 2011).

———. 2007b. Ya somos ALBA [in Spanish]. *El Nuevo Diario* (Jan. 11). http://archivo.elnuevodiario.com.ni/2007/01/11/nacionales/38486 (accessed June 4, 2011).

Rogers, Tim. 2007. Gov't: power blackouts to end Dec. 1. *Nica Times* (Sept. 11).

Román, Jaime Wheelock. 1975. *Imperialismo y dictadura: crisis de una formación social* [in Spanish]. Mexico City: Siglo XXI.

Rostow, Walt Whitman. 1956. The take-off into self-sustained growth. *The Economic Journal* 66 (261): 25–48. ISSN: 00130133, http://www.jstor.org/stable/2227401.

———. 1960. *The stages of economic growth: A non-communist manifesto*. London: Cambridge University Press.

Sánchez, Edwin. 2007. ¿Nicolás Calderón o Augusto César? [In Spanish]. *El Nuevo Diario* (May 27). http://archivo.elnuevodiario.com.ni/2007/05/27/nacionales/49790 (accessed June 2, 2011).

Sandbrook, Richard. 1995. Bringing politics back in?: The World Bank and adjustment in Africa. *Canadian Journal of African Studies* 29 (2): 278-289.

Sandoval, Consuelo. 2007. Posponen instalación de consejos ciudadanos [in Spanish]. *El Nuevo Diario* (July 12). http://impreso.elnuevodiario.com.ni/2007/07/12/politica/53578 (accessed June 4, 2011).

Santos, Theotonio Dos. 1977. Socialismo y fascismo en America Latina hoy [in Spanish]. *Revista Mexicana de Sociologia* 39, no. 1 (Jan.): 173-190. ISSN: 0188-2503, http://links.jstor.org/sici?sici=0188-2503%28197701%2F03%2939%3A1%3C173%3ASYFEAL%3E2.0.CO%3B2-Q.

Schultz, Victoria. 1980. *Women in arms.* movie.

Serrano, Armando Rodríguez, ed. 2007. Censo 2005: Caracterización sociodemográfica del departamento de Managua. Instituto Nacional de información de desarollo. http://www.inide.gob.ni/censos2005/MONOGRAFIASD/MANAGUA.pdf (accessed Apr. 16, 2011).

Silva, José Adán. 2008. Ortega embraces Kremlin. *Inside Costa Rica* (Nov. 1). http://insidecostarica.com/special_reports/2008-11/nicaragua_russia.htm (accessed Apr. 9, 2011).

———. 2010. Tantean a ejército [in Spanish]. *El Nuevo Diario* (Apr. 10). http://www.elnuevodiario.com.ni/nacionales/71959 (accessed June 2, 2011).

Singer, Hans W. 1950. The distribution of gains between investing and borrowing countries. *The American Economic Review* 40 (2): 473-485. ISSN: 00028282, http://www.jstor.org/stable/1818065.

Smith, Steven Kent. 1997. Renovation and orthodoxy: Debate and transition within the Sandinista National Liberation Front. *Latin American Perspectives* 24, no. 2 (Mar.): 102-116. ISSN: 0094-582X.

Smukkestad, Oddvar. 1998. *Den innviklete utviklingen* [in Norwegian]. 2nd ed. Oslo: Gyldendal.

Somoza García, Anastasio. 1976. *El verdadero Sandino o el calvario de las segovias* [in Spanish]. 2nd ed. Managua: Editorial San José.

Der Spiegel. 1980. Alle sollen sich erheben [in German]. *Der Spiegel*, no. 19:183-191. http://www.spiegel.de/spiegel/print/d-143 32124.html (accessed Feb. 27, 2010).

Tatar, Bradley. 2005. Social thought and commentary: emergence of nationalist identity in armed insurrections: A comparison of Iraq and Nicaragua. *Anthropological Quarterly* 78 (1): pp. 179-195. ISSN: 00035491, http://www.jstor.org/stable/4150895.

Taylor, B. W. 1963. An outline of the vegetation of Nicaragua. *Journal of Ecology* 51 (1): pp. 27-54. ISSN: 00220477, http://www.jstor.or g/stable/2257504.

Téfel, Reinaldo Antonio, et al. 2000. *La privaticazión que sangra* [in Spanish]. Managua: Foro Democratico.

Tercer Cine. 1981a. *Sandino, today and forever*. Ed. Jan Kees de Rooy. movie.

———. 1981b. *Thank God and the revolution*. Ed. Wolf Tirado and Jackie Reiter. movie.

The UN Inter-agency Group for Child Mortality Estimation, ed. 2010. Mortality rate, infant (per 1,000 live births). World Bank. http://da ta.worldbank.org/indicator/SP.DYN.IMRT.IN (accessed May 10, 2011).

Tijerino, Frances Kinloch. 2008. *Historia de Nicaragua* [in Spanish]. 3rd ed. Managua: Instituto de Historia de Nicaragua y Centroamérica, Universidad Centroamericana.

Tortuga - Grupo anti-militarista, Elx - Alacant, ed. 2006. Once preguntas y once respuestas sobre Unión Fenosa en Nicaragua. Nov. 8. http: //www.grupotortuga.com/Once-preguntas-y-once-resp uestas (accessed Apr. 27, 2011).

Toynbee, Arnold Joseph. 1927-1930. *Los Estados Unidos, México y Nicaragua* [in Spanish]. Ed. Fernando Solís B. Trans. from the English by Claudia Ferreira. Managua: Aldilá Editor, 2003. ISBN: 999240213X.

Tully, Sheila R. 1997. Nicaraguan memories of sacrifice: Visual representations and contested histories. *Visual Anthropology* 9 (3): 301-323. http://www.informaworld.com/10.1080/08949468.199 7.9966708 (accessed Nov. 4, 2010).

United Nations, ed. 1971. New textile mill to benefit Nicaraguan cotton industry. May 1. http://www.unmultimedia.org/photo/detail.jsp?id=132/132410&key=14&query=Nicaragua&lang=en&so=0&sf=date (accessed June 12, 2011).

———, ed. 1990. ONUCA demobilizes Nicaraguan Resistance forces in Honduras. Apr. 18. http://www.unmultimedia.org/photo/detail.jsp?id=171/171898&key=42&query=Nicaragua&lang=en&so=0&sf=date (accessed June 12, 2011).

United Nations Statistics Division, ed. 2010. Demographic and social statistics: Social indicators. http://unstats.un.org/unsd/demographic/products/socind/health.htm (accessed May 10, 2011).

US Census Bureau, ed. 2009. Trade in goods (imports, exports and trade balance) with Nicaragua. http://www.census.gov/foreign-trade/balance/c2190.html (accessed Nov. 17, 2009).

US Department of Labor, Bureau of Labor Statistics, ed. 2011. Inflation – Consumer Price Index (CPI): Historical Consumer Price Index data. http://www.seattle.gov/financedepartment/cpi/historical.htm (accessed June 19, 2011).

Valenta, Jiri. 1985. Nicaragua: Soviet-Cuban pawn or non-aligned country? *Journal of Interamerican Studies and World Affairs* 27 (3): 163–175. ISSN: 0022-1937, http://links.jstor.org/sici?sici=0022-1937%28198523%2927%3A3%3C163%3ANSPONC%3E2.0.CO%3B2-0.

Vargas, Oscar-René. 2006. *Elecciones 2006: la otra Nicaragua posible* [in Spanish]. Nicaragua: Centro de Estudios de la Realidad Nacional.

Velasco, Andrés. 2002. Dependency theory. *Foreign Policy,* no. 133:44–45. ISSN: 00157228, http://www.jstor.org/stable/3183555.

Veterans Peace Action Team Pre-election Observation Delegation to Nicaragua. 1989. *US-waged "low intensity" warfare in Nicaragua.* travel. Veterans Peace Action Team. http://www.brianwillson.com/u-s-waged-low-intensity-warfare-in-nicaragua/ (accessed Feb. 27, 2010).

Vilas, Carlos M. 1992. Asuntos de familia: Clases, lineajes y politica en la Nicaragua contemporanea [in Spanish]. *Desarrollo Económico* 32 (127): 411–437. ISSN: 0046001X, http://www.jstor.org/stable/3467244.

La Voz del Sandinismo. 2009. Decreto presidencial: Medidas económicas para afrontar crisis financiera internacional [in Spanish] [in Spanish]. Jan. 22. http://www.lavozdelsandinismo.com/nicaragua-triunfa/2009-01-22/decreto-presidencial-medidas-economicas-para-afrontar-crisis-financiera-internacional/ (accessed Nov. 18, 2009).

———. 2011. Una nueva vida para afectados por el nemagón [in Spanish] [in Spanish]. Feb. 26. http://www.lavozdelsandinismo.com/nicaragua/2011-02-26/una-nueva-vida-para-afectados-por-el-nemagon/ (accessed Nov. 18, 2009).

Walker, Thomas W., and Christine J. Wade. 2011. *Nicaragua: Living in the shadow of the eagle.* 5th ed. Boulder, Colorado: Westview Press. ISBN: 9780813343877.

Wall, David L. 1993. Spatial inequalities in Sandinista Nicaragua. *Geographical Review* 83 (1): 1–13. ISSN: 00167428, http://www.jstor.org/stable/215376.

Wallerstein, Immanuel Maurice. 1974. *The modern world system: Capitalist agriculture and the origins of the European world economy in the sixteenth century.* New York: Academic Press.

———. 1997. The rise of East Asia, or the world-system in the twenty-first century. http://www.binghamton.edu/fbc/iwrise.htm (accessed Jan. 20, 2008).

———. 1999. The rise and future demise of world-system analysis. Chap. 13 in *The end of the world as we know it - social science for the twenty-first century,* 192–201. Minneapolis & London: University of Minnesota Press.

Warren, Bill. 1980. *Imperialism: Pioneer of capitalism.* London: Villiers Publications Ltd.

Wikileaks, ed. 2008. 1000 US soldiers in Georgia from Jul 15 to Aug 8 2008. http://www.wikileaks.ch/wiki/1000_US_Soldiers_in_Georgia_from_Jul_15_to_Aug_8_2008 (accessed Apr. 9, 2011).

Williams, Harvey. 1984. An uncertain prognosis: Some factors that may limit future progress in the Nicaraguan health care system. *Medical Anthropology Quarterly* 15 (3): 72–73. ISSN: 07455194, http://www.jstor.org/stable/648793.

Wilm, Johannes. 2009. *La joven revolución Hondureña* [in Spanish]. Ed. PuenteSur. movie. http://www.johanneswilm.org/honduras/ (accessed Nov. 2, 2010).

———. 2010. Cuba: economic changes and the future of socialism: Interview with cuban professor José Bell Lara. *Links International Journal of Socialist Renewal* (Sydney). http://links.org.au/node/1916 (accessed Oct. 31, 2010).

Winters, Donald H. 1964. The agricultural economy of Nicaragua. *Journal of Inter-American Studies* 6 (4): 501–519. ISSN: 08853118, http://www.jstor.org/stable/165000.

World Bank, ed. 2011a. External debt stocks (% of GNI): Nicaragua. http://data.worldbank.org/indicator/DT.DOD.DECT.GN.ZS/countries/NI?display=graph (accessed May 17, 2011).

———, ed. 2011b. World dataBank: Joint external debt hub (JEDH). http://databank.worldbank.org/ddp/home.do?Step=12&id=4&CNO=1174 (accessed May 12, 2011).

———, ed. 2011c. World dataBank. http://databank.worldbank.org/ (accessed Sept. 17, 2011).

World Bank Latin America and Caribbean Regional Office. 1978. *Memorandum on recent economic development and prospects of Nicaragua*. 2061-NI. World Bank, June 30. http://www-wds.worldbank.org/external/default/WDSContentServer/WDSP/IB/1999/09/20/000178830_98101912400072/Rendered/PDF/multi_page.pdf (accessed Aug. 22, 2011).

World Bank Latin America and Caribbean Regional Office. 1981. *Nicaragua: The challenge of reconstruction.* 3524-NI. World Bank, Oct. 9. http://www-wds.worldbank.org/external/default/WDSContentServer/WDSP/IB/2001/11/15/000178830_98101912552056/Rendered/PDF/multi0page.pdf (accessed Aug. 22, 2011).

World Health Organization, ed. 2011. Global Health Observatory Database. http://apps.who.int/ghodata/?theme=country (accessed May 10, 2011).

World Health Orgnization, ed. 2005. Choosing interventions that are cost effective (WHO-CHOICE): Purchasing power parity. http://www.who.int/choice/costs/ppp/en/ (accessed May 10, 2011).

2008. World population prospects: The 2008 revision. Population Division of the Department of Economic and Social Affairs of the United Nations Secretariat. http://esa.un.org/unpp (accessed Apr. 11, 2011).

Index

abortion, therapeutic, xxx, xxxiii, xxxiv, 4, 148, 149, 151, 154, 240
Aguirre Pérez, José Santos, 173, 174, 176
ALBA de Nicaragua, S.A., 78, 97, 110
Alegría, Francisco, 121, 123
Alemán Lacayo, José Arnoldo, 2, 19, 21, 50, 118, 121, 122, 137, 150, 151, 242
Alianza Liberal Nicaragüense, 23, 122, 123, 132, 157, 236
Alonso Moreno, Rigoberto Irurzum, 52
Alternativa Bolivariana para los pueblos de nuestra América, 94, 110, 138
Alvarado Soza, Amada, 194, 195, 200, 201
Amigos, Los, xx, 26, 36, 58, 166, 167, 216
Aminta Arias, Guimar, 31, 157, 193, 197, 204–206
anthropological studies
    1979–90, xxvi
    1990–2007, xxix
        current relevance, xxxi
        destruction, xxix, xxx
    2007–, xxxii
    health care
        2007–, xxxiii
    literacy campaign
        1980s, xxvi
        2007–, xxxiii
    Miskito
        1980s, xxvi
        1990–2007, xxxi
anti-imperialism, xvii, 5, 7, 16, 29, 31–36, 41, 224, 243
Antigua and Barbuda, 94
Argüello, Alexis
    election, 136
    suicide, 136
Asia, 189
    exports to, 96

Barrios Torres de Chamorro, Violeta, 2, 17, 19, 21, 48, 50, 87
Blandón Montenegro, María Antonieta, 154, 155, 157, 192, 197, 202, 204–206, 208
Blandón Robleto, Francisco, 193, 194, 200, 201
Bolaños Geyer, Enrique José, 2, 19, 21, 51
Bolivia, 94
Borge Martínez, Tomás, 7, 10, 77, 79, 225
Bravo Urbina, German, 42
Bukharin, Nicolai, 33
Bulgaria, 14, 82
Bustillo, María Elena, xxv, 180

Calderón Sandino, Augusto Nicolás, 3–5, 7, 29–39, 41, 43, 53, 56, 77, 119, 125, 146, 171, 217, 222

Calderón, Manuel, 123, 129, 130, 134, 135, 164
Campos Montenegro, Mercedes, 191, 192, 199, 205
Carter, James Earl, 12, 81, 100
Castro Estrada, Andrés, 3, 4, 29–31
caudillismo, 254
Central America
  exports to, 96
  imports from, 95
Central Intelligence Agency, xxiv, xxvi, 13
Centro para la Promoción, la Investigación y el Desarollo Rural y Social, 169
Centro Universitario de la Universidad Nacional
  León, 227
Cerna Juárez, Reinaldo Gregorio Lenín, 144, 229
Cerna, Pedro, 160, 161, 163
Chavez, Hugo, 53, 125, 146, 152, 187, 252
Chinandega
  population, xii
Chontales, xx
  border adjustment, xii
Cienfuegos, Víctor, 36, 37
Ciudad Sandino, 131, 173–175
  land occupation, 173, 176
  mayor of, 174
Colombia
  presidential reelection, 251
Comités de Defensa Sandinista, 17, 45, 46, 49, 158, 163
Consejo Supremo Electoral, 132, 181, 182, 254
Consejos de Poder Ciudadano, xviii, xxxiii, 138, 157–164, 166, 169, 179
Contras, xviii, xxiii, xxvi, xxxii, 12, 17, 28, 29, 36, 47, 53, 56, 87, 100, 104, 134, 173–175, 193, 202, 211
Corea, Manuel, 131, 165

Corrales Rivas, Byron, 168
Costa Rica, xi, 50, 69
  border crossing, xiii
  ethnicities of, 213
  Nicaraguan migration to, xiii
  presidential reelection, 251
  tourism, 252
  US military, 253
Council of Mutual Economic Assistance, 86
crime rate, 109
Cuadra Núñez, Arlen Jahoska, 97, 150, 152, 157, 158, 162, 164
Cuba, 7, 11, 12, 15, 17, 26, 46, 56, 62, 80, 82, 94, 110, 131, 157, 187, 195, 207, 234, 241, 245
  government spending, 78
Cutbert Ramírez, José Roberto, 214
Czechoslovakia, 14

Darío, Rubén, 31
Davila, Petronilá, 213
departamental structure, xi
Dependency Theory, 64
  Nicaraguan interest in, xvii
  Radical, 65
  Structural, 64
Development theories, 58
Disnorte, 90
Dissur, 90
Dominica, Commonwealth of, 94

earthquake
  1972, 99
Eastern Europe
  imports from, 95
Ecuador, 94, 251
El Rama, xii, xx, 213
El Salvador, xi, 15, 69
  Nicaraguan involvement with politics of, 47, 81, 138, 243
Empresa Nicaragüense de Alimentos Básicos, 240

Index

Engels, Friedrich, 77
Estelí, 182, 193, 195
    population, xii
    wartimes in, 213
European Union
    exports to, 96
    imports from, 95
export oriented development strategies, 59
exports, xi, 59, 66, 73, 75, 77, 82, 84, 86, 91, 96

First World War, 33, 62
Fitoria, Adolfo, 168
Flores Genet, Raymundo, 174
Fonseca Amador, Carlos, 3, 7-10, 28, 31, 37, 41, 42, 74, 99, 211, 214, 222, 224
Fonseca Galo, Bayardo José, xx, xxi, 42, 163, 166, 216, 217, 220, 231, 232, 234
Fonseca Icabalzeta, Carolina, xx, xxiv, xxv, 29, 163, 218, 220-223, 226, 229-232
Fonseca Terán, Carlos, 28, 33, 35, 36, 79, 97, 110, 123, 132, 144, 149, 150, 152, 153, 157, 158, 162, 164, 243
Fonseca, Fernando, 30, 99, 170
Fonseca, Gloria María, 160, 161
foreign debt
    Nicaragua to others, 83, 88, 89
    United States to Nicaragua, 50, 87, 88
Freie Deutsche Jugend, xix, 194
Frente de Liberación Nacional, 3, 7, 56
Frente Farabundo Martí para la Liberación Nacional, 47, 138, 243
Frente Sandinista de Liberación Nacional
    Consejos de Liderazgo Sandinista, 145
    structure, 144

Garay, Benjamín, 171

García López, Celso Celestino, 47
García Torres, Serafín, 102, 103
gas prices, 114
Georgia, conflict of, xix, 111, 127, 128, 187, 189
Germany, 125, 126, 201, 206-208, 254
    East, xix, xx, 14, 82, 124-126, 131, 165, 185, 189-191, 193-204, 206-208, 234, 245
        socialism, 125
    Imperial, 60, 62
    Nazi, 7
    West, 81, 82, 126, 195, 200, 201
Gini coefficient, 107
government consumption, 78
government spending, 78
Granada, 171
    land occupation, 170, 173
    oligarchs, 226
    population, xii
    Sandinismo in, 171, 211
Gross Domestic Product, 63, 71
    per Capita, 105
Gross National Income
    relation to debt, 88
Grupo Pellas, 75, 79, 87, 97, 100, 111
Guardia Nacional, xxiii
Guerra Popular Prolongada, 9-11
Guevara Montano, Margarita, 43, 44
Guevara, Ernesto, 7, 43, 224
Guharay, Falguni, 164, 168, 169, 238
Guillén, Aracely, 173
Gómez Morales, Félix, 159, 160, 182

Hambre Cero, 93, 106, 170, 186
Hassan Morales, Moisés, 2, 80
health care
    public spendings, 92
    studies of
        1980s, xxviii
        1990-2007, xxx
        2007-, xxxiii, xxxiv

Honduras, xi, xvi, xix, 30, 92, 124, 126, 144, 189
  border crossing, xiii
  government spending, 78
  military coup, 138, 139, 251, 253
    agreement, 251
    US military, 253
Honecker, Margot, xix, 125, 126, 208

Icabalceta Garay, Carolina, xxviii, 35, 49, 56, 101, 102, 151, 153, 164, 221, 222, 231, 240
illiteracy rate, 140
import-substitution, 64, 66, 71, 72
imports, 59, 65, 73, 84, 90
  cultural, 177, 187
infant mortality rate, 92
inflation
  1979–2011, 101
  1980s, 84
Ingenio San Antonio, 79, 253
Instituto de Estudio del Sandinismo, 218
Instituto Nicaragüense de Fomento Municipal, 31, 193
Instituto Nicaragüense de Seguridad Social, 195
insurrection 1979, xx, xxvi, 3, 7, 9, 11, 14, 72, 76, 79, 81–83, 99, 135, 137, 160, 167, 211, 213, 217, 222, 231, 232
Inter-American Development Bank, 81, 82, 89
International Emergency Economic Powers Act, 82
International Monetary Fund, xxix, 46, 61, 87–89, 101, 106, 110, 183, 252

Jinotega
  population, xii
Juventud Sandinista, 131, 132, 193, 194, 202, 221, 222, 225, 229, 232, 245

Juárez, Jacinto, 144

Krenz, Egon, 194

La Prensa
  transport strike, 115
Laguna Perla
  mayor of, 214
Laguna, Agapito, 217
land reform
  1980s, 79, 103
  2007–, 171–175
Leiva Cardoza, William, 166, 167
Lenin, Vladimir Ilyich, 15, 33, 35, 61, 62, 77, 224, 225
Lewites, Herty, 106
León, xix, xxiv, 212, 213, 227, 228, 241, 244
  insurrection, 135
  mayor of, 123
  Movimiento Renovador Sandinista, 239
  population, xii
  Sandinismo in, 211, 214–216, 219, 227, 232, 234
  transport strike, 114, 115
  wartimes in, 213
Liberal governments, 17, 50, 57, 86
literacy campaign
  1980s, 193
    anthropological studies of, xxvi
    East German help, 125
    remembering, 219
    results, 204
    US response, 13
  2007–, 219
    anthropological studies of, xxxiii
    goals, 204
    participation, 220
    results, 140
  illiteracy rate 1979–2009, 140
Lobo Sosa, Porfirio, 251
Luxemburg, Rosa, 33, 62, 66

López Centeno, José Francisco, 97
López Pérez, Rigoberto, 3, 6

Managua, xix–xxiv, xxxi, 35, 36, 38, 43, 47, 48, 52, 114, 117, 118, 123, 124, 128–131, 133, 137, 138, 146, 155, 160, 161, 165, 168, 169, 174, 176, 177, 179, 192–194, 205, 211, 216, 220, 222, 223, 227, 228, 232, 233, 235, 239, 241, 251
   1990s, xxix
   earthquake, 99
      1972, 74
   economic development, 74, 86
   mayor of, 3, 106, 118, 122, 136, 231
   migration to, 74
   municipal elections 2008, 132
   population, xii
   road to east coast, xi
   rotondas, 118, 119
   Sandinismo in, 214
   shopping centers, xvi, 230
   street gangs, xxxi
   structure of, 118
   wartimes in, 213
Martí, Farabundo, 36
Martínez, Armando, 41, 155, 156
Marx, Karl Heinrich, xvii, 35, 41, 62, 63, 65, 77, 224
Masaya, 76
   population, xii
Matagalpa, 192–195, 206
   population, xii
   Riogrande de, 141
   wartimes in, 213
Matargo Diez, Ana Milagro, 221
Mendieta, Ossiel, 190, 191, 196–198, 206, 208
Mercado Común Centroamericano, 72
Metrocentro, xvi, 230
   rotonda, 97, 118, 131

Mexico, 3, 26, 34–36, 38, 56, 82, 107, 108, 146, 252
   government spending, 78
   imports from, 95
   Partido Revolucionario Institucional, 56, 252
Micheletti Baín, Roberto, 251
Ministerios
   Agropecuario y Forestal, xx, 93, 249
   1980s, 170
   Comercio Exterior, 79
   Educación, 141
   Salud, 149
Miskito, xxvi, xxxi, xxxii
modernization theory, 59
monopoly state-capitalism, 62
Montealegre Rivas, Eduardo, 80, 122, 123, 132, 133, 137
   Vamos con, 122
Morales, Evo, 146
Movimiento por el Rescate del Sandinismo, 117, 138
Movimiento por Nicaragua, 251
Movimiento Renovador Sandinista, xxiii, xxxii, xxxiii, 21, 110, 117, 118, 121–124, 127, 133, 134, 137, 138, 144, 149, 150, 168, 176, 178, 179, 236, 238–245, 251
Murillo, Rosario, 23, 125, 144, 148, 158, 163, 169, 179, 226, 229
mystique, revolutionary, xxvi

Nella, Blanca María, 162
neoliberalism, 61
   16 years of, 3, 23, 50, 86, 187, 199, 202, 221, 232, 236, 245
Nueva Guinea
   population, xii

Oficina de Ética Pública, 139, 192
oil crisis
   1974, 74
Ometepe, 213

Organization of American States, 251
Ortega Saavedra, José Daniel, xii, xvii, xviii, xxxii, 2, 9, 10, 12, 17, 20-24, 40, 44, 47, 50, 53, 80, 83, 91, 93, 94, 97, 104, 106, 108, 110, 111, 113-117, 121, 124-126, 128, 132, 137, 138, 143, 144, 146-150, 152, 154, 155, 157, 158, 169, 172, 179, 180, 183, 185, 187, 189, 192, 193, 203, 205, 206, 209, 211, 214, 216, 226, 229, 230, 233, 234, 238, 241-243, 251, 254
Ortega, Humberto, 19, 33, 50

pacto, el, xxxiii, 24, 122, 137, 149-151, 241
Panama
  exports to, 96
  imports from, 95
Panama Canal
  Nicaraguan alternative to, 18, 69
Partido Liberal Constitucionalista, xxxiii, 19, 23, 28, 118, 122, 123, 132, 133, 137, 150, 151, 157, 176, 179, 241, 242
Partido Liberal Independiente, 6, 137
Partido Resistencia Nicaragüense, 173
Partido Socialista Nicaragüense, 7, 41, 44, 72
Petrocaribe, 138
Petróleos de Venezuela, S. A., 97
Piñata, la, 86, 104, 111
population, xi
  growth, xi
primitive accumulation, 65
privatization, 86
  reversal, 93

Quezada Picado, Freddy Enrique, 234, 235, 237

Ramos, Ninfa Patricia, 132, 222, 223, 229, 230

Ramírez Mercado, Sergio, 2, 80
Reagan, Ronald, 12, 61, 81, 82, 100
Región Autónoma del Atlántico Norte, xii
Región Autónoma del Atlántico Sur, xi
  border adjustment, xii
renal insufficiency, 97
Rios Juarez, Erick Saul, 138, 139, 177, 225, 226, 229
Rocha Castro, Carlos Alberto, xxvii, 168, 177, 214
Rostow's phase model, 60, 103
Ruiz, Víctor, 195, 196, 198, 203
Russia, xix, 62, 111, 127, 128, 187, 189, 208, 209, 245, 253
  imports from, 95

Saint Vincent and the Grenadines, 94
Salmerón Vásquez, Helen Maydelin, 215, 218
Sampson Davila, Rigo, xxiv, 36, 213
Santamaria Rosales, Gerardo Antonio, 220
Second World War, 71
self-determination, nations' right of, 5, 33, 35
Selva Gonzales, Rogelio Antonio, 193, 202, 203, 206
Servicio de Información Mesoamericano sobre Agricultura Sostenible, xxi, xxvii, 157, 168, 169, 186, 233, 237, 238
Siuna
  population, xii
Sobalvarro Baldelomar, Francisco Isidoro, 216
socialism
  21st century, xvii, 143, 152, 157, 183, 187
  antidote to, 251
  Cuban, 187
  East German, 125, 126
Somozas, 2, 3, 5-7, 10, 11, 14, 29, 39-43,

Index

56–58, 69, 71, 72, 74–77, 79, 81, 84, 97, 98, 101, 104, 112, 115, 129, 135, 137, 189, 211, 222, 227, 238
  economics, 71
Soviet Union, 6, 12, 15, 16, 18, 33, 41, 42, 46, 48, 53, 55, 62–64, 83, 86, 100, 128, 186, 188, 189, 196, 198, 208, 209, 214, 234, 238, 243, 245
state-capitalist transition periods, 62
Structural Adjustment Programs, 61
Sweden, 78

Telica, 240
Tendencia Proletaria, 9, 10, 44, 45, 76
Tendencia Tercerista, 9, 10, 44, 77
Terán, Ariel, 134, 135
Thatcher, Margaret Hilda, 61
Tipitapa
  population, xii
Torres, Daisy, 136
trade balance, 85
transport strike, 114, 115
Téllez, Dora María, 118, 120, 121

undernourishment, 87
unemployment rate, 108
United Kingdom, 82, 254
United States
  exports to, 96
  government spending, 78
  imports from, 95
Universidad Centroamericana, 227
Universidad de Managua–León, xxi
Universidad Nacional Autónoma de Nicaragua, 192, 220, 222, 231
  León, 117, 120, 127, 227, 228, 232, 239
Unión Fenosa, S.A., 90, 93, 104
Unión Nacional de Estudiantes de Nicaragua, 223, 227–229
Unión Nicaragüense Americana, 251

urbanization, xi
US House of Representatives, 12, 80
Usura Cero, 93, 106

Varela Vilchez, Douglas Augusto, 117, 123, 178
Vargon, Ronald, 241, 242
Venezuela, 53, 94, 97, 110, 111, 138, 152, 169, 187, 245, 251, 252
  aid to Sandinistas, 114
  exports to, 96
  imports from, 95
  oil deal, 115

Wheelock Román, Jaime, 28, 67, 68, 71, 76, 77
World Bank, 61, 75, 80, 83, 88, 105, 109

Zelaya López, José Santos, 2, 4, 29, 30, 68, 69, 98, 112
Zelaya Rosales, José Manuel, 124, 125, 127, 138, 251
Zeledón Rodríguez, Benjamín Francisco, 3, 4, 30, 32

CPSIA information can be obtained
at www.ICGtesting.com
Printed in the USA
LVOW10s1303211116
513915LV00016B/527/P